A FORTUNE YET

GARLAND REFERENCE LIBRARY
OF THE HUMANITIES
(VOL. 1421)

A FORTUNE YET
Money in the Art of
F. Scott Fitzgerald's
Short Stories

Bryant Mangum

GARLAND PUBLISHING, INC. • NEW YORK & LONDON
1991

Library of Congress Cataloging-in-Publication Data

Mangum, Bryant, 1943–
   A fortune yet : money in the art of F. Scott Fitzgerald's short
stories / Bryant Mangum.
      p. cm. — (Garland reference library of the humanities ; vol.
1421)
   Includes bibliographical references and index.
   ISBN 0–8153–0083–2 (alk. paper)
   1. Fitzgerald, F. Scott (Francis Scott), 1896–1940—Knowledge—
Economics. 2. Money in literature. 3. Short story. I. Title.
II. Series.
PS3511.I9Z684   1991
813'.52—dc20   91–9442
                                               CIP

Printed on acid-free, 250-year-life paper
Manufactured in the United States of America

For my mother
Alice Bryant Mangum
and in loving memory of my father
G. C. Mangum, Jr.

Contents

Expanded Table of Contents

xv

Acknowledgments

The idea for this book originated in Matthew J. Bruccoli's first Fitzgerald seminar at the University of South Carolina. He has provided help and encouragement in countless ways, and I am enormously grateful to him for his support. On this project in particular he has never been too busy to read my work-in-progress and comment on it. I wish also to thank the members of that seminar, William R. Anderson, Jennifer McCabe Atkinson, and James L. W. West III, for their help and their friendship.

I would also like to acknowledge an enormous debt to E. B. White scholar Rebecca M. Dale, without whom I suspect this book would never have been finished. She has been through every draft with a sharp editorial eye and improved the manuscript every time she touched it. Among many other things, she compiled the index for this volume, and I deeply appreciate her valuable suggestions, her hard work, and her patience.

I am grateful to Maurice Duke, my colleague at Virginia Commonwealth University, for his continued encouragement and support. Jackson R. Bryer of the University of Maryland and Scott Donaldson of the College of William and Mary have been generous with their time and expertise. Paula Ladenburg, my editor at Garland, has been a pleasure to work with. Parts of this book appeared in different form in *Critical Survey of Short Fiction* and *Critical Survey of Long Fiction*. I wish to thank Salem Press for allowing me to use this material.

I also wish to thank Dave Smith, Lynn Graham, Donna Chenault, Gary Sange, Eleanor Bonnoit, Frances Yeatman Gunter, Richard Layman, and Mary E. Goolsby.

I especially want to thank my children Skipper, Bronhed, Wrenn, and Charlotte for their graceful acceptance of my neglect during the preparation of this book. My wife Sally is the best reader there is, and she read every draft with care. I thank her for making this book possible.

Introduction

In his introduction to *The Price Was High: The Last Uncollected Stories of F. Scott Fitzgerald* (1979), Matthew J. Bruccoli observes that "After a quarter of a century of intensive Fitzgerald criticism, the significance of the stories in his career is still not generally understood." Jackson R. Bryer notes the astonishing fact that, as of 1979, only twenty-two of Fitzgerald's 178 stories had been treated in full chapters or essays. Since 1979 this number has increased only at the rate of approximately two each year. John A. Higgins's *F. Scott Fitzgerald: A Study of the Stories* (1971) is the single book to date which analyzes every Fitzgerald story. And only two other books are devoted exclusively to Fitzgerald's short stories. One of these is Bryer's *The Short Stories of F. Scott Fitzgerald: New Approaches to Criticism* (1982), which contains essays written for the collection by well-known scholars in the field and provides original ways of looking at previously neglected concerns in Fitzgerald's stories. The other book, Alice Hall Petry's *Fitzgerald's Craft of Short Fiction* (1989), treats all of the stories contained in the four authorized collections that appeared in Fitzgerald's lifetime.

One area that has been largely ignored in the examination of Fitzgerald's stories is that of the complex financial and artistic role that they played in his development as a professional writer. The study that follows examines all of Fitzgerald's stories in the context of their composition, marketing, and publication history in an attempt to provide an overview of the ways in which Fitzgerald learned to write for money while using the magazines for which he wrote as a workshop for his art.

Note: References in the text are to the first magazine printings, except in the cases of the apprenticeship stories. When each story is mentioned for the first time it is followed in parentheses by date of composition, place of first magazine publication, date of publication, price received before commission, and the title of the volume for those stories contained in one of the four authorized story collections published in Fitzgerald's lifetime. These collections are abbreviated as follows: *Flappers and Philosophers*, F&P; *Tales of the Jazz Age*, TJA; *All the Sad Young Men*, ASYM; *Taps at Reveille*, TAR.

A Fortune Yet

1

Fitzgerald and Literary Economics

From the beginning critics have argued that Fitzgerald prostituted his talent by writing slick magazine fiction when he could have devoted his energy to the production of more novels. Consequently, his career is often viewed as a study in literary schizophrenia. In a 1935 review of *Taps at Reveille*, T. S. Matthews mirrored the contemporary critical opinion that Fitzgerald's short stories were weaker than his novels because they were written for popular audiences: "Scott Fitzgerald is supposed to be a case of split personality: Fitzgerald A is the serious writer; Fitzgerald B brings home the necessary bacon. . . . There seems to be a feeling abroad that it would be kinder not to take any critical notice of the goings-on of Fitzgerald B, since his better half is such a superior person and might be embarrassed."[1] Margaret Marshall, surveying Fitzgerald's achievement a month after his death, concluded that he did not fulfill his early promise, partly because he could not resist the high prices that the *Saturday Evening Post* was willing to pay him for "short stories about glamorous and, today, boring girls, and boys who are not even glamorous."[2] Arthur Mizener also sees the stories as Fitzgerald's inferior work: the creative output of Fitzgerald B. According to Mizener, the short stories caused Fitzgerald regularly to compromise his artistic integrity, a practice which resulted in moral conflicts that would "haunt his career from beginning to end."[3]

But Fitzgerald's career as a short story writer is not dissociated from and irrelevant to his career as a novelist. Despite the financial successes of *This Side of Paradise*, which earned over $11,000 during the first two years of publication, and *The Beautiful and Damned*, whose royalties in the first year of publication amounted to over $12,000, he found that in order to earn a regular income as opposed to a sporadic—and in terms of the Fitzgeralds' spending habits, moderate—one, he needed to produce marketable short stories. Beginning in 1924 the stories became and remained the backbone of his income. During the year in which *The Great Gatsby* appeared, Fitzgerald earned $11,025 from short stories as opposed to the $3,952 he received in royalties that year for all of his novels combined. In 1930, $25,529 of his $29,331 income came from his short story writing. Fitzgerald's stories provided the money that enabled him to remain a novelist, particularly in the "barren years" between *The Great Gatsby* and *Tender Is the Night*, years filled with stories for which he was consistently paid high prices.

Early in his career Fitzgerald became aware of the difficulties involved in writing things that were good while at the same time supporting himself by producing marketable fiction. "May Day," a fine 1920 novelette, earned only $200, while a weak, reworked *Nassau Literary Magazine* story, "His Russet Witch," earned $810 in that same year.[4] Any conflict that this might have created in his mind, however, was short-lived. From the beginning his goals as a writer were clearly defined. He wanted to write good novels and he wanted to make a lot of money. Fitzgerald expressed his feelings to his literary agent, Harold Ober, about selling stories to the *Saturday Evening Post*: "But, by God + Lorimer, I'm going to make a fortune yet," he wrote in early 1922.[5] Approximately two years later he gave Ernest Hemingway his reasons for writing stories for the slicks. According to Hemingway, "He [Fitzgerald] said it was whoring but that he had to do it as he made his money from the magazines to have money ahead to write decent books."[6]

The primary function of the short stories, then, was to provide the financial means that enabled Fitzgerald to remain a professional writer. A central question is whether he would have written more novels if he had not spent so much time writing stories for money. But given his near-mania for rewriting, given the amount of time that the composition of a novel like *Tender Is the Night* required, and given the amount of money needed to keep the Fitzgerald household in operation, the practical function that the stories served is clear. They could be written quickly—"The Camel's Back," Fitzgerald claimed in his introduction to *Tales of the Jazz Age*, took only one day to write—and with much less effort than his novels. The big magazines, therefore, provided him with a well-paying job with fringe benefits: while living on the money from his most recent stories, he could put on the kind of sustained drive necessary to write *The Great Gatsby* or *Tender Is the Night*.

Aside from seeing the stories solely as the means by which he "would make a fortune" and get enough "ahead to write decent books," Fitzgerald also learned to use the magazines as a workshop for his novels. This central literary function of the stories is usually dismissed in a few words. Critics occasionally point to a well-known story such as "Winter Dreams" as an example of a story that can be associated with a novel, but, in fact, most of Fitzgerald's stories can be directly linked with a particular novel. More often than not, the novels are surrounded by groups of stories in which he experimented with themes, subjects, and techniques that he would later use in novels.[7] Also, stories written after certain novels show him treating material that he had used in that novel in a different way. Indeed, a study of the cluster stories—those stories which are associated with particular novels because of similarities of theme, subject matter, and technique—is important in any examination of Fitzgerald's development as a writer.[8]

When one considers that Fitzgerald, between 1919 and 1940, wrote 178 stories[9] and made from them approximately one-half of his lifetime earnings as a professional writer, the important role that the stories play in his overall career becomes obvious. Looking back on those months late in 1919 after *This Side of Paradise* had been accepted, he describes the beginning of his career as a professional writer: "While I waited for the novel to appear, the metamorphosis of amateur into professional began to take place—a sort of stitching together of your whole life into a pattern of work so that the end of one job is automatically the beginning of another."[10] Some of Fitzgerald's writing jobs were better than others, some made more money than others, and some were more fun than others; but each is important as a link in the chain of his maturation as a writer. The writer of *This Side of Paradise* did not simply blossom into the author of *The Great Gatsby* and *Tender Is the Night*. He worked a lot in between. The stories, particularly his tailoring of them for particular buyers, provide "a more orderly writer's notebook" through which his development as a professional writer can be followed, almost literally, month by month.

****

Fitzgerald was a serious craftsman who depended on his craft for his livelihood. The problems which existed for him—and they exist for any literary artist who is also a professional writer—are indicated by William Charvat in his study of the profession of authorship in America:

> The terms of professional writing are these: that it provides a living for the author, like any other job; that it is a main and prolonged, rather than intermittent or sporadic, resource for the writer; that it is produced with the hope of extended sale in the open market, like any

article of commerce; and that it is written with reference to buyers' tastes and reading habits. The problem of the professional writer is not identical with that of the literary artist; but when a literary artist is also a professional writer, he cannot solve the problems of the one function without reference to the other.[11]

Fitzgerald had three major markets: the book publishing industry from which he earned approximately $120,000; the magazine market, which netted for him over $250,000; and the movie industry, from which he made over $110,000.[12] From an artistic viewpoint the book industry was the most important, and it was also the market that brought in a relatively small amount of money. The least important for its contribution to Fitzgerald's artistic development was the movie industry, which, in terms of money earned for actual time spent working, was the most profitable.[13] In 1938 alone he made some $50,000 writing for the movies.

Standing between these two outlets for his work was the magazine market.[14] It served neither a purely artistic purpose as did the book industry, nor did it act solely as a financial resource as did the movie industry. The big magazine market functioned in both of these capacities. Between 1920 and 1936 Fitzgerald earned $289,612—a yearly average of $18,000—from the sale of his stories to popular magazines. The fact that he was a popular writer in his time is clear. His daughter notes in her introduction to *Six Tales of the Jazz Age and Other Stories* that the significant increase in price—from $500 for "The Camel's Back" in 1920 to $2,000 for "The Adjuster" in 1925—"is a tangible measure of my father's remarkable and rapid success."[15] With the last of these, the prices of Fitzgerald's stories had just begun to climb to the high mark of $4,000 per story that he began receiving from the *Post* in 1929.[16]

Fitzgerald's career as a writer of magazine fiction breaks logically into three periods: 1919-1925, those years during which he shopped around for markets and published stories in most of the important periodicals of the times; 1925-1933, the central period characterized by a close association with the *Saturday Evening Post*—a relationship which almost precluded his publication of stories in other magazines; and 1934-1940, a period beginning with the publication of his first *Esquire* story and continuing through a subsequent relationship with that magazine which lasted until his death. During the first of these periods he published thirty-two stories in ten different commercial magazines, two novels (*This Side of Paradise* and *The Beautiful and Damned*), two short story collections (*Flappers and Philosophers* and *Tales of the Jazz Age*), and one play (*The Vegetable*). In the second period he enjoyed the popular reputation he had built with readers of the *Post*, and he published forty-seven of his fifty-eight stories which appeared during this nine-year period in that magazine; the remaining eleven were scattered through five different magazines. Also in the second period Fitzgerald published *The Great Gatsby*, his third short story collection (*All the Sad Young Men*), and he delivered *Tender Is the Night* to Scribners. In the third period he lost the large *Post* audience and gained the smaller *Esquire* audience. Of the forty-four Fitzgerald stories to appear between 1934 and his death, twenty-eight appeared in *Esquire*. In addition to *Tender Is the Night*, which was completed and delivered before his relationship with *Esquire* began, he published one short story collection (*Taps at Reveille*), and he wrote the incomplete *The Last Tycoon* in the *Esquire* years. Thirteen stories, nine of which have appeared in *Esquire*, have been published since his death.

One conclusion to be drawn from a summary of Fitzgerald's professional career—and it is supported by the closer study which follows—is that he was at his best artistically in the years of his greatest popularity. During the composition of *The Great Gatsby*, Fitzgerald's commercial fiction was in such demand that large magazines such as the *Post*, *Metropolitan*, and *Hearst*'s competed for it. *Tender Is the Night* was written during the time when his popularity with slick magazine readers was at its all-time high point: in 1929 and 1930, important years in the composition of *Tender Is the Night*, he published fifteen stories in the *Post*. For the first six of these he was paid $3,500 per story, and the last nine brought $4,000 each. In sharp contrast to the 1925-1933 stories, which are characteristically of an even, high quality, and many of which are closely related to the two novels of this period, the stories of the *Esquire* years are, in general, undistinguished. In addition, with the exceptions of "Discard" and "Last Kiss," the stories written in this period have little relation to his last "serious" work, *The Last Tycoon*. No amount of wishing alters the basic fact that Fitzgerald wrote *Esquire* stories because he could no longer write *Post* stories. The *Esquire* years constitute a low point, from both a popular and an artistic standpoint, in his career. They are years during which Fitzgerald lost the knack of pleasing the large middle-American reading public and at the same time produced very little serious fiction.

2

The Apprenticeship Period
(1909-1918)

The fashionable myth that Fitzgerald mismanaged his genius and squandered his talent from the beginning of his career goes something like this: Following the overnight success of *This Side of Paradise*, he promptly mortgaged his literary soul to the popular magazines, wrote stories between drinks to make his monthly payment to a middle-brow reading public, and ignored the serious side of his talent. The facts show otherwise. Fitzgerald had much clearer ideas about the management of his talent and the permanent record of his literary achievement than is generally acknowledged. As he expressed it to Edmund Wilson, his ambition was to be "one of the greatest writers who ever lived";[1] and part of his job, as he saw it, was to get as much of his best work as possible between hard covers.

To understand the role of Fitzgerald's magazine work in the creation of what he would have considered his literary legacy (his hardbound works), it is important to realize that he regarded his commercial magazine stories as drafts of work in progress. He treated magazine contributions as some authors treat penultimate typescripts—as material that he would either revise for publication in hardbound volumes or strip for phrases and ideas which he would integrate into later stories or novels. This use of the magazines as a workshop for his novels is especially evident in his *Post* stories surrounding *Tender Is the Night*, as it is also evident in subtler ways in the stories which cluster around *The Great Gatsby* and *The Beautiful and Damned*. Less often discussed in critical studies of his work is the fact that the stories' workshop function can be found in the "apprentice fiction," which anticipates *This Side of Paradise*; and perhaps more important, that one can trace through his early school and college fiction the development of aesthetic principles which Fitzgerald would spend the rest of his life refining.

Fitzgerald's apprenticeship began in October, 1909, with the publication of "The Mystery of the Raymond Mortgage" in St. Paul Academy's *Now and Then*. It ended with the October, 1917 publication

9

in the *Nassau Literary Magazine* of "The Pierian Springs and the Last Straw." During this seven-year apprenticeship, four Fitzgerald stories appeared in *Now and Then*, three in the *Newman News*, and six stories in the *Nassau Literary Magazine*. One difficulty in making connections between the apprentice stories and Fitzgerald's mature fiction, as John Kuehl notes, results from the fact that the "points of similarity . . . are scattered rather than clustered; no one juvenile work shares themes, characters, and techniques with any single work written during maturity."[2]   Several clear patterns of development in Fitzgerald's maturation as a writer can, however, be seen by following the apprentice stories chronologically. To appreciate the way that these patterns operate in the juvenile stories, it is necessary to look first at what will become the foundation of Fitzgerald's mature talent and then to examine the ways in which these patterns evolve in the apprentice stories.

Fitzgerald's Material, His Stamp, and Double Vision

"The test of a first-rate intelligence," Fitzgerald remarked in the 1930's, "is the ability to hold two opposed ideas in the mind at the same time, and still retain the ability to function."[3]   At his best—in *The Great Gatsby*, in *Tender Is the Night*, in the unfinished *The Last Tycoon*, in parts of his first two novels, *This Side of Paradise* and *The Beautiful and Damned*, and in scores of short stories—he demonstrates the kind of intelligence he describes, an intelligence characterized by what Malcom Cowley calls "double vision." Double vision denotes two ways of seeing: it implies the tension involved when Fitzgerald sets things in opposition in such a way that the reader can, on the one hand, sensually experience the event about which Fitzgerald is writing, immersing himself emotionally in it, and yet at the same time retain the objectivity to stand back and intellectually criticize it. The foundation of double vision is polarity—the setting of extremes against each other; the result in a fictional work is dramatic tension.

The major themes of Fitzgerald's mature works derive from the resolution of tension when one idea (usually embodied in a character) triumphs over another. The common denominators in his fiction are the subjects with which he most often deals: youth, physical beauty, wealth, and potential or "romantic readiness"—all of which are ideals to him.   Set against these subjects are their opposites, as they are possessed by antagonists: age, ugliness, poverty, squandered potential. If such conflict and resulting tension is the stuff of which all fiction is made, Fitzgerald's characters, partly because of the themes he deals with and partly because of his skillful handling of point of view, rarely experience choices as obvious or clear-cut to the main characters as they may be to a detached observer. It is Fitzgerald's main gift that he can, in his best work, draw the reader into a web of emotional attachment to a character, as he does to Daisy through Gatsby, while simultaneously allowing the reader to inspect the complexity of the web, as he does through Nick.

For the origins of his double vision it is natural to look at those facets of Fitzgerald's early life which presented him with the polarities and ambiguities that would furnish the subjects and themes of his art. Down the street from Fitzgerald's boyhood home on Summit Avenue in St. Paul lived James J. Hill, the multimillionaire empire builder referred to by Fitzgerald in "Absolution" and by Gatsby's father in the last chapter of *The Great Gatsby*. The Fitzgerald family, nearly in sight of such wealth, lived moderately on the interest from his mother's inheritance, taking pains not to disturb the capital; for Fitzgerald's father, in spite of his idealistic gentility and an ancestral line that linked him to the Maryland Scott and Key families, was unable to hold a good job. When Fitzgerald was sent East to boarding school and then to Princeton, it was with his mother's money, less than a generation earned, and with considerably less of it than stood behind most of his classmates. While Fitzgerald, a child with sensitivity, intelligence, and good looks—qualities possessed by most of his heroes and heroines—was impressed with the importance of money and the graceful living of the leisure class, he was limited by the fixed income of his family. In addition, he watched his father, an idealist unable to compete in a materialistic world, become defeated.

With this kind of early life, Fitzgerald was left unprepared for the series of events in his life which formed the basis of much of his later fiction. Two of these stand out: his romantic attachment to Ginevra King, a wealthy Chicago debutante who in his words, "ended up by throwing me over with the most supreme boredom and indifference";[4] and his relationship with Zelda Sayre, who broke their engagement (because he was not rich enough or famous enough at the time) before finally marrying him after Scribners accepted his first novel for publication. Fitzgerald emphasizes the importance of the Ginevra King episode in particular and of biographical material in general in his essay "One Hundred False Starts": "We have two or three great and moving experiences in our lives. . . Then we learn our trade, well or less well, and we tell our two or three stories—each time in a new disguise—maybe a hundred, as long as people will listen."[5] The subjects and themes from those experiences formed what he called "my material."

Through Ginevra King, Fitzgerald saw the opportunity to be accepted into the wealth that the King family represented. However, her father did not conceal his "poor boys shouldn't think of marrying rich girls" attitude, recorded in Fitzgerald's *Ledger*; and when Fitzgerald was "thrown over" in favor of an acceptable suitor with money and social position, he saw the rejection as a personal one. It was this experience, coupled with his near-loss of Zelda and their subsequent, complex relationship that he would write about over and over, "each time in a new disguise." In addition to his "material," the subjects of youth, wealth, and beauty that derive from the Ginevra King and Zelda Sayre experiences, he describes an attitude which grows out of experiences like them and which he identifies as his "stamp": "Taking things hard—from Ginevra to Joe Mank. That's the stamp that goes into my books so that people can read it blind like Braille."[6]

The Apprentice Fiction

While it is too simple to suggest that these facets of Fitzgerald's talent evolved in neat, easily defined stages, their development coincides with particular phases of his apprenticeship. Specifically, he is more concerned with point of view in the earliest group of stories, written for the St. Paul Academy's *Now and Then*, than he is in many of the later apprentice stories. All four stories published in *Now and Then* possess a detachment and objectivity that will later form the basis of Fitzgerald's double vision. The *Newman News* stories, by contrast, reflect greater concern with subject matter than with technique: the *homme manqué*, or failed man, the *femme fatale*, and the indolent rich, for example, which Fitzgerald later identified as part of his "material," appeared for the first time in this group of stories. As he moves into the Princeton stories, a mood which he labels as "taking things hard" (his "stamp") comes to characterize his writing. In the last of the *Nassau Literary Magazine* pieces, "The Pierian Springs and the Last Straw," there is a more skillful fusion of the three major aspects of Fitzgerald's talent than in any previous story; it is the best of the juvenilia and the story which predictably signals the end of his apprenticeship.

Fitzgerald's earliest short story, written when he was thirteen, relies on the form and subject matter of the detective story, which he appears to have known well by this time. "The Mystery of the Raymond Mortgage" has the standard ingredients of the genre: a murder to be solved, a bungling police captain to be upstaged by a bright detective, a missing document to be found, and puzzles to be solved. Fitzgerald's departures result from what seem to be oversights. The mortgage document which gives its name to the story, for example, is mentioned once and never brought up again; and the reason for the original murder is never addressed. Chief Egan, a bungling police captain, is mystified when he discovers that John Syrel, a reporter for the *Daily News,* has solved the mystery surrounding the deaths of Miss Agnes Raymond and her family's reputedly honest servant. Syrel guides the captain to a hotel room in which are found the lover of the dead Miss Raymond and Miss Raymond's mother, who has committed suicide shortly before the arrival of Syrel and Captain Egan. Syrel had deduced the truth before the late Miss Raymond's boyfriend revealed it: Gregson, the servant, had killed Miss Raymond, which prompted Mrs. Raymond to kill Gregson and escape with her daughter's boyfriend, only to take her own life.

After one glance at the many absurdities and unresolved strands of the story, one might pass it off simply as an amateurish counterfeit of Sir Arthur Conan Doyle or Edgar Allan Poe. But the story is more than this because Fitzgerald manages in it to create a believable and consistent point of view. Narrated from the chief's first person viewpoint, the story maintains his perspective throughout. The reader goes into no mind other than the chief's, and Fitzgerald requires all other characters to reveal their thoughts only through dialogue. Perhaps the most interesting feature of this viewpoint, essentially the first person participant viewpoint, is that the narrator here is not the story's hero, but rather is one who chronicles the hero's success. The point of view has high potential for irony since there is always a discrepancy between what the hero knows and what the narrator knows. The dramatic possibilities of this point of view appealed to Fitzgerald, and he returned to it over and over, among other places, in *The Great Gatsby,* "The Rich Boy," and *The Last Tycoon.* "The Mystery of the Raymond Mortgage," in which the reader can participate in the excitement through the chief and also analytically come to understand the facts, presents the earliest evidence of Fitzgerald's double vision.

The two brief *Now and Then* stories which follow, "Reade, Substitute Right Half" and "A Debt of Honor," achieve objectivity in dramatic situations through Fitzgerald's use of the objective, third person point of view. "Reade, Substitute Right Half" recounts the moment of glory when Reade, a bench warmer, is surprisingly called into a game and makes a touchdown on a pass interception. Again in this story Fitzgerald does not violate the point of view established at the beginning. When Reade is called to come from the bench, the reader observes from the stands: "Pulling off his sweater, a light haired stripling trotted over to the coach."[7] By sharply focusing the narration on Reade and yet refusing to allow the reader to know his thoughts except as they are expressed in dialogue, Fitzgerald creates at once a situation of intimacy and distance. At the beginning the crowd shouts "Hold! Hold! Hold!" and at the end "Reade! Reade! Reade!"—a device which cleverly brings the reader from identification with the crowd to identification with Reade and creates the effect of split vision.

Fitzgerald uses a similar device in "A Debt of Honor." Private Sanderson, who has fallen asleep on guard duty and who is ordered shot, is given a reprieve by General Robert E. Lee. In dialogue he assures Lee that he will make the army proud of him. The reader soon sees him dead through the eyes of searchers who make it to the enemy-occupied house which Sanderson has heroically burned: "There on the floor, beside the mattress he had set fire, lay the body of him who had once been John Sanderson, private, third Virginia. He had paid his debt."[8] Again Fitzgerald has split the narrative focus without changing the third person point of view. The reader first becomes involved in Sanderson's plight and sympathizes with him. Then he must see Sanderson through the eyes of his fellow soldiers who survive and with whom the reader must finally identify since they are the only ones left alive. In both of these third person narratives, the dramatic tension results from Fitzgerald's control of point of view.

In "The Room With the Green Blinds," the final *Now and Then* story, Fitzgerald returns to the first person narrator, a grandson of Robert Calvin Raymond, who recently inherited a house and a fortune from his grandfather. Through a series of improbable events and sweeping changes in location, the narrator discovers that one room in the house is occupied by John Wilkes Booth, who has been given sanctuary by Raymond's grandfather, a dedicated Confederate. Raymond discloses this fact to Georgia Governor Carmatle, and Carmatle at last kills Booth. Curiously, although the story pretends to be Raymond's, Carmatle is, in fact, the hero who comes and makes the house and the room with the green blinds, which has housed Booth, habitable for the narrator. Again, as in "The Mystery of the Raymond Mortgage," Fitzgerald creates a situation filled with dramatic irony by establishing a first person narrator who finally is telling the story of a hero.

Since no drafts of the *Now and Then* stories survive, it is impossible to know how much Fitzgerald experimented in his earliest stories with various points of view or how conscious he was of maintaining a consistent viewpoint. The early *Now and Then* stories suggest that the first person participant viewpoint came most naturally to him and its refinement served as a catalyst in the development of his double vision.

Two of the three stories written during Fitzgerald's fifteenth and sixteenth years and published in *Newman News* ("A Luckless Santa Claus" and "The Trail of the Duke") suggest a shifting concern in his writing, from technical considerations of point of view evident in the *Now and Then* stories to a discovery of the leisure class material that will later become his trademark. The third story, "Pain and the Scientist," a brief spoof on Christian Science, is of negligible literary worth and interest. Fitzgerald introduces "A Luckless Santa Claus" (which he dated as Christmas, 1912) through a first person narrator who notes in the first paragraph that, "I am getting ahead of my story," and adds in the second the phrase "as I have said before."[9] The narrator then vanishes, not to be seen again. The story he narrates concerns an unlikely situation in which wealthy Harry Talbot is commanded by his insolent girlfriend to go into the streets of New York and give away twenty-five dollars. "Why, you can't even spend money, much less earn it,"[10] she tells him before ordering him to see if he can, at least, give it away. Dorothy's plot, a thinly veiled attempt to undermine Talbot's sense of worth, backfires when Talbot decides to spend the remainder of Christmas Eve with the beneficiaries of his generosity. The story's major interest lies in its introduction for the first time in Fitzgerald's writing of the *femme fatale* after which many of his fictional creations will later be patterned. In "A Luckless Santa Claus," though, Dorothy's attractiveness, which is only hinted at, does not sufficiently counterbalance her insolence; and the reader is more interested in the Christmas Eve tour of the city that Talbot's adventure provides than he is with the Talbot-Dorothy conflict. Such will not be the case in such later stories as "The Offshore Pirate" in which Ardita Farnham's beauty offsets her impertinence.

"The Trail of the Duke" (1913), like "A Luckless Santa Claus," revolves around the whim of a wealthy *femme fatale* who sends her boyfriend, Dodson Garland, into the streets searching for "the Duke," the name—unknown to Garland—of her dog. The trivial plot is counterbalanced by the energy of descriptive passages like the following, which foreshadow Fitzgerald's mature prose: "It was a hot July night. Inside, through screen, window and door fled the bugs and gathered around the lights like so many humans at a carnival, buzzing, thugging, whirring. . . . In the flats that line upper New York, pianos (sweatting [*sic*] ebony perspiration) ground out rag-time tunes of last winter and here and there a wan woman sang the air in a hot soprano."[11]   In passages like this, scattered through these two best Newman School stories, are to be found the earliest hints of Fitzgerald's prose genius.

As the St. Paul Academy and Newman School fiction indicates, at least two major ingredients of Fitzgerald's prose style—double vision and his material—had been, at least partly, formed by the time he entered Princeton in the fall of 1913. Fitzgerald marked the origin of a third ingredient, his "stamp" of "taking things hard," with the loss of Ginevra King. In fact, "the mood of loss and regret" that will inform the stories of his sad, young men of the early 1920's and the stories surrounding *Tender Is the Night* does not appear in his writing until he has met Ginevra King (on 4 January 1915) and there are forebodings that he will lose her. "The Ordeal," later reworked and published in the *Smart Set* as "Benediction,"[12] is a transition story which bridges the gap between the school stories and what he came to consider his first mature work, "The Spire and the Gargoyle." "The Ordeal" is concerned with abstract evil which becomes real to a young man about to take his vows for the priesthood. The internal struggle is projected onto the flame of an altar candle, which represents the fire of passion and which continues to flicker, finally going out. The young man gazes into a stained glass window depicting St. Francis Xavier, wins his spiritual struggle, and goes on to take his vows. Though written in the third person, "The Ordeal" focuses sharply on the mental processes of the novice priest and is the first story in which Fitzgerald deals in the abstract with the quality of evil. There are, in the story, suggestions that the main character's struggle involves giving up a woman to whom he has been sensually attracted. Thus Fitzgerald begins to make here connections between sensual beauty, wealth, and evil. When he reworked the story for *Smart Set* he introduced the novice's sister as one who embraces a sensual life in contrast to the one her brother is about to choose.

In "The Spire and the Gargoyle" (February 1917), Fitzgerald's stamp, "taking things hard," appears for the first time. The mood of loss that results from the main character's failure to pass the exam that would allow him to remain at Princeton is associated with the gargoyle, personified by the preceptor who grades his examination; and the gargoyle stands watch over the campus spires which point heavenward, suggesting the limitless possibilities that the main character could have realized. "The Spire and the Gargoyle" becomes the first in a series of lost Eden stories, prompted by Fitzgerald's actual failure at Princeton during his junior year and by the unsatisfactory ending of his romantic relationship with Ginevra King.

The idea of life experience resulting in the creation of art reappears in a story "Tarquin of Cheepside," later published in *Smart Set* (as "Tarquin of Cheapside"), which pictures a student's garret and has Shakespeare intrude after having committed the rape of Lucrece. The main character, without realizing fully what he is doing, provides a sanctuary in which Shakepeare can transform into art the rape that he has just committed.

"Babes in the Woods," which is closely related to his play *The Debutante* and which Fitzgerald revised and included in the Amory/Isabelle section of *This Side of Paradise*, explores a den scene in which the hero's line is so complicated that by the time he gets to the suggestion that he and Isabelle kiss, it is too late. At the precise moment that the kiss is to occur, they are interrupted by intruders from the party. The frustration causes Isabelle later in the night to beat her pillow into a "lucurious [sic] lump."[13]

"Babes in the Woods" occupies an anticipatory position in Fitzgerald's lost Eden cycle. Isabelle and Kenneth, in Fitzgerald's words, are "distinctly not innocent, nor were they particularly hardened."[14] They exist in an uncertain no man's land, capable either of resisting the fall from innocence, as does the novice priest in "The Ordeal," or of moving irreversibly into experience as does Clay Harrington Syneforth, the hero of the next *Lit* story, "Sentiment—and the Use of Rouge." Syneforth, a young Englishman and an idealist, has come home on furlough from the war to find that his sister and his dead brother's ex-girlfriend Eleanor have become morally reckless, symbolized by their use of rouge. Eleanor convinces Clay to take her to his rooms, where he is hypnotically seduced by her charm. After returning to the front and receiving a wound, he finds all the ideas and images in his mind have been "muddled" by his trip home. The end of the story finds him at the edge of death, but he observes that "he had stopped living in the station at Rochester"[15] where he had left Eleanor. The reader is left to wonder if he has perhaps died from moral shock, a conclusion that Fitzgerald foreshadows in the story's double-edged opening line: "This story has no moral value."[16]

"Sentiment—and the Use of Rouge" brings to a conclusion the *Lit* stories in which Fitzgerald develops his signature or "stamp," experimenting with various emotional responses to the condition of lost innocence. In the best of the apprentice stories, "The Pierian Springs and the Last Straw," his double vision, his material, and his stamp come together to produce a narrative which is, in many ways, as mature an artwork as *This Side of Paradise*. Most immediately obvious in the story is Fitzgerald's return to the first person narrator-observer point of view that he had not worked with since the *Now and Then* stories. He uses this point of view in "The Pierian Springs" to establish a distance between the narrator and the story's hero, Uncle George. The reader first encounters George through stories the narrator's parents told about his adventures and his dissipation. The central part of the story, however, is revealed through dramatic scenes actually witnessed by the narrator. In these scenes the reader sees through the narrator's eyes the pitiful condition to which George has been reduced by a *femme fatale* similar to Dorothy Harmon from "A Luckless Santa Claus." The last decade of George's life—which he stopped living one night at "sixteen minutes after ten" when he was twenty-one—has been spent mourning the loss of a woman, now widowed, who had rejected him. In the presence of the narrator, the widow verbally abuses George for the last time and he finally comes back to life. In what the narrator calls "an inartistic sixth act," George and Mrs. Fulham elope and live happily ever after, the marriage curing not only George's drinking but also his desire to write novels.

This Side of Paradise:
"The Collected Works of F. Scott Fitzgerald"

When Scribners accepted *This Side of Paradise* on 16 September 1919, what would become a familiar creative cycle came full circle for the first time. The cycle is one in which Fitzgerald experiments with subjects, themes, and techniques in short stories before working them out in final form in a novel.[17] The function that the undergraduate and school publications served for *This Side of Paradise* is similar to the one which the *Post* will come to serve for *Tender Is the Night*. One general characteristic of the apprentice fiction which links it with *This Side of Paradise* is subject matter: the world through which Amory Blaine moves, peopled with glamorous, erudite, and youthful members of the leisure class, is essentially the same as the world of Harry Talbot ("A Luckless Santa Claus") and Dodson Garland ("The Trail of the Duke"). But more specifically, entire works are lifted from the pages of the *Nassau Literary Magazine*: "Babes in the Woods" and *The Debutante*, both of which appeared in the *Smart Set* after their initial appearance in the *Lit*, were incorporated into *This Side of Paradise*; and the *Lit* story "The Spire and the Gargoyle" informs the mood of the "Spires and Gargoyles" section in the novel. So extensive were Fitzgerald's borrowings from his undergraduate fiction for *This Side of Paradise* that one reviewer called the novel "The collected works of F. Scott Fitzgerald."[18] And while it is true that Fitzgerald's use of previously written episodes may help account for the loose structure of *This Side of Paradise*, much of the novel was new and moved ambitiously beyond anything he had done before.

Writing in 1938 about the subject matter of his first novel, Fitzgerald alludes to its origins in his experience: "In 'This Side of Paradise' I wrote about a love affair that was still bleeding as fresh as the skin wound on a haemophile."[19] The love affair that he refers to is his relationship with Zelda Sayre; and it is but one of many episodes from his own life—the courtship with Ginevra King is another—that are loosely tied together in *This Side of Paradise* to form a "quest" novel or *Bildungsroman*, which unlike the novel of "selected incident" is a novel of "saturation." That is, the quest novel is one in which the hero takes on experiences until the saturation point is reached, and by virtue of the hero's coming to this point he reaches a higher level of self-awareness. Fitzgerald's use of this matrix obviously allowed him to blend in episodes about which he had already written. In *This Side of Paradise*, Amory Blaine, the hero and thinly veiled Fitzgerald persona, reaches this point when, at the end of the novel, he rejects all of the values that have been instilled in him, embraces socialism, and says, "I know myself . . . but that is all."[20]

Edmund Wilson called the novel "a gesture of indefinite revolt,"[21] a comment intended as a criticism of the novel's lack of focus. The social historian, however, would see the phrase as a key to the novel's value, which view would cast Amory in the role of spokesman for the vague rebelliousness of a generation, in Amory's words, "grown up to find all gods dead, all wars fought, all faiths in man shaken."[22] As Malcolm Cowley has noted, "More than any other writer of these times, Fitzgerald had the sense of living in history. He tried hard to catch the color of every passing year, its distinctive slang, its dance steps, its songs . . . its favorite quarterbacks, and the sort of clothes and emotions its people wore."[23] John O'Hara, in his introduction to *The Portable F. Scott Fitzgerald*, recalls the impact of *This Side of Paradise* on his generation: "A little matter of twenty-five years ago I, along with half a million other men and women between fifteen and thirty, fell in love with a book. . . . I took the book to bed with me, and still do, which is more than I can say of any girl I knew in 1920."[24] By Fitzgerald's own account, the novel made him something of an "Oracle" to his college readers; and largely on the strength of *This Side of Paradise*, he became the unofficial poet laureate of the Jazz Age.

Yet, the value of *This Side of Paradise* for those interested in Fitzgerald's development as a writer goes beyond its worth as a novel of growth or as a social document. In it are contained stories which he had already written and which take on new meaning in the context of Amory's quest. And moreover, in *This Side of Paradise* there are germs of the novels that he will write, which is to say that by the time of its completion, Fitzgerald's major subjects were cast and marked with his stamp, "taking things hard." Amory takes hard the breakup with the young, wealthy, and beautiful Isabelle (from "Babes in the Woods"). He takes hard his rejection by Rosalind by going on an extended drunk. Event after event in the novel shows Amory taking hard the absence of wealth and the ephemerality of beauty, an attitude which Fitzgerald had already expressed not only in "The Spire and the Gargoyle" but also in "Sentiment—and the Use of Rouge." With subject matter, themes, and his stamp already formed, he needed to find a point of view by which he could distance himself, more than he had through Amory, from his material. To experiment with this, he needed a workshop, an outlet for his work in progress.

3

Exploring the Market
(1919-1924)

In the twelve months that followed the acceptance of *This Side of Paradise* Fitzgerald found the workshop he needed in both the *Smart Set* (which had already published the revised *Lit* piece, "Babes in the Woods") and in the *Saturday Evening Post*. These magazines had nearly opposite editorial policies and extremely different kinds of readers. Taken together, they provided an ideal workshop in which he could explore very different facets of his talent during his first years as a professional writer. Between 1919 and 1924, he published seven stories in the *Smart Set*. In addition to "Babes in the Woods," *Smart Set* published two other revised *Lit* stories: "Benediction" (which had appeared in the *Lit* as "The Ordeal") and "Tarquin of Cheapside" (which Fitzgerald misspelled in the *Lit* as "Tarquin of Cheepside"). The first two of these are important in the development of his reputation as the flapper's historian; and because both stories were too daring at the time for a middle-American magazine such as the *Post*, their publication in the *Smart Set* points to the role of this magazine in his early career. It gave the Fitzgerald flapper her first exposure to the public, and it was the first magazine to allow him to show the serious side of his talent by publishing stories like "May Day," which were also unacceptable to popular magazine audiences.

During the time that Fitzgerald's work appeared in the *Smart Set*, the magazine had a monthly circulation of 22,000 and sold for thirty-five cents a copy. It was edited by George Jean Nathan and H. L. Mencken and had published work by such authors as D. H. Lawrence, James Branch Cabell, and Theodore Dreiser and included literary reviews by Mencken and dramatic criticism by Nathan, in addition to the novels, plays, satires, and burlesques by writers such as Aldous Huxley, Ben Hecht, and Dreiser. Under the editorship of Mencken and Nathan, the *Smart Set* was a champion of realism and naturalism in writing and a strong critic of middle-class values.[1]

Fitzgerald's reasons for wanting to publish in the *Smart Set* are not difficult to understand. When "Babes in the Woods" appeared in

September 1919, he had published no other work in a commercial magazine. With *This Side of Paradise*—accepted by Scribners on 15 September 1919—scheduled for publication early in 1920, he needed the exposure he would get from the *Smart Set* before the appearance of his novel. But it was the quality of this exposure that most interested him. In late 1919 the *Post*, whose payments for contributions were much higher than the *Smart Set*'s, accepted "Head and Shoulders." In addition to the more than one million readers of the *Post* to whom Fitzgerald's name might be familiar when the novel appeared, he added with the *Smart Set* audience another possible 22,000 who would read the novel critically.[2] It is noteworthy, then, that the way for *This Side of Paradise*—the only Fitzgerald book to be both a critical and popular success—was prepared by the prior publication of two stories, "Head and Shoulders" and "Myra Meets His Family," in the most popular of American magazines, and three stories, "Babes in the Woods," "Benediction," and "Dalyrimple Goes Wrong," in one of the most prestigious journals in America.

Clearly this was part of Fitzgerald's strategy. In discussing advertising plans for the novel with Maxwell Perkins, Fitzgerald was aware of the nature of his reputation at that point: "Those stories I sold to the *Post* will start to appear Feb. 21st. I have *Dalyrimple & Benediction* in the current *Smart Set*. . . ."[3] And in discussing the reception of the book he stated to Perkins that he planned to publish three more stories in *Smart Set* because "I want to have Mencken & Nathan hot on my side when my book comes out."[4] It was beside the point that the *Smart Set* paid only "$40 apiece": he was using the magazine to ready the way for his book, and that emerges as the primary function of that magazine in the formative stage of his literary career. From the beginning, he was known both to the selective *Smart Set* readers as well as to critically unselective readers of such a popular magazine as the *Post*—audiences who, though they knew Fitzgerald, would not have known each other.

The *Smart Set* also served another important function: it published two of the best stories that Fitzgerald ever wrote, "May Day" and "The Diamond as Big as the Ritz." These stories were unsuitable for most of the slicks because both were too long, and, certainly, "May Day" was too realistic. If either had been published in the *Post*, it would have undergone perhaps massive cuts and revisions. With this in mind, he wrote to Harold Ober concerning "The Diamond as Big as the Ritz": "If the *Diamond in the Sky* is still unsold I wish you'd offer it to *Smart Set* as a novelette. Any other magazine would cut it to pieces before they published it anyway."[5]

The thing that differentiated Fitzgerald's *Smart Set* fiction from his popular fiction, however, was not simply that it was of superior quality. The *Post*, for instance, published at least one of his finest stories: "Babylon Revisited." His *Smart Set* stories were unlike his stories which appeared in the large magazines because of a fundamental difference between the readers of that magazine and those readers of the majority of American periodicals of the time: audiences of the slicks wanted entertainment, at the expense of enlightenment through exposure to brutalities or complexities of experience. In theory, if not always in practice, the *Smart Set* readers wanted precisely the opposite.

All seven of Fitzgerald's *Smart Set* stories appeared during the 1919-1924 period of his magazine career, and their diversity suggests another aspect of the *Smart Set* market. The magazine accepted not only flapper stories ("Babes in the Woods") like those one might expect to find in the *Post*, but also serious, realistic stories ("May Day") and stories of biting social satire ("The Diamond as Big as the Ritz"). In addition to the variety of subjects Fitzgerald could explore in the *Smart Set*, he was allowed to pursue them in as many or as few words as he wished: "Tarquin of Cheapside," the shortest, is 2,500 words long, while "May Day," the longest, is 20,000. One might argue that Fitzgerald could have produced much more work of the quality of "May Day" and "Diamond as Big as the Ritz" if he had not been so concerned with making money; the *Smart Set* paid only $200 for the 20,000-word "May Day." On the one hand, he did have to make money to continue writing; on the other hand, the body of *Smart Set* stories suggests that other pressures from that magazine audience, if he had written regularly for it, might have been just as "damaging" to his novel writing as any he ever experienced from the *Post* audiences. Mencken's preference for naturalistic fiction helps account for Fitzgerald's flirtation with naturalism and thus for the pessimistic determinism that flavors such stories as "Dalyrimple Goes Wrong," as well as his novel, *The Beautiful and Damned*. Certainly the aloof wittiness and cynicism of the group of *Smart Set* stories are uncharacteristic of Fitzgerald's mature long fiction. Yet these are the qualities which bind his *Smart Set* stories together and set them apart from most of the other stories in the canon.

"Babes in the Woods" (January 1917; *Smart Set*, September 1919; $30),[6] the first Fitzgerald story to appear in a commercial magazine, contains many of the ingredients of the early Fitzgerald flapper story which readers of the big-circulation magazines would come to demand. In it Isabelle, a sixteen-year-old "speed" who has come to spend the Christmas holidays with her wealthy cousin, Elaine Hollis, has a short, inconsequential flirtation with Stephen Palms, a college man who "stayed over a day from college" just to see Isabelle. The story line is uncomplicated, with much less action than later *Post* flapper stories. A summary of the action indicates how little of it there is, especially when compared with the *Post*'s "The Offshore Pirate," a heavily plotted story. The heroine Isabelle looks down the stairs, at the beginning of the story, hoping to see the feet that belong to Stephen Palms, whom she has not met. As she stands there, she recalls the events leading up to her visit and the planned encounter with Stephen which is to follow. When she goes downstairs and, at last, meets him, they go to the dimly-lit den of the clubhouse. Here, they are interrupted just as they are about to kiss for the first time. Stephen leaves immediately to return to school, while Isabelle goes back to the Hollis home and mutters "Damn!" at having been deprived of this chance to kiss her boyfriend of several hours.

The story in its bare essentials seems designed for a popular audience; and, although it is more daring than any of the early Fitzgerald *Post* stories, it resembles many of Fitzgerald's slickest stories. Isabelle is an early version of one of the first *Post* flappers, Bernice ("Bernice Bobs Her Hair"). There are, however, three distinct types of women that fall into the general category of the Fitzgerald flapper; two of these types appear first commercially in the *Smart Set*. The first is a young girl about sixteen, like Isabelle and Bernice, who is fresh, attractive, and still under the direct influence of her family. She must gear her actions, at least partly, to the conventions of her relatives; and her family is inevitably wealthy: she always makes her debut in a major city.

The second variation of the Fitzgerald flapper is older and less restricted by her family: she, like Lois of "Benediction," Betty Medill of "The Camel's Back," and Ardita Farnham of "The Offshore Pirate," is older than the "Isabelle" characters—nineteen or so—and differs from her mainly in her degree of liberation. In addition, she may or may not be wealthy, and she may or may not be acquainted with the social code which she is constantly breaking.

The pure flapper, who incorporates the qualities of the first two, is one clearly delineated, though not in the *Smart Set*, in Myra ("Myra Meets His Family"): "When Myra is young, seventeen or so, they call her a 'wonderful kid' [Isabelle; Bernice]; in her prime—say nineteen—she is tendered the subtle compliment of being referred to by her name alone [Lois; Ardita]; after that she is a 'prom trotter' or 'the famous coast-to-coast Myra.'"[7]

These distinctions are important on several counts: from the viewpoint of social history, they help in defining the loose term "flapper," and point to a stereotype in American fiction in the earliest stage of its gestation. From an artistic viewpoint, they explain the appeal to very different readerships of the flapper "type," which constitutes a group of entertaining characters that a variety of audiences would pay to see created and placed in various situations over and over again.

The entertainment value of "Babes in the Woods" derives from its characterization of the "wonderful kid" Isabelle. By clearly focusing his narrative on her, Fitzgerald reveals the workings of this particular type's mind. However, sophisticated readers would not have been amused if he had been less than ironic in his presentation of the den scene with a sixteen-year-old flirt and a man-about-campus. When Fitzgerald says, "They had both started with good looks and excitable temperaments, and the rest was the result of certain accessible popular novels and dressing-room conversation culled from a slightly older set,"[8] the reader knows that Fitzgerald's view is ironic. Isabelle's final "Damn!" can, then, be viewed as humorous. Thus, he has set up for laughter the idea of young love in a country club setting. In doing so he has reinforced the bias of the *Smart Set* readers: romantic love is a suitable subject for fiction only if it is treated ironically. But one needs merely to read "Jacob's Ladder," "The Love Boat," or any of a number of Fitzgerald's later *Post* stories dealing with romantic love to know that he could also treat the subject seriously.

Yet, in "Babes in the Woods" Fitzgerald is so convincing in presenting the glamour as well as the naiveté of his heroine, that *Smart Set* readers had to become at least partly involved with her or else miss the impact of the story's irony. To some, Fitzgerald's involvement with the character—with her beauty and her charm—may seem to undercut his final ironic stance toward her. But just as much of the success of *Tender Is the Night* depends on Fitzgerald's skillful control of Rosemary's viewpoint in Book One of the novel, so does the relative success of his irony in "Babes in the Woods" depend on his control of Isabelle's point of view. It is this authorial stance that makes "Babes in the Woods" a *Smart Set* story; had he presented the story without irony and taken a sympathetic view of Isabelle, the story would have been close in subject matter and technique to many of his early *Post* stories.

"Benediction" (October 1919; *Smart Set*, February 1920; $40; *F&P*), a revision of the *Nassau Literary Magazine* story "The Ordeal,"[9] shows Fitzgerald working with a new character type that would soon become familiar to *Post* readers.   Different in many ways from Isabelle, "Benediction's" heroine, Lois, is older, more introspective, more philosophical.   In the story she faces a choice between a life within the church and one in the outside world with no rules, social or religious. She is drawn briefly to the church during an encounter with her brother Keith, who is studying to become a priest.   True to the preferences of the *Smart Set* readers, Lois chooses the outside world.   But Fitzgerald added another ironic touch to the story: the decision to opt for the world is presented ironically as a kind of religious experience.   In a Benediction service she faints after seeing something come out of the altar candle—Fitzgerald's symbolic representation of evil.   After she regains consciousness, Lois seems torn between believing the experience a genuine religious one and believing it to be an explainable psychological event.   She speaks to her brother about the non-Christian beliefs of her boyfriend, Howard, a character whose disposition, though not his beliefs, is likened to Keith's.   According to Howard, "Christ was a great socialist,"[10] Lois tells Keith.   And although she wants Keith to help her decide between a religious life and a worldly one, he remains non-committal.   Her final decision to go to Howard—whether they will be married or simply lovers is not clear—signifies her choice of the world and consequent rejection of those things Keith believes in.

"Benediction," therefore, attacks organized religion, specifically the Catholic Church, as a force which causes people to waste their youth; and it glorifies the young.   Keith has spent much of his life studying for the priesthood, and the reader is led to believe that his youth was wasted on religion; Lois, on the other hand, is living her youth instead of taking care of her sick mother.   "Youth shouldn't be sacrificed to age, Keith," she says.[11]   Thus Fitzgerald establishes a tension between the Christian life and the worldly life and resolves it by having his prom-trotter Lois select the latter after an ironic conversion in the chapel.   However, Keith in his "sweetness" is so attractive to Lois that the tension remains until her final spur-of-the-moment decision to join Howard.   The reader can only suspect that if she had chosen the church, the story might have been a *Post* story.

Whereas the entertainment value of "Babes in the Woods" depends almost solely on Fitzgerald's exploration of a young debutante's mind at work—that is, on character development—and "Benediction" relies on the choice of a pretty girl to remain worldly—character development plus anti-establishment philosophy, "Dalyrimple Goes Wrong" (September 1919; *Smart Set*, February 1920; $35; *F&P*) entertains primarily because of the naturalistic philosophy it embodies.   Not only is the glamour and intrigue of a debutante's love absent from the story, but its hero, Bryan Dalyrimple, presents a drab figure who even lacks the money which might have given him sparkle. However, Fitzgerald deliberately makes his hero undistinguished in order to enhance his deterministic moral that "evil is only a matter of hard luck, or heredity—and—environment, or 'being found out.'"[12]

The story's Bryan Dalyrimple decides that he will never advance beyond the stock room of the Theron G. Macy Company, and after being passed over for several raises in salary he becomes a burglar during his spare time away from the Macy store. After his break-ins have gained notoriety for the anonymous burglar—Dalyrimple is never caught—he is called into the office of the store owner, Mr. Macy, who tells him, for no obvious reason, that he plans to put Dalyrimple into the State Senate. According to Macy, Dalyrimple had "the stuff that wins out."[13]

The interplay of hereditary and environmental forces stressed by Fitzgerald in this story coupled with Dalyrimple's random good fortune make the story naturalistic. The naturalistic formula was a tested one, and though Fitzgerald could probably have counted on no other magazine in America to publish "Dalyrimple Goes Wrong," he could be reasonably sure the *Smart Set* would. He felt that "Dalyrimple" was, at its date of composition (September 1919), "the best story I ever wrote,"[14] and it is significant that Fitzgerald thought originally the story would be suitable for the *Post*.[15] Clearly he was in the process of exploring the market, and his misconception about "Dalyrimple" indicates that he had a good deal to learn at that point.

"The Smilers" (September 1919; *Smart Set*, June 1920; $35),[16] written the same month as "Dalyrimple Goes Wrong," further illustrates Fitzgerald's uncertainty about the tastes and preferences of the various commercial magazine audiences. Like "Dalyrimple Goes Wrong," "The Smilers" is cynical and pessimistic. Sylvester Stockton, the story's protagonist, remains puzzled as to why people smile when they have no apparent reason. He assumes that all "smilers" are shallow people who do not know that life is full of hardship. The reader, however, discovers that each person who has smiled at Stockton has a serious personal problem. To the audience, therefore, the particular smilers in the story actually are shallow since they smile for no reason; but Stockton has no way of knowing this. Ironically, he becomes the most superficial character in the story: one whose cynicism is as hollow as blind optimism may be in others. After *Scribner's Magazine* rejected "The Smilers," Fitzgerald asked the Reynolds Agency to sell it to another magazine. When Harold Ober, who was a partner in the agency and who began handling Fitzgerald's work in November 1919, had no luck with the story, Fitzgerald himself sold it to the *Smart Set*. After his experience with "The Smilers" Fitzgerald began to be more conscious of the kinds of stories the public wanted. A question that he asked Ober in December 1919 indicates his growing awareness of the requirements of the commercial magazines: "Is there any market at all for the cynical or pessimistic story except the *Smart Set* or does realism bar a story from any well-paying magazine no matter how cleverly it's done?"[17]

The features of the early *Smart Set* stories which distinguished them from other of Fitzgerald's first short fiction—the *Post* stories, for example—were these: they could be cynical; they could be naturalistic; they could be critical of society; and they could be flippant about romantic love. Fitzgerald's early *Post* stories, on the other hand, were never cynical, though they were occasionally less than happy; they were never naturalistic; certainly, they were never openly critical of the near-Puritan virtues which made the *Post* the mouthpiece of middle America; and seldom were they less than serious about romantic love. It was the philosophical or intellectual bias of the early *Smart Set* stories which earmarked them for their audience. And it was almost solely for their ability to entertain by reinforcing the intellectual bias of that audience—not for their artistic brilliance—that these stories were saleable.

Didactic Stories in *Scribner's Magazine*

The two Fitzgerald stories published in *Scribner's Magazine*, both written before May 1919, are didactic stories which resemble, in many ways, the *Smart Set* stories. In "The Cut-Glass Bowl" (October 1919; *Scribner's*, May 1920; $150; *F&P*) Fitzgerald uses a bowl to symbolize the life of his heroine, Evelyn Piper, because it "was as hard as you are and as empty and as easy to see through."[18] The bowl takes on added significance, however, after Evelyn's daughter loses a hand, and Harold, Evelyn's husband, becomes a drunkard: it becomes "fate . . . the flight of time and the end of beauty."[19] In "The Four Fists" (May 1919, *Scribner's*, June 1920, $150, *F&P*) Fitzgerald also uses a symbol—Samuel Meredith's lumpy chin—to show the reader that lessons must often be learned the hard way; in Meredith's case it took four fists to teach him how to behave. The main weakness of "The Four Fists" is one that will later characterize the stories which mark Fitzgerald's decline in popularity with *Post* readers in the middle 1930's: he subordinates the entertainment value of the story to its message—a quality of "The Four Fists" which links it with the weak *Smart Set* story, "The Smilers."

Both stories appealed to *Scribner's*, which paid little but encouraged writers in the Scribner stable like Hemingway, Thomas Wolfe, and Fitzgerald to experiment with their art; a magazine which enjoyed a reputation as the journal for "educated readers."[20] The 200,000 readers of *Scribner's*, unlike the two million *Post* readers, would likely appreciate Fitzgerald's use of an object and its shattering to symbolize the life of an aging woman, just as they could be receptive to the idea that certain acts in life, such as Meredith's getting hit, take on symbolic value for the person involved. Both of the stories are weak—Fitzgerald described "The Four Fists" as "a mere plant, a moral tale which utterly lacks vitality."[21] One can be reasonably certain that if Fitzgerald had not sold the two stories for $150 each to *Scribner's*, he would have offered them to the *Smart Set* for less than $50 each.

Early *Post* Stories:
The Flapper Comes to Middle America

Located opposite the *Smart Set* and *Scribner's* in terms of literary prestige was the *Saturday Evening Post*, a magazine which paid its contributors well and accurately mirrored popular American reading tastes. On 21 February 1920 the *Post* published its first Fitzgerald story, "Head and Shoulders";[22] on 6 March 1937 "'Trouble'" appeared as the last. During his seventeen-year association with the magazine, Fitzgerald contributed a total of sixty-five short stories. Of these, eleven appeared during the 1919-1925 period.

When the *Post* published "Head and Shoulders," the magazine's president was Cyrus H. Curtis, who channelled money from his prosperous *Ladies' Home Journal* into the *Post* until the latter became the largest mass-circulation magazine in America.[23] Its circulation rose from 2,000 in 1899 to 3,000,000 in January, 1937.[24] Under the editorship of George Horace Lorimer, who served during this thirty-seven year period, the *Post* became an institution of conservatism operating to reinforce "the middle-class sanity," that is, to reinforce the biases of "the economically and morally controlling class in the American community."[25] The magazine during the years Fitzgerald contributed to it sold for five cents a copy and contained only those things Lorimer felt would be "acceptable to the Post audience." And Lorimer was "the final judge of what was good and what was acceptable."[26]

Fitzgerald, early in his career, reportedly voiced directly to Lorimer his disapproval of magazines like the *Post*: "American magazines have always published work of mediocrities and nobodies. They've taken no note of real genius. . . . It may be fifty years before anybody, except a few of us, even knows that Frank Norris ever existed."[27] But the *Post* roster reads like a "Who's Who in American Fiction": Stephen Crane, Theodore Dreiser, Stephen Vincent Benét, William Faulkner, Frank Norris, Sinclair Lewis, Ring Lardner, John P. Marquand, and James Gould Cozzens are a few whose work appeared in the *Post*. The most important reason that so many good writers contributed to the magazine was that it paid well: in one year during the Depression, 1931, Fitzgerald earned $28,800 by selling eight stories to the *Post*; DeVoto maintained he knew "a good many" who made from $20,000 to $50,000 a year writing for slicks like the *Post*.[28]

The precise audience for whom *Post* authors had to gear their work is difficult to define. In a contemporary analysis of the magazine during the 1920's, Leon Whipple characterized the audience in this way: "Everybody—high-brow, low-brow, and mezzanine; the hard-boiled businessman and the soft-boiled leisure woman; the intelligentsia, often as a secret vice. . . . You read it—and I."[29] Such a claim may be extravagant, but it emphasizes the wide variety of readers who might read a *Post* author. The thrust of the writer's appeal, though, needed to be aimed at the center of the audience described by Whipple—the average, middle American for whom the magazine itself primarily existed.

Lorimer's own prescription for stories clearly dictated the kind of fiction the *Post* wanted and got: "In every number . . . stories unite with the Post's editorials and articles to portray American life—its ideals, its struggles, its defeats, and its successes, in a way that has made it recognized as the dominant representative American publication not only at home but in every country abroad."[30] At first it seems ironic that Fitzgerald was able to fit himself into the blueprint of a magazine so clearly dedicated to mirroring the status quo. His *Smart Set* stories openly criticized the American Dream, while his four complete novels, in varying degrees, are also indictments of it. Whether or not he compromised his ideals and prostituted his talent by writing regularly for a magazine whose policies appear to contradict the basic statements of his novels is a question which must arise in any consideration of Fitzgerald's career as a professional writer. In theory Fitzgerald, the artist, does not belong in the *Post*; but Fitzgerald the professional writer had to support an expensive wife and a child, not to mention his own inclination to spend large sums of money. In short, Fitzgerald at once shared the American Dream and criticized it.[31] He resolved this major problem of professional authorship by choosing not to breach openly, in most of his early short fiction written with the *Post* in mind, those questions concerning contradictory or conflicting American values. And so, in a magazine for middle America he became the specialist in upper class life—an historian of the wealthy who could make his chronicles as amusing to the average citizen as they were sometimes, perhaps, tragic to him. In the two periods that follow, he was able to extend the boundaries of those things which Lorimer considered "acceptable"; his *Post* stories which cluster around *Tender Is the Night* become progressively more serious in subject and tone than any of the early *Post* stories such as "The Camel's Back." His reputation as a *Post* writer, though, was formed on the basis of his ability to deal in an intimate and entertaining way with two main subjects: youth and wealth.[32] Youth, primarily the flapper, became the topic of almost every early Fitzgerald story, and as he wrote to Ober, "I know the magazines only want Flapper stories from me—the trouble you had disposing of *Benjamin Button* + *The Diamond as Big as the Sky* showed that."[33] If the flappers themselves were not wealthy, Fitzgerald found a way of displaying them credibly against a backdrop of money; and as John O'Hara puts it, "he knew the forks."[34] Fitzgerald's popular reputation, in fact, is grounded in those first *Post* stories in which he chronicles flapperdom and the wealthy with a kind of authenticity—a surface realism—that is a first requirement of a *Post* author.

The first story, "Head and Shoulders" (November 1919; *Post*, 21 February 1920; $400; *F&P*), entertains with a gimmick—the trick ending. In the story, Horace Tarbox, child prodigy and Yale graduate student at age seventeen, falls in love with singer-dancer-actress, Marcia Meadow. After they are married—"The sensation in academic circles both at Yale and Princeton was tremendous"[35]—Marcia begins writing "Sandra Pepys, Syncopated," while Horace becomes a star trapeze artist at the Hippodrome. The label "Head and Shoulders" originally developed as an allusion to their roles when they were first married: Horace was the head and she the shoulders. That title becomes blatantly ironic when newspapers print it with authoress Marcia as the head and trapeze artist Horace the shoulders—a role reversal that will apparently remain for the rest of their lives.

In "Myra Meets His Family" (December 1919; *Post*, 20 March 1920; $400), Fitzgerald again uses a gimmick. But this time, he added to his story a flapper, "the famous coast-to-coast Myra."[36] After being tricked into believing that her fiance's hired actors are members of his immediate family, Myra tricks him into believing she will marry him although he has deceived her; but, in fact, she slips quietly out of his life and into a cab, where she signals her cousin to "Tell the driver 'Biltmore,' Walter"[37]—a last laugh for this woman who would not allow herself to be deceived, even by the man that she wanted to snare as a husband.

"The Camel's Back" (January 1920; *Post*, 24 April 1920; $500; *TJA*), too, uses a trick device—the marriage at a costume party of Perry Parkhurst, who was posing as a camel's head, to Betty Medill, a flapper disguised as a snake charmer, in a mock ceremony that turns out to be authentic. As in "Myra Meets His Family," the heroine is an impetuous flapper whose presence in the story makes the hero's wild masquerade seem almost plausible and, consequently, entertaining. The next *Post* flapper story, "Bernice Bobs Her Hair" (January 1920; *Post*, 1 May 1920; $500; *F&P*), is concerned primarily with the steps by which one becomes a popular "wonderful kid" as opposed to a plain visiting cousin. The story, again, turns on a trick when Bernice, who has been persuaded by her cousin to have her hair bobbed, slips into the cousin's room during the night and, in turn, cuts her hair.

"The Ice Palace" (December 1919; *Post*, 22 May 1920; $400; *F&P*) shares little with Fitzgerald's other early *Post* fiction, but its publication history reveals information about *Post* editorial policies and the possible effects of these policies on Fitzgerald's story writing. "The Ice Palace" was written, according to him, in December 1919. In an undated letter to Fitzgerald which must have arrived shortly before 30 December 1919, Ober reports that the *Post* has bought "The Ice Palace."[38] The magazine, however, did not publish the story until 22 May 1920, and at this time they placed it strategically between two issues that contained the flapper stories, "Bernice Bobs Her Hair" and "The Offshore Pirate"; both appeared in May 1920. Fitzgerald's interest in this story, its disposal by Ober, and its delayed publication provide insight into the direction his magazine career began to take from the time "The Ice Palace" was written. The *Post* had apparently been hesitant about accepting the story at first, and Fitzgerald wrote to Ober: "I had an idea that the Post was going in strongly for local color and atmosphere stories—and I suppose that the 8,000 word length is hard to dispose of elsewhere."[39] Having written it almost to order for the *Post*, he was disappointed that they had not published it by mid-March 1920: "It was the 2nd story you sold 'em + I'm quite depressed about it," he wrote to Ober.[40] Fitzgerald naturally would have wanted a good, serious story such as "The Ice Palace" seen by as many people as possible before the publication of *This Side of Paradise* (26 March 1920).

The story provides excellent local color in its treatment of stereotypes one might find in the small town of Tarleton, Georgia: Sally Carrol Happer with her near-obsessive concern for the Confederate dead could have grown up only in the South, and only a writer who knew the South and its women well could have recorded so sensitively her inevitable return from her fiancé's "Northern City" to Georgia. And the atmosphere of both regions which Fitzgerald creates in the story was, no doubt, one of the main reasons that it appealed to the *Post*. More basic to the story's theme than the atmosphere of North and South is the explicit conflict that goes a step beyond a simple contrast between the two regions. The characters are victims of geographical determinism: there is no more question that Harry Bellamy must live his adult life in the North than there is doubt that Sally Carrol could live nowhere except the South. Love, then, becomes a function of geography—a belief that is not only unromantic, but also very close to being naturalistic, and thus, questionable material for a *Post* audience.

Fitzgerald's concern that the *Post* may have "buried" the story, therefore, is understandable. He planned to mine Tarleton, Georgia, for a series as indicated by the two other Tarleton stories, "The Jelly-Bean" (*Metropolitan*, May 1920) and "The Last of the Belles" (*Post*, 2 March 1929).[41] If the *Post* was unsure about the acceptability of North-South contrasts for its audience, then Fitzgerald needed to know it.

"The Offshore Pirate" (*Post*, 29 May 1920; $500), in the direct line of the flapper stories published before "The Ice Palace," is a masterpiece of entertainment in which Fitzgerald employs numerous slick devices and gimmicks. Ardita Farnham, victim of the piracy, is an exemplary Fitzgerald flapper. "She was about nineteen, slender and supple, with a spoiled, alluring mouth and quick gray eyes full of radiant curiosity."[42] The only family that Ardita has is a wealthy uncle who delights in her impertinence to him and on whose yacht she spends most of her time inventing schemes to alleviate her chronic boredom. She wants to go to Palm Beach to meet a mysterious suitor who has promised her a famous Russian bracelet, and she tells her uncle to "either take me to Palm Beach or else shut up and go away."[43]

Ardita is reminiscent of Fitzgerald's other *Post* flappers such as Betty Medill, Myra, and Bernice; but she is more defiant, more adventurous, wealthier, and more attractive than any of these.[44] Moreover, her men will go to wilder extremes for her than even the masquerading Perry Parkhurst would go to win Betty Medill's favor. By accentuating the eccentricities of his standard *Post* heroine

Fitzgerald is able to make acceptable to *Post* readers a story that is nearly as implausible as "The Diamond as Big as the Ritz."

But perhaps an even more important feature of "The Offshore Pirate" which makes it an outstanding *Post* story lies in its treatment of the all-American competitiveness theme. The pirate, Toby Moreland, is wealthy and he belongs to approximately the same social class as Ardita. Being unable to offer her anything that she did not already have, Moreland uses his ingenuity in inventing a scheme to hijack the Farnham yacht with Ardita aboard, thus winning out over his competitors. After he has sworn to Ardita that the plot "was entirely a product of [his] own brain," she asks Moreland to "lie to me just as sweetly as you know how for the rest of my life."[45]

This is not to say, however, that an average *Post* reader would have wanted his daughter to grow up to be like Ardita. Instead, the veil of wealth that Fitzgerald places between the reader and the characters in "The Offshore Pirate" serves also as a kind of morality veil which places the characters, at least partly, beyond middle-class American values. They may become bored; they can even lie. However, these things had better be done in the name of love and preferably the characters should finally show some kind of allegiance to the free enterprise system as Moreland does in his competitive quest for Ardita.

In "The Popular Girl" (November 1921; *Post*, 11 and 18 February 1922; $1500), Fitzgerald creates suspense by having another flapper, twenty year old Yanci Bowman, plan an elaborate scheme by which she hopes to win Scott Kimberly, a twenty-five year old New Yorker. Yanci and Scott meet each other at a country club dance and go for a midnight ride after he has driven Yanci's drunken father home. Later when the father dies, Yanci is left penniless, but she tries to give the wealthy Scott the impression that she can afford to travel all over the country to keep her engagements: that she can afford to be a popular girl. Though Scott has known about Yanci's financial situation all along, he has loved her anyhow. Fitzgerald remarked after "The Popular Girl," for which he earned a raise from the *Post*,[46] that "I've learned my tricks better and am now technically proficient."[47]

From this early period of exploration several distinct patterns emerge. In the first year of his career Fitzgerald wrote under the idealistic assumption that his good stories would sell; and he was correct. The *Smart Set* bought most of them and gave him a small fee. The light, frothy stories, he found, were bought and published more readily by the *Post*. With these stories, Fitzgerald made his early reputation as the historian of youth, particularly the flapper, and the wealthy.   Popular magazine readers came to know him by this trademark.

Flappers and Philosophers

When *Flappers and Philosophers* (September 1920), Fitzgerald's first collection of short stories, was published, bookbuyers were able to see both the side of his talent that he had shown to *Post* readers and the one that he had shown to the *Smart Set* audience. The collection accurately reflects the kind of work Fitzgerald had been doing in his short stories during his first year as a professional writer. Four of the stories are *Post* stories, two are *Smart Set* stories, and two are *Scribner's* stories. Just as Fitzgerald's 1920 *Post* stories had been light stories about flappers, the stories in *Flappers and Philosophers* which were taken from the *Post* are also light: "The Offshore Pirate," "Head and Shoulders," and "Bernice Bobs Her Hair." The single exception is "The Ice Palace"—the best of Fitzgerald's 1920 *Post* stories and the best in the collection.   The selections included from the *Smart Set* are representative of the different kinds and different quality of Fitzgerald's contributions to this magazine: the first *Smart Set* story in *Flappers and Philosophers*, "Benediction," is both serious and good; the second, "Dalyrimple Goes Wrong," is serious but weak. The two remaining stories in the collection, "The Cut-Glass Bowl" and "The Four Fists," are *Scribner's* stories, and they illustrate the point that Fitzgerald, as one would expect of an author in the Scribner stable, built didactic stories around controlling symbols.

Of the thirteen stories available for inclusion in *Flappers and Philosophers*, then, Fitzgerald chose eight that demonstrated all sides of his talent visible to magazine readers in 1919 and 1920. After seeing both the "popular" and "good" Fitzgerald in one volume, almost half of the contemporary reviewers who wrote about *Flappers and Philosophers* reacted favorably, concluding that Fitzgerald wrote well about his chosen subjects: the young and the wealthy.[48] Those who praised the collection most highly were often those still under the spell of *This Side of Paradise*, and they were extolling the virtues of that novel as much as they were reacting critically to the stories themselves. Many of the mixed reviews criticized the unevenness of the volume and pointed to the two different sides of Fitzgerald's talent displayed in *Flappers and Philosophers*. Mencken, reviewing the book for *Smart Set*, predictably selected a *Smart Set* story, "Benediction," as the best story in the group: "From 'Benediction' the leap to 'The Offshore Pirate' and other such confections is like the leap from the peaks of Darien to the slums of Colon."[49]   His comment here reflects the general tone of the mixed reviews. Heywood Broun, writing for the "Books" section of the *New York Tribune*, perceptively selected "The Ice Palace" as the outstanding story in the volume, a story which "brought a sudden conviction that F. Scott Fitzgerald did have something to say and knew how to say it."[50]

The Beautiful and Damned Cluster Stories:
"The Meaninglessness of Life"

In the two-year period separating "The Offshore Pirate" (May 1920) from Fitzgerald's last *Smart Set* story, "The Diamond as Big as the Ritz" (May 1922), Fitzgerald embraced the naturalistic philosophy both in the stories of this period and in his second novel, *The Beautiful and Damned*.   Edmund Wilson, in a 1922 critical appraisal of Fitzgerald's work, analyzed the causes of what seemed a radical shift in his philosophy during this time: "In college, he had supposed that the thing to do was to write biographical novels with a burst of energy toward the close; since his advent into the literary world, he has discovered that another genre has recently come into favor: the kind which makes much of the tragedy and what Mencken has called 'the meaninglessness of life.'"[51] On one level, Wilson's implication is that Fitzgerald, in turning to naturalism, was doing what he thought was in literary vogue; on another level the implication is, perhaps, that his flirtation with naturalism owed something to Mencken's influence. The *Smart Set* under Mencken's editorship had been the only magazine receptive to Fitzgerald's naturalistic stories, which may have provided mild encouragement for him to continue writing them. Whatever the cause, Fitzgerald's stories leading up to and away from *The Beautiful and Damned* exhibit the "meaninglessness of life" philosophy, which meant that they wouldn't be published by the *Post*. *The Beautiful and Damned* cluster stories, whose kinship to the novel is primarily of philosophical bias and mood, were either (a) *Smart Set* stories, which appeared in that magazine because they were unsuitable for magazines that paid higher prices or (b) stories written under contract for popular magazines other than the *Post*.

Late *Smart Set*

Two of the three final *Smart Set* stories are artistically brilliant. Few would deny that "May Day" (March 1920; *Smart Set*, July 1920; $200; *TJA*) and "The Diamond as Big as the Ritz" (October 1921; *Smart Set*, June 1922; $300; *TJA*) are among the best stories that Fitzgerald ever wrote. "May Day" is perhaps the single outstanding achievement to come out of Fitzgerald's experimentation with naturalism. Predictably, both stories went to the *Smart Set* by default: the better paying magazines wanted neither of them. And while Fitzgerald contends in "A Table of Contents" to *Tales of the Jazz Age* that "The Diamond as Big as the Ritz" "was designed utterly for my own amusement,"[52] his correspondence with Harold Ober about the story indicates that he hoped and believed that it would also amuse readers of a magazine that paid well: "I am finishing a two part story which should be good for the *Post*."[53] Later in acknowledging the *Post*'s rejection of it, he suggests to Ober that *McCall's*—a magazine that paid well and had a large circulation[54]—might buy it: "As to *The Diamond in the Sky*. I was sorry the Post refused but I can understand. It might interest Burton Rascoe of Mccaulls or Harry Sell. . . ." And only "as a last recourse Nathan of *Smart Set* would take it for a novelette. . . ." After at least two rejections, Harry Sell "[could not] get through Scott Fitzgerald's 'The Diamond in the Sky'"[55]—therefore it wound up with the *Smart Set*. The route by which "May Day" travelled on its way to the *Smart Set* is not known, but Fitzgerald, no doubt, also tried to market it elsewhere first.

These two stories were suitable to the *Smart Set* for reasons that are perhaps clearer now than they were to Fitzgerald at the time. The *Smart Set*'s preferences, based on its publication of the four previously discussed Fitzgerald stories, combine to make a formula. Those ingredients already established—cynicism, urbane humor, social criticism, determinism—help set the boundaries of the *Smart Set* formula. In short, those subjects generally tabooed by the middle class constituted suitable material for *Smart Set* fiction. The formula, therefore, was restrictive primarily in the limitations that it imposed on subject matter. It was much less restrictive in prescribing the length of a given story: Fitzgerald needed only to call a long story a novelette and have the typist designate simple section breaks as chapter breaks before submitting it to the *Smart Set*.[56] And moreover, *Smart Set* could take a heavily plotted story ("Dalyrimple Goes Wrong") as well as one with very little action ("Babes in the Woods").

Given the *Smart Set*'s preference for particular subjects and given the absence of length restrictions, both "May Day" and "The Diamond as Big as the Ritz" were, if unintentionally, made to order for that magazine. *Smart Set* billed "May Day" as "A Complete Novelette By F. Scott Fitzgerald (Author of 'This Side of Paradise')."[57]   "The Diamond as Big as the Ritz" was featured on the cover of the magazine as "A Complete Novelette by the Author of 'The Beautiful and Damned'";[58] preceding the text, Fitzgerald is cited as "Author of 'This Side of Paradise,' 'The Beautiful and Damned,' etc."[59]   But the early *Smart Set* stories had many of the ingredients of "May Day" and "The Diamond as Big as the Ritz"; and these two grew logically out of the early stories, in many ways products of *Smart Set* audience taste.

In "May Day" Gordon Sterrett, a once promising artist whose luck and money have run out, tries to borrow money from his old Yale classmate Philip Cory[60] so that he can pay a girl who is blackmailing him. The money would free him to renew his courtship with his old girlfriend Edith Braden, a respectable socialite. Cory will not lend him the money he needs, however, and Sterrett wakes up one morning after a drunken night married to Gloria Hudson, the blackmailer. The story ends with Sterrett's buying a gun and ammunition, presumably so that he can shoot himself.[61]

Though there is comic relief in the subplot of the Mr. In and Mr. Out episode, the story is primarily cynical and pessimistic.   Edith Bradin's socialist brother, Henry, an editor of the *New York Trumpet*, is cynical about the American system; Gordon Sterrett is cynical about life.   Fitzgerald himself appears cynical here about traditionally hallowed illusions such as the legendary loyalty of an old college roommate: Philip Cory is anything but loyal to Sterrett.   Even the college games like the "Mr. In and Mr. Out" game are presented, not as humorous diversions, but rather as pathetic remnants of an awkward adolescence.   And in the mob scene the characters become "simple apes"—a naturalistic tinge reminiscent of "Dalyrimple Goes Wrong." The elements conspire to produce a somber tone much akin to that of *The Beautiful and Damned*. But such cynicism was not out of place in the *Smart Set* as it would have been in *The Post*, nor was it unprecedented in Fitzgerald's early stories which appeared in the *Smart Set*.

Another familiar ingredient of "May Day" is the heroine Edith, a debutante with many qualities in common with Lois of "Benediction." Edith is attractive, bored, and very temporarily in love with Gordon. Like Lois, she has a brother with enough moral consciousness for both of them. Fitzgerald pictures Edith's attachment to Gordon in the first part of the story as selfish and hopelessly unrealistic, but it is as genuine a bond as she is capable of forming. Edith brings glamour to the story, as her type does to many stories that follow "May Day," but significantly here she functions artistically as a force to make Gordon's suicide credible. Edith, unlike the early *Post* flappers such as Ardita Farnham, is more than an ornament to set off another's sparkle. She is one of Fitzgerald's flappers who does not work chiefly in this entertaining capacity.

For all of its ties to the early *Smart Set* stories, many elements in "May Day" also demonstrate the influence of popular readers' tastes, an indication that Fitzgerald was beginning to reconcile the extremes in his fiction. The main story line of "May Day," the Gordon Sterrett story, is heavily plotted and, in some respects, points ahead to the *Post* stories that surround *Tender Is the Night*: Dick Ragland in "A New Leaf" (*Post*, 4 July 1931) leads an alcoholic life and commits suicide, which closely allies him to Sterrett. In addition, Fitzgerald's elaborate treatment of the college amusements—the Mr. In and Mr. Out game, the drunken party at the Biltmore—had entertained popular audiences and would entertain them for years to come: for example, "The Camel's Back" (*Post*, 24 April 1920) and "Rags Martin-Jones and the Pr-nce of W-les" (*McCall's*, July 1924).

"Tarquin of Cheapside" (February 1917; *Smart Set*, February 1921; $50), which first appeared in the *Nassau Literary Magazine* as "Tarquin of Cheepside" and was then published in *Smart Set* a month after "May Day," bears little resemblance to any of Fitzgerald's other stories; *Smart Set* readers would, no doubt, have been puzzled that the author of "May Day" was also the writer of "Tarquin of Cheapside." The only characteristic of the story which made it saleable even to the *Smart Set* was its "cleverness" or "cuteness." In the story, "Soft Shoes" is chased through the streets of London, intrudes upon Wexel, a scholar in the midst of reading *The Faery Queen*, and finally persuades Wexel to allow him to hide in his attic. After Soft Shoes's pursuers have come and gone he descends from the attic, writes "The Rape of Lucrece," and vanishes just as the reader realizes that he is Shakespeare. The story is one of the weakest and most atypical in the Fitzgerald canon as the summary suggests. The story indicates both the wide variety and uneven quality of stories that were acceptable to the *Smart Set*.

In "The Diamond as Big as the Ritz," written during the serialization of *The Beautiful and Damned*, Fitzgerald is still toying with the question of audience. He had hopes that a popular magazine would buy it[62] but it was not a slick story, despite its entertaining and ingenious plot line. In the story John T. Unger from the small

Mississippi town of Hades accepts an invitation from his St. Midas School friend, Percy Washington, to go home with him during a vacation. When they arrive Unger discovers that Percy Washington's claim that his family owns a diamond as big as the Ritz-Carlton Hotel is true. If the world found out about their diamond mountain, the bottom would fall out of the diamond market because there would inevitably be a fear that the market could be flooded at any time with Washington diamonds. Unger, with his knowledge of the diamond, is held hostage by the family. He finally escapes when the mountain is discovered by airplane pilots; and as they begin to converge on the diamond, Braddock Washington, Percy's father, blows up the entire mountain along with himself, his wife, and son. Two daughters, Jasmine and Kismine, escape with Unger and will presumably go with him to Hades—which he tells them not to confuse with the old place that was abolished long ago.

In offering the story to the big magazines Fitzgerald was attempting to sell a powerful indictment against materialism by disguising it as fantasy.[63] Braddock Washington's bribe to God is a corruption of the sacred American values of wealth and beauty embodied in the diamond. The things which anticipate this bribe—the atrocities carried out in the name of protecting the diamond; the dehumanization of Kismine, Jasmine, and Percy by the Washington wealth—simply prepare the reader for Braddock's final sellout to Baal.

An interesting feature of the story, though, in terms of its low market value, is that the story contains in large doses those ingredients which *Post* editors would become anxious to buy in smaller parcels: the vivid representation of the rich, as Fitzgerald records the lushness of Washington's El Dorado; the beautiful, callous rich girl portrayed in Kismine; and the didactic statement that those guilty of wrongdoing must be punished. Here Fitzgerald demonstrates that the American Dream come true leads to blasphemy, an unappealing conclusion for many *Post* readers who preferred to believe that an alliance between materialism and twentieth-century Puritanism was good. Although *Post* readers would consider Washington's death necessary as punishment for his immorality, at the same time they would, deep down, admire his gigantically protective gesture toward the free enterprise system. Fitzgerald, however, was clearly naive in believing that the story might be bought by a popular magazine.

In the process of publishing *Post* rejects during the time that Fitzgerald was learning exactly how to compose a *Post* story, the *Smart Set* served important functions in his development as a professional writer. The *Smart Set* offered a last resort for Fitzgerald, particularly during the time of the composition of *The Beautiful and Damned*: at no time while he was learning to make a living from his writing did he need worry that he could not publish his work somewhere. In serving this function for Fitzgerald, the *Smart Set* played the same role in his career that the little expatriate magazines played in Hemingway's early career.

Contract Stories: Naturalism in the Slicks

The second group of stories which reflect the mood and philosophy of *The Beautiful and Damned* grew out of a contract that Fitzgerald signed on 27 May 1920 with *Metropolitan*, a magazine which was in constant financial difficulty and went into receivership before Fitzgerald's contract was fulfilled. By the terms of the contract, *Metropolitan* would have first refusal on the next six stories he wrote. For each of them the magazine would pay $900. If *Metropolitan* refused six stories, however, Fitzgerald would have the right to sell three stories to the *Post*, after which *Metropolitan* would again have an option on Fitzgerald's next six stories. Under this contract Fitzgerald submitted five stories, one of which was refused, before the magazine went into receivership. Submitted and accepted were "The Jelly Bean," "His Russet Witch," "Two for a Cent," and "Winter Dreams." Rejected was "The Curious Case of Benjamin Button."

Though there is no correspondence to indicate why Fitzgerald signed the contract with *Metropolitan*, the obvious answer is that it provided money and a steady market for his stories. The *Metropolitan* contract itself and the stories Fitzgerald submitted under this contract pose several questions. If he was determined to make a fortune with the help of Lorimer, why did he commit a year's work to another magazine, especially after the *Post* had bought six of his stories in less than a year before he made the arrangement with *Metropolitan*? No answers to this question can be positively documented because there is no correspondence to indicate the circumstances surrounding the contract. Several reasons, however, suggest themselves. The first one is money. In order to obtain Fitzgerald's work *Metropolitan* was willing to outbid the *Post*: the most the *Post* had been willing to pay him was $500 per story; *Metropolitan* offered and paid $900 for each of the stories it published. From the contract, then, Fitzgerald earned a raise of $400 per story. Perhaps, too, he was attempting to show the *Post* editors that his work was in demand and thus succeed in gaining an increase from that magazine. The next story bought by the *Post*, the two-part story "The Popular Girl," brought $1,500—representing an increase of $250 per segment over his last single *Post* story. Fitzgerald, then, used the *Metropolitan* contract to jockey for a higher position with the *Post* and in the meantime guaranteed himself a set sum to live on during the composition of *The Beautiful and Damned*.

The nature of the stories submitted under the *Metropolitan* contract suggests another reason that Fitzgerald may have been open to an arrangement with that magazine. It allowed him a good deal of leeway in terms of the length and subject matter of his stories, leeway that made *Metropolitan* a good workshop for *The Beautiful and Damned*. The lengths of the *Metropolitan* stories ranged from 3,700 words ("Two for a Cent") to 10,000 words ("His Russet Witch"); and the dramatic frameworks ranged from near-fantasies ("His Russet Witch") to realistic stories ("The Jelly-Bean") and, finally, to sad, romantic stories about lost youth ("Winter Dreams").

There is much to suggest, in fact, that the *Metropolitan* contract represented a rebellion against the restrictions that the *Post* placed on Fitzgerald: it had published, with one exception, flapper stories. The exception was "The Ice Palace," and the *Post* had delayed its publication by several months. In view of the *Post*'s delay, it is understandable why Fitzgerald submitted "The Jelly-Bean," the second story in the Tarleton trilogy,[64] to *Metropolitan* under the new contract.

The *Metropolitan* stories are, in general, somber stories, much like *The Beautiful and Damned* in mood. And unlike the *Post* stories, they have unhappy endings. "The Jelly-Bean" (May 1920; *Metropolitan*, October 1920; $900; *TJA*) is characteristic, in many ways, of these stories. Jim Powell, by nature a loafer, resolves temporarily to make something out of his life after he has become infatuated with flapper Nancy Lamar. But in a drunken moment she runs away with her fiancé, whom she does not love, thus causing Jim to feel "right sick" and return to his idle life.

It is true that Nancy is a *Post*-type flapper in the line of Betty Medill, and it is also true that the local color is reminiscent of the *Post*'s "The Ice Palace"; it is, after all, part of the same Tarleton package.[65] In "The Jelly-Bean," however, Fitzgerald does not focus the narrative on the girl in order to entertain his audience. Rather, she becomes a vehicle through which he expresses the unpleasantness that can result from irresponsibility, a theme which links the story with *The Beautiful and Damned*. In "The Ice Palace" romance and realism conspire to produce what is essentially a happy ending: the South is the only place where Sally Carrol could have finally been happy, just as Harry Bellamy could only have been content in the North. Fitzgerald's realistic portrayal of both regions in "The Ice Palace" functions as a foreshadowing device that makes the outcome credible and, if not totally happy, at least acceptable to popular as well as critical audiences. In "The Jelly-Bean" the realistic portrayal of the region and its colorful and typical idler provides the basis for a sadder commentary on human nature. At the end, Nancy is unhappily situated in a marriage she would not have chosen sober, and Jim is denied the opportunity to step out of his stereotyped and unproductive role as a loafer. But even sadder, Jim is unable to see that Nancy would not have been worth the effort.

With "The Jelly-Bean" Fitzgerald did not discover a new creative vein—the story is too closely akin in outlook to "Benediction" and "May Day." But with the publication of the story in *Metropolitan* Fitzgerald managed for the first time to place one of his "unpleasant" tales in a popular magazine, and though *Metropolitan* had clearly expected *Post* stories from him, its editors immediately recognized that they were displaying a new kind of Fitzgerald ware to popular readers as the headnote to "The Jelly-Bean" indicates:

> A year or two ago Scott Fitzgerald was a student at Princeton, apparently unknown and unknowing. Today he is welcomed as the most promising comer among fiction writers in this country. Readers of his first novel, "The Other Side of Paradise," have gleaned the impression of a youth who was able, with the greatest charm and expressiveness, to tell about himself, and still more about the young American flapper. Here is a new story which shows another side of Fitzgerald's realistic gift.[66]

This was not true, of course, if *Metropolitan* readers had been familiar with the *Smart Set*. But few *Metropolitan* readers would have known this side of Fitzgerald.

Fitzgerald took this editorial stance as a cue to fulfill his contract by submitting additional cynical, clever, *Smart Set*-type stories. The occasion for the sadness in each story is lost youth. Merlin Granger in "His Russet Witch" (November 1920; *Metropolitan*, February 1921; $900; *TJA*) becomes a pathetic old man who is all the more miserable at age sixty-five when he tries to understand exactly what Alicia Dare, his temptation personified, has actually stood for in his allegorical life. "Understanding," he says, "is allowed to us old people—after nothing much matters."[67] Anthony Patch, who has prematurely become old by the end of *The Beautiful and Damned*, could say the same thing. And in "Two for a Cent" (September 1921; *Metropolitan*, April 1922; $900) both Hemmick and Abercrombie, in spite of the fact that one is poor and the other rich due to an ironic twist of fate, are left sitting together on a porch in their old hometown musing nostalgically on their lost youth.[68]

The *Metropolitan* contract gave Fitzgerald latitude to experiment with his "realistic gift" and paid him well as he did it. However, when he carried the experimentation with the lost youth idea into the realm of the fantastic, *Metropolitan* rejected the story—"The Curious Case of Benjamin Button" (February 1922, *Collier's*, 27 May 1922, $1,000), which was then published by *Collier's*, a general-interest weekly with approximately 2,500,000 readers.[69] This fantasy carried Benjamin Button from age sixty backward in life to the crib. Fitzgerald remarks that one reader was prompted after reading the story to write: ". . . of all the pieces of cheese I have ever seen you are the biggest piece."[70] What actually had happened to Fitzgerald was that he was testing the limits of the popular reading public to see how far he could go without offending them. The test resulted in one of the bleakest periods in Fitzgerald's story writing career. It began with the *Metropolitan* contract, continued with "The Lees of Happiness" (July 1920; *Chicago Sunday Tribune*, 12 December 1920; $750; *TJA*)[71]—the tale of Jeffrey Curtain's decline from popular writer to vegetable—and ended with *Collier's* publication of "The Curious Case of Benjamin Button."

The things Fitzgerald gained from this bleak period were these: he made $5,350 for the seven stories in a three-year period, much of which helped carry him through *The Beautiful and Damned*; he broadened his popular reading public and, in addition, demonstrated to them that he could write about things other than the American flapper; he tested the popular audiences with realism ("The Jelly-Bean") and with fantasy ("His Russet Witch"); and finally, he found two new themes with which most of these stories are concerned—lost youth and crushed ideals.

It is difficult to account for the bleak period in Fitzgerald's career which finally culminated in *The Beautiful and Damned* except to say that he was testing in it the limits of a formula for human behavior which reduced man to a stimulus-response mechanism and which pictured him as a pawn of forces and circumstances over which he had very little control, the aging process being the most pernicious one. *The Beautiful and Damned* is Fitzgerald's last major test in his fiction of that theory, a theory that he finally could not accept. On the one hand, Fitzgerald posits the theory that life is meaningless; and yet Anthony's life is given meaning by his quest for money, not to mention that his hedonistic philosophy can be practiced only when there is enough money. Certainly Gloria, who is sane and happy at the novel's end, does not seem much impressed by life's meaninglessness; and the reader is left with the feeling that Anthony, when the advantages that his inheritance can offer him are evident, will recover from his flight into insanity. The effect of the ending is to leave the reader with the impression that Fitzgerald had not thought the theme carefully through—or that he had not taken the ideas in the novel seriously. On a deeper level, it indicates that Fitzgerald's attempt to embrace the naturalistic philosophy that had worked its way through the stories into *The Beautiful and Damned* had died a natural death before the novel was completed.

Tales of the Jazz Age

During the seven months of the serialization of *The Beautiful and Damned* in *Metropolitan* (September 1921-March 1922), Fitzgerald had written four stories: "The Popular Girl," "Two for a Cent," "The Curious Case of Benjamin Button," and "The Diamond as Big as the Ritz." In the six months separating the book publication of the novel from the publication of his second short story volume, *Tales of the Jazz Age* (22 September 1922), he wrote only one story, "Winter Dreams," which he later called an early version of *The Great Gatsby*. This novel, then, was already beginning to take shape in Fitzgerald's mind by the time *Tales of the Jazz Age* appeared. The stories in the collection either look backward to light subjects characteristic of Fitzgerald's 1920 *Post* stories or they mirror the disenchantment which marks his short stories between "May Day" and "The Diamond as Big as the Ritz."

A majority of the contemporary reviewers of *Tales of the Jazz Age* reacted favorably to the book. Twenty-one of the thirty-seven reviews located by Bryer are favorable, six are mixed, and ten are unfavorable.[72] Fitzgerald's descriptive "Table of Contents" for the collection was universally liked by those who reviewed the book favorably, and many of these reviewers were impressed by the humor in the stories. Robert Garland, who characterized Fitzgerald as "profoundly foolish, ironically wise," went on to observe with reference to the humor in the collection, that "The world of the short story has turned out to be young Fitzgerald's literary safety valve."[73] The mixed reviews, like those of *Flappers and Philosophers*, criticized the unevenness of the volume, pointing, as expected, to the flapper stories like "The Camel's Back," on one extreme, and "May Day" on the other. Several reviewers were very much aware of the fact that Fitzgerald had already received high prices for many of the stories in the collection, one observing that he was making "financial hay while the popular sun is shining."[74] Those critics who particularly disliked the volume—the reviewer for the *Minneapolis Journal*, for example—complained generally about Jazz Age morals reflected in the book, noting that "If one could hold a burning match to the mouths of most of Mr. Fitzgerald's characters, they would burn with a pale blue flame."[75] Stephen Vincent Benét predicted accurately what the net effect of *Tales of the Jazz Age* and its critical reception would be on Fitzgerald's reputation: "It shows neither that Fitzgerald is a flash in the pan nor that he is a constellation."[76]

In one sense, then, *Tales of the Jazz Age* provided a good indicator for bookbuyers of the direction that Fitzgerald's career as short story writer was taking: his stories after the publication of *Flappers and Philosophers* were becoming increasingly serious, as stories like "May Day" show and as several reviewers noted.   In another sense, the collection proved a bit misleading to bookbuyers who had not closely followed Fitzgerald's magazine career from 1920 to 1922. The balance of serious and light stories in *Tales of the Jazz Age* suggests a similar balance in his magazine work; there was not.   Five of the six light stories in *Tales of the Jazz Age* were written before 1921.   In choosing such stories as "The Camel's Back" for inclusion in the collection, Fitzgerald minimized his experiments with naturalism and, in effect, prolonged his reputation as the flapper's historian.

A Workshop for *The Great Gatsby*

Critics have marvelled that the author of *This Side of Paradise* and *The Beautiful and Damned* could, in less than three years after the publication of the latter, produce a novel of the stature of *The Great Gatsby*. As should be clear by now, Fitzgerald's novels do not so much represent isolated bursts of creative energy as they are tangible endpoints for themes, characters, and ideas that have been developing in magazine stories which anticipate the novels.

A constant is Fitzgerald's prose genius, evident as early as the "ebony perspiration" passage in "The Trail of the Duke" and apparent even in the weakest commercial stories.   Also constant are the subjects that Fitzgerald knew well and stayed with from the early stages of his apprentice fiction: wealth, youth, and beauty.   What did change between the creation of *This Side of Paradise* and *The Great Gatsby* was Fitzgerald's perspective on his material and his ability to objectify his attitudes toward it.   In 1925 Fitzgerald was more than five years removed from his relationship with Ginevra King, a time lapse which gave him the distance to be Nick Carraway, the novel's "objective" narrator. Yet he was also near enough in memory that he could recall, even relive, the seductiveness of her world; that is, he was still able to be the romantic hero, Jay Gatsby.   In effect, he had reached the pivotal point in his life that allowed him to see clearly through the eyes of both Gatsby and Nick.

The steps by which he developed the technical skill to present authentically both points of view can be followed through the magazine fiction that appeared between the publication of *Tales of the Jazz Age* (22 September 1922) and *The Great Gatsby* (10 April 1925). Specifically, Fitzgerald used three different markets that he had carefully cultivated during the first two years of his career. One of these was the "contract" market, which he had learned to use during the composition of *The Beautiful and Damned* to experiment, having some assurance that *Metropolitan* would buy the stories, with themes he was shaping for the novel. In the two years leading up to *The Great Gatsby* he negotiated a similar contract with Hearst's *Cosmopolitan*,[77] and he used the stories written under this contract to develop a perspective on, among other things, the wealthy insider/poor outsider theme around which the Daisy-Gatsby relationship in the novel revolves. Another market became the *Post*, to which Fitzgerald had contributed only one story ("The Popular Girl") since May 1920. The *Post* was well-suited to serve as an outlet for Fitzgerald's "studies" on the American Dream, which is the backbone not only of Gatsby's vision but of Mr. Gatz's and Wilson's as well. Fitzgerald published four success stories treating this subject, sometimes bittersweetly, in the *Post* in 1924. Another market for the *Gatsby* workshop stories was *American Mercury*, essentially a glossier *Smart Set*, which was by then defunct. *American Mercury* and *Metropolitan* published the two most important Gatsby cluster stories, "Absolution" and "Winter Dreams." Those looking for a magical change that accounts for the artistic leap between *The Beautiful and Damned* and *The Great Gatsby* will find the closest thing there is to it in the stories written for these three markets.

Contract Stories in *Hearst's International*

The second magazine to publish Fitzgerald's fiction under contract was *Hearst's International*, one of the numerous magazines owned by William Randolph Hearst. In 1911, Hearst had bought the magazine, then ten years old and called *World Today*. After purchasing it, Hearst was told by advisers that unless the editorial policies were changed the magazine could never reach more than 200,000 readers. And so, in order to appeal to a larger number of people, *Hearst's International* became a monthly packed with fiction, the quality of which was viewed generally as inferior to that of other slick magazines. In 1925 *Hearst's*

International was absorbed by its sister publication, Hearst's *Cosmopolitan.*[78]

The Fitzgerald stories that appeared in *Hearst's International* were written under the terms of a contract made with *Cosmopolitan*, signed on 26 December 1922. The arrangements were these: *Cosmopolitan* paid Fitzgerald $1,500 for an option on his story output during 1923; and according to the agreement they were to buy at least six stories at $1,875 per story. The following four stories were published by *Hearst's*: "Dice, Brassknuckles & Guitar," "Hot & Cold Blood," "Diamond Dick and the First Law of Woman," and "The Baby Party." Two stories "'The Sensible Thing,'" and "Rags Martin-Jones and the Pr-nce of W-les" were accepted by *Hearst's* under the contract but were returned in exchange for "Diamond Dick and the First Law of Woman" and "The Baby Party." An additional two stories, "Our Own Movie Queen" (chiefly Zelda Fitzgerald's work),[79] and "One of My Oldest Friends" were submitted and rejected.

In this group of stories written under contract, Fitzgerald began an about face from the "atypical" Fitzgerald stories of *Metropolitan*, *Collier's*, and the *Chicago Sunday Tribune*. Much of the interest of the stories written specifically with *Hearst's* in mind—and this includes one reject accepted by *Liberty* and another published by *McCall's*—arises from the fact that Fitzgerald began a return to the popular material that had proved successful in earlier *Post* stories. But he does so with a significant alteration: the stories are more realistic; his heroines, with few exceptions, are less glossy, and his men occupy the center stage.

"Dice, Brassknuckles & Guitar" (January 1923; *Hearst's*, May 1923; $1,500) illustrates what this new brand of story was like. This Tarleton, Georgia-related story provides a convenient gauge, not necessarily of Fitzgerald's maturation as an artist, but certainly of his growing mastery of the art of pleasing the reader. The Tarleton stories serve, in fact, as a miniature chronicle of his development of a keen sense of audience: "The Ice Palace" (*Post*, 22 May 1920), though finally published by the *Post*, was delayed perhaps because of its sophistication; "The Jelly-Bean" (*Metropolitan*, October 1920) was too realistic and contained too little sentimental relief to ever satisfy the readers of the highest paying slick magazines, though it had been acceptable to *Metropolitan* as displaying a new side of Fitzgerald; but "Dice, Brassknuckles & Guitar" distills the most popular ingredients of both of the other Tarleton stories.

Hearst's editors captioned the story "A *Typical* Fitzgerald *Story*"[80] and further commented about it: "*F. Scott Fitzgerald Holds the Mirror up to Youth.*"[81] If readers did not know some of Fitzgerald's darker

Smart Set and *Metropolitan* stories—"May Day" or "His Russet Witch," for example—the captions would ring true to the story. And in fact, the story represents, on Fitzgerald's part, a swing back to his earlier *Post* material: youth and wealth. Amanthis is, in many ways, a typical *Post* flapper: she is eighteen, a debutante, and pretty. But she is very warm toward Jim Powell, who could never have become a part of her way of life, though he succeeds in winning her admiration just as Jim Powell of "The Jelly-Bean" wins Nancy's. And in addition to the flapper, Fitzgerald also draws on the glamourous wealthy of Southampton and places Jim, a boy from Tarleton, Georgia, and his Negro body servant Hugo against the backdrop of the socially elite. Also, just as he had done in "The Offshore Pirate," Fitzgerald pays homage to the hard-work, success ethic that, to a degree, Toby Moreland had subscribed to. Jim establishes a school to instruct budding socialites in the use of "brass knuckles, debutante-size,"[82] and their fashionable men in the art of throwing dice and playing the guitar; and one of the reasons that he works so hard in the school is to win for Amanthis the opportunity to mix with the wealthy—a birthright Jim is unaware she already possesses. The story then has the blue-chip *Post* ingredients, and in that sense it is "a typical Fitzgerald story."

It also has extras that mark the distance Fitzgerald had come as a professional writer in the two-year period that separates this story from its merely amusing *Post* counterparts. Beneath the entertaining fireworks there is a serious message. Jim heads back to Georgia and, in effect, rejects the elite in whose circle he had tried to make a place for himself and Amanthis. If his departure in a dilapidated jalopy is humble, it provides, nonetheless, a powerful indictment of the rich. And, of course, this allies the story closely with *The Great Gatsby*. Also important to this study is the fact that Fitzgerald has learned to use his most serious material as a core over which to sprinkle glitter. "The Diamond as Big as the Ritz" comes closest, in terms of submerging a serious subject in froth, to doing what "Dice, Brassknuckles & Guitar" does for the first time in a popular magazine: its glossy surface effectively camouflages the core of the story. Casual readers need only read it as one in which "Fitzgerald Holds the Mirror up to Youth." It stands up well as a very entertaining story, in many ways at once a *Smart Set* story and a *Post* story.

The two other *Hearst's* stories do not demonstrate this quality as well. "Hot & Cold Blood" (April 1923; *Hearst's*, August 1923; $1,500; *ASYM*), "Fitzgerald's Story of a Good Fellow,"[83] stands as a serious story in which Fitzgerald deals, in a fashion, with the concept of emotional bankruptcy. "You're—eternally—being used! I thought I married a man—not a professional Samaritan who's going to fetch and carry for the whole world!" Jacqueline Coatesworth tells her husband.[84] But, unlike Dick Diver in *Tender Is the Night*, Coatesworth has a very successful marriage, not in spite of, but because he was a "hell of a nice fellow"[85]—a superficial covering over on Fitzgerald's part of one of his most complex subjects.

"Diamond Dick and the First Law of Woman" (December 1923; *Hearst's*, April 1924; $1,500) is strictly entertaining. It includes the gimmick of an amnesiac who comes to his senses to find that he has, in fact, been married all along to the infinitely desirable Diana Dickey (Diamond Dick), a wife who has waited patiently for his full recovery.

"'The Sensible Thing'" (November 1923; *Liberty*, 5 July 1924; $1,750; *ASYM*), one of the stories written for *Hearst's* under contract but finally rejected by the magazine, suggests however that Fitzgerald was attempting within the framework of his *Hearst's* contract to blend the popular and the serious as he had done in "Dice, Brassknuckles & Guitar." *Liberty*, one of the three major general interest weekly magazines—the other two were the *Post* and *Collier's*[86]—headnoted "'The Sensible Thing'": "YOUTH, its bitter and its sweet, its tragic partings and its glad reunions, its passions and its calculation—all these are in this warm, colorful, wholly human short story."[87]   The headnote capitalizes on Fitzgerald's reputation as an authority on youth.   The story is one of young love: George Rollins[88] is as much in love with Jonquil Cary as Fitzgerald was with Zelda Sayre. It is, in addition, a success story: Rollins succeeds financially on a larger scale than even Rip Jones ("The Third Casket," *Post*, 31 May 1924). And at the end Rollins and Jonquil Cary can enjoy their love with "all the time in the world" before them.[89]

The story, though, for all of its slickness and all of the entertainment its love-success plot provides, is serious. Discouraged from marrying Jonquil because, according to her, he hasn't enough money, Rollins leaves her at the peak of their love (a clear link with *The Great Gatsby*) and after succeeding in the business world returns to find that he has succeeded in buying the rest of her life with his new-made money; but he has in the process forfeited the most beautiful time of their lives: "April is over, April is over. There are all kinds of love in the world, but never the same love twice."[90]   To *Liberty*'s readers this may have provided the emotion which made the story acceptable; but the story is not merely a sentimental story about young love.   It documents a realistic exchange of values: George Rollins gives up seventeen months of his life to purchase the right to enjoy his love for Jonquil in "all the time in the world." In the process he has lost, in fact, an irrecoverable period in his relationship with Jonquil.

The first two *Hearst's* contract stories, though one was rejected, show Fitzgerald as a professional working to satisfy, at once, his needs as an artist and his requirements as a breadwinner. In some ways "Dice, Brassknuckles & Guitar" and "'The Sensible Thing'" show him at the most ambitious peak in his career as a writer of magazine fiction: he tried to have it both ways. And for a time he did: he earned a total of $3,200 for these two works; with "'The Sensible Thing'" he added to the canon one of his best stories.

In "Rags Martin-Jones and the Pr-nce of W-les" (December 1923; *McCall's*, July 1924; $1,750; *ASYM*), contracted by *Hearst's* but rejected and bought by *McCall's*, he falls back on the sure thing—a flapper story. It concerns John Chestnut, who rigs a plot to ensnare wealthy Rags Martin-Jones by staging a meeting for Rags with a Prince of Wales impersonator. Thanks to his new money and ingenuity, Chestnut succeeds in winning her and they presumably live happily ever after. Of their love, Rags says: "Wrap it up; Mr. Merchant. . . . It looks like a bargain to me."[91] This story is one in which Fitzgerald imitates the ingredients of "The Offshore Pirate"—a flapper, a lover's willingness to go to wild extremes for her, and the wealth they both have—to entertain in his earlier manner. And it succeeds as an amusing, "typical Fitzgerald story." *McCall's*, a woman's magazine with a rising circulation of two million in 1927[92] which had featured such female writers as Willa Cather and Edith Wharton,[93] described "Rags Martin-Jones and the Pr-nce of W-les" thus: "The writer who discovered the Flapper tells how one of them acts when she meets a real prince—in this, one of the best love stories of the day."[94]

Post Success Stories

As Fitzgerald moved toward completion of *The Great Gatsby*, he returned to the *Post*, which had helped launch his reputation in 1920 as the flapper's historian. Instead of returning with variations on the subject of the flapper, however, he became a resident authority on the American Dream, publishing in the *Post* in 1924 four stories about success and American business. Clearly he was authenticating in these success stories the perspective that would inform not only Gatsby's point of view in the novel, but also that of the other characters, like Mr. Gatz and Wilson, who subscribe to the Dream. The stories themselves are less significant than the insight they provide into Fitzgerald's increasing awareness of the workshop potential of the *Post*, which would become his main outlet for fiction during the composition of *Tender Is the Night.*

The first *Post* success story, "Gretchen's Forty Winks" (January 1924; *Post*, 15 March 1924; $1,200; *ASYM*), pictures Roger Halsey's competitive drive to succeed, illustrated by his willingness to sacrifice forty days and forty nights to his work, as quite admirable. For it, he gains success, wealth, good health, and the admiration of his wife Gretchen. In "The Third Casket" (March 1924; *Post*, 31 May 1924; $1,750) a successful sixty-year-old businessman, Cyrus Girard, offers his business to the one young man who can tell him how to best spend his time after he has given away his business. When Rip Jones, who even has the "wrong name," finally suggests that Girard will never be happy unless he continues to work, Rip is made a partner in the business. And as an extra bonus he also wins the boss's daughter. This story is a successful fantasy in that it manages to appeal to the dreams of every young businessman who would like to inherit a lucrative business, and also to every older businessman who, like Girard, would prefer to feel at sixty that "I got twenty good years in front of me."[95]

"The Unspeakable Egg" (April 1924; *Post*, 12 July 1924; $1750) begins with a newspaper announcement of the engagement of Van Tyne and Fifi, a couple whose success seems assured by their secure place among the social elite. In a variation of the hard-work, success ethic, the story shows that even the wealthy must use ingenuity and imagination to retain their happiness within the social order. Van Tyne, whose family founded the Society for the Preservation of Large Fortunes, must demonstrate to Fifi, a member of that society, that he is exciting and imaginative enough to marry her. To do this he masquerades as a social misfit—an unspeakable egg—and gains the admiration of Fifi, who had broken their engagement because she thought he was too dull. By shocking her family with what appears to be anti-social behavior, he becomes acceptable to her; and both seem sufficiently imaginative to enter into a successful marriage.

In "John Jackson's Arcady" (April 1924; *Post*, 26 July 1924; $1,750) Fitzgerald presents a sentimental view of a businessman who has begun to feel that his productive years are over. Younger than Girard, John Jackson looks back longingly at his youth and even tries to regain the affection of his boyhood sweetheart; but he grows cynical because he cannot go back to the past. The cynicism, however, is short-lived when Jackson overhears numerous testimonials in his behalf; it appears that his life has had a positive influence on everyone with whom he has come into contact. At the end, "he could stand anything now forever."[96]

There is a progression in the success stories from the energetic success drive of Roger Halsey, to the application of the hard work ethic by both the young Rip Jones and the older Cyrus Girard, to the final temporary disenchantment with this ethic in John Jackson. Whereas the early Fitzgerald stories entertained a wide variety of readers with frivolities, gimmicks, trick endings, and glossy flappers, the group of success stories is aimed at a narrow audience of those who enjoy reading about American businessmen. To entertain this audience, Fitzgerald fulfilled their wishes, anticipated their fears and dispelled them, and always confirmed the deeply-rooted belief that hard work is a panacea.

"Winter Dreams" and "Absolution": Preliminary Sketches for *The Great Gatsby*

One of the most accurate gauges of Fitzgerald's learning to use the magazines as workshops for his novels is found in the two stories that are most closely associated with *The Great Gatsby*. Whereas he had used his stories almost haphazardly in the creation of his first two novels—lifting stories from the *Nassau Literary Magazine* and incorporating them whole into *This Side of Paradise*, and later testing moods of despair that he would carry to a low point in *The Beautiful and Damned*—he began consciously to see the workshop potential of the short stories and apply it to his novel writing with "Winter Dreams" and then in a more specialized way with "Absolution."

In a letter to Maxwell Perkins, Fitzgerald describes "Winter Dreams" (September 1922; *Metropolitan*, December 1922; $900; *ASYM*) as "A sort of 1st draft of the Gatsby idea."[97] Indeed, the parallels between Dexter Green and Jay Gatsby are striking.[98] Dexter falls in love with wealthy Judy Jones and devotes his life to making the money that will allow him to enter her social circle. His idealization of her is closely akin to Gatsby's feeling for Daisy Buchanan. Gatsby's idealized conception of Daisy is the motivating force that underlies his compulsion to become successful, just as Dexter's conception of Judy Jones drives him to amass a fortune by the time he is twenty-five. The theme of commitment to an idealized dream that is at the core of "Winter Dreams" and *The Great Gatsby* and the similarities between the two men point up the close relationship between the story and the novel.

But important differences in Fitzgerald's methods of constructing short stories and novels also emerge from these closely related works. Much of the effectiveness of *The Great Gatsby* lies in the mystery of

Gatsby's background. No such mystery surrounds the early life of Dexter Green. "Winter Dreams" opens with a description of Dexter as a caddy at the Lake Erminie Golf Club. In addition, we are told that his father "owned the second best grocery store in Dillard" and could not afford to send Dexter to a good Eastern school.[99] Judy Jones's father, on the other hand, was a wealthy summer resident, and Dexter often caddied for him. When Dexter meets Judy his position is one of subservience, and from their initial encounter he is motivated to overcome his inferior position. Fitzgerald's documentation of Dexter's quest for financial success is thorough. At twenty-three Dexter borrows $1,000 "on his college degree and his steady eye"[100] and by the age of twenty-seven he owns the largest chain of laundries in his section of the country. Fitzgerald presents Judy as a stereotype of the very rich: callous and spoiled by wealth. Dexter's attachment to her—despite his protestations to the contrary—seems mainly a craving for the social class to which Judy belongs. Daisy, by contrast, is more believable than Judy. The fragments of her past with Gatsby, such as the bathtub letter scene and the details provided by Jordan, make her more than simply an emblem of upper class life.

Another contrast between *Gatsby* and "Winter Dreams" is that in "Winter Dreams" Dexter's disillusionment occurs quite suddenly. When he learns that Judy is no longer pretty, his dream is immediately shattered: "The dream was gone. Something had taken it from him . . . the moonlit veranda, and gingham on the golf links and the dry sun and the gold color of her neck's soft down. . . . Why these things were no longer in the world!"[101] Because his enchantment could be shattered so quickly, Dexter's commitment to Judy seems of less magnitude than Gatsby's commitment to Daisy. Gatsby's disenchantment could only occur gradually. When he is finally able to see Daisy, "the colossal significance of [the green] light . . . vanished forever."[102] But "his count of enchanted objects" had only diminished by one. Even toward the end of the novel there is no way of knowing that Gatsby was completely disenchanted with Daisy. Nick's statement that "perhaps he no longer cared"[103] leaves open possibilities of interpretation that are closed at the end of "Winter Dreams." While Dexter can cry at the loss of a dream, Gatsby dies, and the reader is left to imagine which fragments of his dreams about Daisy survive.

The expansiveness of the novel allowed Fitzgerald to make Gatsby and his dream believable while he could maintain the mystery of Gatsby's past and the origins of his dream. Fitzgerald could not do this as well with Dexter in "Winter Dreams." As the first major story which is closely associated with a novel, "Winter Dreams" served the important function of showing Fitzgerald that he could work in the popular magazines with segments of the material he was shaping for his novels.

The relationship between "Absolution" (June 1923; *American Mercury*, June 1924; *ASYM*) and *The Great Gatsby* is more complex. In a letter to Perkins, Fitzgerald refers to "Absolution": "I've had to discard a lot of *The Great Gatsby*—in one case 18,000 words (part of which will appear in the Mercury as a short story)."[104] And further, in a letter to John Jamieson, Fitzgerald relates that "It might interest you to know that a story of mine, called 'Absolution,' in my book *All the Sad Young Men* was intended to be a picture of [Gatsby's] early life but that I cut it because I preferred to preserve the sense of mystery."[105]

Critics have used these few bits of information as a springboard into elaborate comparisons of "Absolution" and *The Great Gatsby*.[106] Bruccoli notes that "There has been reckless speculation" about the relationship of the story to the novel,[107] concluding that the story was probably a prologue to a lost early draft of the novel.[108] Fitzgerald had spent little time working on *Gatsby* during 1922 and 1923, while he and Zelda lived in Great Neck. Much of his energy had gone into work on his play *The Vegetable* which failed in November 1923. During the winter of 1923-24 he had written short stories to finance a summer of uninterrupted work on the novel. When he returned in April 1924 to what he refers to as the novel "with a Catholic element," he probably is referring to an early draft of *The Great Gatsby*, the draft of which "Absolution" was a "prologue."[109]

The information that "Absolution" offers about Gatsby's background is significant, it appears, in establishing the image that Fitzgerald had at a very early stage of his conception of him, and comparison should be made with this in mind. Rudolph Miller comes from a small Midwestern town, grows up in a strict Catholic home, and ultimately rejects the rigid value system of the Catholic Church. Miller frees himself at the age of eleven from a conflict that had always paralyzed his father. The older Miller's "two bonds with the colorful life were his faith in the Holy Roman Catholic Church and his mystical worship of the Empire builder, James J. Hill."[110] It is not surprising that he was a man incapable of making decisions, because the bonds directly conflicted with each other. The story reveals that "he had never in his life felt the balance of any single thing in his hands," because "for twenty years he had lived alone with Hill's name and God."[111] Young Miller rejects this sort of dual allegiance by first creating an imaginary person who is free to dream because he is immune to the rules of the Catholic Church. And his final rejection of the value system follows an encounter with a priest who is also trapped by a need to dream and the impossibility of doing so as a representative of the Church. To the degree that Gatsby's background is Rudolph Miller's, it is characterized by a shattering of the illusions that he had about the Church. He ultimately realizes that "There was something ineffably gorgeous somewhere that had nothing to do with God."[112] In rejecting the Church, Rudolph Miller frees himself to dream the American dream of success. His dream could certainly be extended to Gatsby's worship of Daisy Buchanan: one of the "gorgeous" things that "had nothing to do with God."

Read in association with *The Great Gatsby*, "Absolution" adds to the novel by showing that at least in an early working out of Gatsby's character, his behavior was the result of a revolt against traditional standards. But even if the story were, in fact, a prologue to the final version of the novel, its inclusion would have weakened the novel. The facts of Gatsby's past, had they been known to readers of the novel, would have diminished his stature as a tragic figure, and the suspense that Fitzgerald creates by gradually revealing bits of information about him would have been undercut by the information in "Absolution."

Considered as a separate work of art, "Absolution" skillfully defines the conflict of a young boy who is resisting his natural impulses because he has been taught that they are evil.[113] His father has told him that if he does not adhere to the discipline imposed by the Church "the next thing you'll begin to lie and steal, and the *next* thing is the *reform* school!"[114] On a deeper level the story is a struggle of man against the opposing forces of traditionalism and a faith in the American dream of success; the former is represented by the Church and the latter by James J. Hill. Rudolph Miller's father is paralyzed by the tension these forces create. But the tension is resolved at the end of "Absolution" by Rudolph's decision to reject the pull of traditionalism in favor of a search for the fulfillment of a dream.

"Absolution" clearly functioned in a unique way in the composition of the novel. It provides information about the book as Fitzgerald visualized it in an early draft, and since the early drafts do not survive, this information is available from no other source. Fitzgerald's publication of the story illustrates his ability to salvage what might have been a "discard" of some of his best writing, and its exclusion from the novel shows him to be a selective craftsman. Unlike most other stories in the canon, "Absolution" was not composed as a business venture. There is no evidence to suggest that Fitzgerald offered it to anyone but the *American Mercury* (though he may have offered it to the *Post* as he later did in the *American Mercury* story "Crazy Sunday"), and he did not enter the price he received for it in his ledger.

The success of *The Great Gatsby* depends on Fitzgerald's ability to transfer to the reader the same kind of vision that he himself had: the ability to believe simultaneously in the possibilities of several opposing ideas at various levels of abstraction. On the most concrete level, the reader must believe that Gatsby will and will not win Daisy, a symbol of the American ideal. On a more general level, he must believe that anyone in America, through hard work and perseverance, can and cannot gain access to the best America has to offer. Until Daisy's final rejection of Gatsby in chapter eight of the novel, the reader can, indeed, believe in both alternatives because he has seen them both from the perspective of Gatsby, who believes, and from the point of view of Nick, who wants to believe but intellectually cannot.

To see how Fitzgerald developed the technical skill necessary to present credibly both alternatives, it is helpful to isolate two qualities of his talent and retrace their development through various "types" of his magazine stories. The first of these qualities can be characterized by the phrase "surface realism." Even in Fitzgerald's earliest apprentice fiction he demonstrated a close attention to detail which enabled him to create, with words, realistic portraits. But as Edmund Wilson observed, Fitzgerald "plays the language entirely by ear,"[115] which added a sensory dimension to his descriptions and accounted, in part, for the "something extra" he gave popular magazine readers, as is illustrated by this description of the Moonlight Quill bookshop in "His Russet Witch": "Merlin Granger stood up and surveyed the wreck of the bookshop, the ruined volumes, the torn silk remnants of the once beautiful crimson lamp, the crystalline sprinkling of broken glass which lay in iridescent dust over the whole interior. . . ."[116] Early, Fitzgerald learned to catch the glitter and sparkle of the exotic subjects that he had chosen for his material and easily satisfied the popular magazine audience's craving for concrete detail while, in the process, giving them more than they paid for with displays of verbal fireworks. Fitzgerald's popular stories, which Mencken called "confections," remind one of the dazzling bazaar scene that John M. Chestnut creates for Rags Martin-Jones, in which he constructs just for her amusement a roof-garden cabaret called the "Hole in the Sky," augmented with bands playing from adjacent rooftops. After the scene is over and Rags learns that it was staged simply for her pleasure, she asks, "Was the whole thing just *mine*. . . . Was it a perfectly useless, gorgeous thing, just for me?"[117] One feels that Fitzgerald's early popular magazine stories, like Chestnut's creation and like Toby Moreland's hijacking scheme, have been performed for the sheer delight of the performance. And there is always about them a touch of genius. These were the "confections" to which Fitzgerald treated his early popular audiences. This side of Fitzgerald's gift is evident in magazines like the *Post*, particularly in 1919 and 1920.

Different from his talents as a surface realist, who involves the reader in many dimensions of experience at the sensory level, are Fitzgerald's abilities as a symbolist—as one who abstracts an idea from its concrete context. Perhaps the earliest demonstration of this quality is "The Spire and the Gargoyle," which Fitzgerald considered his first "mature" work. In this story, both spire and gargoyle work on a more abstract than literal level. Other heavily symbolic stories are "The Cut-Glass Bowl" and "The Four Fists," stories which are didactic and suffer from their preaching tone. The subordination of the literal story line to the symbolic content dictated that they go to magazines such as the *Smart Set* or *Scribner's*. An exception is the fantasy "The Diamond as Big as the Ritz," which is an expression of the symbolist quality of Fitzgerald's talent and one of his best stories.

In following Fitzgerald's magazine stories from 1921 to *The Great Gatsby*, one discovers pockets of stories in which Fitzgerald begins to achieve balance between realism and symbolism. These stories, though not always Fitzgerald's best stories, are nevertheless the most important in the development of the mature style of *The Great Gatsby*, "Babylon Revisited," and *Tender Is the Night*, which succeed on many levels. These stories were written under contract, which meant that Fitzgerald knew the popular audience for which he was writing and, at the same time, felt enough security from the contract to write as his artistic conscience dictated.

By the end of the 1919-1925 period Fitzgerald had become a successful popular magazine writer; in the nine years that followed, he published fifty stories in the *Saturday Evening Post*, the most popular magazine in America. In terms of his career as a professional writer, this meant several things: he had learned to read the pulse of the largest magazine-reading audience in the nation and by economic necessity had geared his short story output to their specifications; he had established a group of followers from this audience to which he would always feel a moral obligation; and he had faced the economic reality that in order to earn a regular income writing for the slick magazines one needed, at least verbally, to espouse the American Dream. The mere stimulus of having to perform regularly, if not against one's will, then partly against one's convictions, could certainly have posed questions early in Fitzgerald's career, the answers to which he argues, most notably, in *The Great Gatsby*.

Fitzgerald wrote Ober that "My novels are not like my stories at all."[118] They are, however, interdependent: when a writer is able to convince three million Americans that success is directly proportional to hard work and dedication, as Fitzgerald does, for example, in "Gretchen's Forty Winks," and then to show America as a wasteland where labor, love, and ingenuity result in disillusion and death (*The Great Gatsby*), and go from there to write fifty-four more stories for the three-million-reader *Post* audience, he has become a skillfully selective craftsman. In Fitzgerald's case his craftmanship for popular magazines gave him the financial stability that enabled him to demonstrate he was also a serious novelist—the most important function of these magazines in the early period of his career.

4

The *Saturday Evening Post* Period
(1925-1933)

During the second phase of Fitzgerald's career (1925-1933), he published a total of fifty-eight stories in six different magazines. Forty-seven of these appeared in the *Saturday Evening Post*, one in *Hearst's International*, four in *Woman's Home Companion*, four in *Red Book*, one in *Century*, and one in *American Mercury*. Three of these magazines—*Woman's Home Companion*, *Red Book*, and *Century*—were new markets. In this period, rather than spreading his stories through several of the large, mass-circulation magazines, he concentrated on the *Post*. Fitzgerald's earnings from stories in these years was $163,601, nearly four times greater than his income from three novels ($46,896). The figures suggest how popular Fitzgerald was during this central period of his life; in addition, they indicate how little, comparatively speaking, bookbuyers were willing to spend on his novels. The makeup of his audience during these nine years of the composition of *Tender Is the Night* is easier to define. Therefore, the direction that his short-story writing took is more easily explainable, and the patterns are more predictable than in the first six years of his professional career. An overview of these years suggests the following patterns: immediately following *The Great Gatsby*, Fitzgerald did not return to the light, frothy stories of college men, college games, and debutantes on which he had founded his popular reputation ("The Camel's Back," for instance); nor did he turn out success stories like "Gretchen's Forty Winks" or "John Jackson's Arcady," stories which made the *Post* regard him as "their kind of writer"; and he did not, with the exception of "The Rich Boy," concern himself solely with the customs and frivolities of the wealthy as he had in such stories as "The Offshore Pirate," "The Unspeakable Egg," or "Rags Martin-Jones and the Pr-nce of W-les." He did not pigeonhole himself as the chronicler of any single segment of society; instead, his stories, in this period particularly, cut sharply across the social scale marked at one end by Charles David Stuart ("The Pusher-in-the-Face"), night cashier at Cushmael's Delicatessen, and at the other by Anson Hunter ("The Rich Boy"). As John O'Hara remarked: "[b]ut Scott wasn't only a man who better than anyone else wrote about the rich. Actually most of his work was about the middle class, your family and mine."[1]   The stories in this period show Fitzgerald working within every social class except the lower class, exercising in the *Post* and other magazines a latitude to experiment outside the narrow framework of youth, wealth, and success. He had gained this latitude, in part, through the *Metropolitan* and *Hearst's* contracts: his stories written under these contracts had proven to the *Post* that he was capable of writing popular short fiction on a variety of topics, serious as well as light.

Fitzgerald found that his stories were in demand during the 1919-1924 period.   However, instead of writing what he knew from experience would sell for a guaranteed income, he took advantage of the popularity he had gained through the *Post* and wrote serious stories for other magazines that allowed him to specify the kind that he wrote. By 1925 he was in the position of controlling the market rather than being controlled by it.   This climate of freedom fostered not only the serious non-*Post* stories like the "The Rich Boy," but also the serious *Post* stories such as "One Trip Abroad" and "Babylon Revisited." The ways in which he chose to use this freedom determined, to a large extent, the subjects and themes of his short fiction between 1925 and 1934. Generally, the stories pointed in one of four general directions: (a) back to the subject of disillusionment in marriage reminiscent of *The Beautiful and Damned*, but also suggestive of *Tender Is the Night* (e.g., "The Adjuster"); (b) backward to the theme of lost youth and subsequent disillusionment characteristic of *The Great Gatsby* (e.g., "The Love Boat"); (c) forward to the theme of emotional bankruptcy which characterizes Dick Diver in *Tender Is the Night* (e.g., "One Trip Abroad"); or finally, (d) back to the subject of adolescence dealt with in *This Side of Paradise* (e.g., The Basil Duke Lee and Josephine Perry stories).   Moreover, within these subjects Fitzgerald began experimenting with locale: he began writing stories set on foreign soil ("A Penny Spent"), in Riviera waters ("Love in the Night"), as well as on American soil ("Jacob's Ladder," "Crazy Sunday").

In this second period Fitzgerald ceased to be a specialist on topical subjects, as he had been a specialist on the subject of the flapper, for example, and he became a social commentator on those subjects, American and foreign, that he chose to explore, thus trying out his *Tender Is the Night* material before he finally put it into book form. And most of this experimentation was done in the *Post*, the magazine of which Fitzgerald became a virtual employee during the composition of *Tender Is the Night*. In addition, during the 1930-1931 period the economic role that the *Post* played assumes major importance beyond its workshop function: as Fitzgerald needed more money to pay Zelda's hospital bills, the *Post* became a dependable source, and Fitzgerald increased his output to meet their needs.

A Profitable Interlude: February 1925-May 1927

During the year of the publication of *The Great Gatsby* and in the year that followed, three of the eleven published Fitzgerald stories appeared in the *Woman's Home Companion*; three in *Red Book*; one in *Hearst's International*; and the remaining four in the *Post*. *Hearst's* story, "The Baby Party," was written under the terms of the contract discussed in the previous chapter and was thus directed to a specific buyer. The *Woman's Home Companion* and *Red Book* stories, on the other hand, served approximately the same purpose for Fitzgerald in 1925 and 1926 that the *Smart Set* had served in 1920, the year of *This Side of Paradise*'s first publication: they accepted stories that Fitzgerald could sell to no one else, either because they were too weak or because the material was too gloomy for the *Post*. *Woman's Home Companion* served the first of these functions while *Red Book* served the latter. Like the 1920 *Smart Set* stories, the *Woman's Home Companion* and *Red Book* stories range in quality from the very weak ("The Pusher-in-the-Face," *Woman's Home Companion*, February 1925) to one of his best ("The Rich Boy," *Red Book*, January and February 1926). The *Woman's Home Companion* stories are examples of the kinds of stories that were simply not good enough for the *Post*—a feature of which Fitzgerald was often very much aware.

Between February 1925 and May 1927, *Woman's Home Companion* published four Fitzgerald stories: "The Pusher-in-the-Face," "One of My Oldest Friends," "Not in the Guidebook," and "Your Way and Mine." This magazine like its chief competitor, the *Ladies' Home Journal*, was conceived "as a service magazine for women."[2] Edited by Gertrude Battles Lane from 1911 through 1940, the magazine's circulation during this period rose from over 700,000 to 3,500,000. When Fitzgerald's work first began appearing in the magazine, each of the monthly issues contained, in addition to its usual eight short stories, regular sections such as "Gardening," "Home Furnishing," "Handicraft and Embroidery," and "Fashions"—features primarily directed to and written by women. There is no evidence, however, to suggest that any of the stories that Fitzgerald contributed to the *Woman's Home Companion* were written with that magazine—or, in fact, with any woman's magazine—in mind. On the contrary, "One of My Oldest Friends" had been written for and accepted first by *Hearst's* under contract and had been returned in exchange for another Fitzgerald story.[3] Although Fitzgerald stipulated to Ober that the revised version of this particular story not be offered to the *Post*,[4] it is logical to assume that the other three *Woman's Home Companion* stories—"The Pusher-in-the-Face," "Not in the Guidebook," and "Your Way and Mine" (May 1927)—were written for any large magazine, including the *Post*, which was willing to buy them. Fitzgerald did not sit down to write with the idea of turning out "women's stories."

The *Woman's Home Companion* stories are bound together by the fact that they are all escape stories and all but the first story deals with disillusionment in marriage. In the first story, "The Pusher-in-the-Face" (March 1924; *Woman's Home Companion*, February 1925; $1,750), Charles David Stuart, the "small, somewhat shriveled, somewhat wrinkled" hero has none of the glamour that would qualify him for the role of rescuing knight; but he does have qualities to which many wives could have easily and quickly related. During a matinee performance, this ordinarily meek man pushes a garrulous, middle-aged woman in the face; his only provocation was that she continued to talk through the performance, thus distracting him. Fitzgerald uses the incident to catch the attention of his readers, who may at first have disapproved of Stuart's action, though he becomes a sympathetic character as the story progresses. The woman Stuart has pushed charges him with assault, but after the particulars of the case are aired, Stuart is released by the judge, who declares his "assault justified." The hero, at that point, returns to his job as night cashier at Cushmael's restaurant and shoves in the face a customer who makes a pass at one of the waitresses with whom Stuart has been secretly in love for years. When it turns out that the customer he has pushed in the face is a criminal wanted by the police, Stuart becomes the delicatessen hero and wins the favor of his waitress-girlfriend.

In the *Woman's Home Companion* stories which follow, the escape routes are more realistic; and, in addition, Fitzgerald addresses himself directly to the problem of unhappiness in marriage—a topic with which he carefully worked in such *Tender Is the Night* cluster stories as "The Rough Crossing" and finally in the novel itself. "One of My Oldest Friends" (March 1924; *Woman's Home Companion*, September 1925, $1,750), the *Hearst's* reject, suggests that marriages and friendships will be threatened when a third party like Charley Hart ceases to be satisfied with his role of friend and tries to become the lover of his "oldest friend's" wife. Marion was loyal to Michael in the face of Charley's passes; and Charley loses face when he is forced to ask Michael for a loan, the sum of which Michael could spare but which he refuses to loan Charley until he is able to make the grandstand play of literally saving Charley's life while handing him the sum that he had requested. Unfortunately, nothing helps to bring back the sparkle to Michael and Marion's marriage, a relationship doomed merely to endure in stagnation.

In "One of My Oldest Friends" Fitzgerald suggests for the first time in a slick magazine that, even with loyal partners, marriages can be happy only in a qualified sense. He wrote Ober about this story, "I don't know what to think of it but I'd rather *not* offer it to the *Post*."[5] Whether the *Post* would have accepted it is questionable; the story offers a glum view of marriage. It also has other features that the *Post* would have considered unsuitable—for example, the cryptic ending at which point the reader cannot know if there has been, in fact, a supernatural experience. But whether the *Post* would have bought it or not is less important than the groundwork that its publication in *Woman's Home Companion* laid for the *Post*'s policy of accepting Fitzgerald's bittersweet stories on the not-so-blissful state of marriage: "The Love Boat" and "Magnetism" are two *Post* stories in which Fitzgerald treats this subject.

In "Not in the Guidebook" (February 1925; *Woman's Home Companion*, November 1925; $1,750), Fitzgerald offers divorce as an alternative to Milly Cooley's lamentable situation. Milly, the pretty, young wife of an American war hero, is deserted in France by her shiftless husband who has used Milly's small inheritance to buy them a boat ticket overseas. After being attacked by two Frenchmen who apparently planned to rob her, Milly is rescued by Bill Driscoll, an American tourguide who recognizes that Milly is American by her "Brooklyn moan." After saving her, Driscoll takes her along with him on his directed tours of places "not in the guidebook," and he gradually falls in love with her. When Milly's missing husband Jim, who had been jailed for drunkenness and disorderliness after he abandoned Milly, finally shows up, Driscoll has little trouble convincing her that Jim did not, in fact, distinguish himself in the war. The reader must assume that Milly divorces Jim, because she and Driscoll marry the following spring. Whereas in "One of My Oldest Friends" Fitzgerald had described a marriage threatened by a hint of potential infidelity and only partly salvaged, he pictured in "Not in the Guidebook" a marriage torn apart by one partner's desertion.

In the final story of this group, "Your Way and Mine" (February 1926; *Woman's Home Companion*, May 1927; $1,750), Fitzgerald elaborates on another kind of pressure that can threaten marriage: the pressure that a wife can bring to bear on a husband by spending more money than he can make. Stella McComas is advised by her husband's partner that to make her husband work harder, she might try spending money more extravagantly. "You might," the partner tells her, "give him a few more bills to pay. Sometimes I think an extravagant wife's the best inspiration a man can have."[6] Stella then goes immediately to a real estate agent and signs the contract for a sixty-thousand dollar home on Long Island. Her husband Henry does begin to work harder, but he has an emotional breakdown working in the city while his wife and daughter Honoria are enjoying the summer home. This story, however, provides more than a comment on marriage. Henry gets well, resets his own pace for working, and succeeds in amassing a large fortune. He is thus able to moralize that an individual—not his wife or business partner—should determine the best way of doing things for himself. And there is a difference, Henry says, "between your way and mine." To view the *Woman's Home Companion* stories as a group is to isolate and thus define some of the qualities that distinguish Fitzgerald's bad commercial fiction from his good. Each of the stories has some redeeming quality which makes it saleable in a high-priced market, but the strong points are often undercut by weaknesses, as the plot summaries suggest. For example, the coincidence of Michael's ("One of My Oldest Friends") actually singling out the one telephone pole by which Charley is standing and the last minute rescue before the train passes obscure whatever serious message Fitzgerald might have succeeded in conveying. And the same is true of "Not in the Guidebook." Who, after all, could believe that of all the soldiers in the American army, Milly would be rescued by the only one who could prove positively that her husband was a fraud and a liar?

In these *Woman's Home Companion* stories, however, Fitzgerald was treating the subjects of infidelity and disillusionment in marriage—by exploring the causes and discussing the symptoms—and he was drawing similar conclusions to the ones he would present in *Tender Is the Night*: the suggestion that an "old friend" could cause a marriage to deteriorate (Charley Hart-Tommy Barban); and the idea expressed in "Not in the Guidebook" that divorce is sometimes the only solution (Dick-Nicole). While the *Woman's Home Companion* stories, then, do not attest to a lack of seriousness on Fitzgerald's part, they do catch him in the process of trying to tailor a new, serious subject to the specifications of slick magazine readers—these stories in particular representing the earliest and, perhaps, crudest attempts. Fitzgerald's status as a beginner in the profession in 1920 made it necessary that he almost give away his weak stories then; his name alone in 1925 made it possible for him to earn high prices—the *Woman's Home Companion* stories each brought $1,750—for stories just as weak as many of the *Smart Set* stories had been and also nearly as poor as many of the $250 *Esquire* stories of the late 1930's. In many ways the *Woman's Home Companion* stories are potboilers in the truest sense of the word: he wanted stories like "Not in the Guidebook" seen by as few people as possible, but as he told Ober, "I know its saleable and I need the money."[7]

Of the same quality as the *Woman's Home Companion* stories is "The Baby Party" (February 1924; *Hearst's*, February 1925; $1,500; *ASYM*), written in "a single all-night session."[8] For this story Fitzgerald draws on the lost youth material that is characteristic of the early *Metropolitan* stories such as "His Russet Witch" (February 1921), "Two for a Cent" (April 1922), and "Winter Dreams" (December 1922), but with a difference. In "The Baby Party" Fitzgerald focuses the narrative on a middle-class social situation involving a man, his wife, and their baby. On the occasion of a neighbor's birthday party there is a squabble over babies, and husband-father John Andros fist-fights to protect his daughter against the insults she has received from the neighbors. Unlike Alicia Dare ("His Russet Witch")—the baby's counterpart who faded out along with old Merlin Granger—little Ede offers to Andros a permanent embodiment of his lost youth; and through fighting for her, he feels that he will never lose it: "He had it now. He possessed it forever. . . ."[9]

Hearst's packaging of "The Baby Party" provides an interesting commentary on Fitzgerald's contemporary, popular reputation. The story was billed as "A Fable for Fathers by F. Scott Fitzgerald who is one,"[10] and this is precisely the kind of comment that suggests how difficult it must have been for Fitzgerald's contemporaries to separate the work from the man. When a reader bought a magazine containing a Fitzgerald story, he was also buying whatever legends were, for the moment, associated with Fitzgerald's name. In fact, Fitzgerald invited such comparisons of his work and his life, and most of his best magazine fiction from "'The Sensible Thing'" to the Basil Duke Lee stories is intensely autobiographical. Most readers were conscious of the fact that Fitzgerald's life was closely related to his fiction, and the *Hearst's* headnote simply suggests that magazine editors helped readers make these connections.

While the *Woman's Home Companion* functioned as a marketplace for Fitzgerald's weakest stories that followed *The Great Gatsby*, *Red Book* served as a place in which he could display his more serious and, in the case of "The Dance," his more experimental short fiction. Unlike the *Smart Set*, which had functioned in the same capacity in 1920, *Red Book* paid Fitzgerald well for his contributions.[11] This magazine in the mid-1920's was a monthly devoted primarily to publishing fiction in quantity. The September 1925 table of contents suggests the orientation of the magazine: sandwiched between an Art Section at the beginning and a section of four essays on topical subjects at the end were three novel serializations and ten short stories—a good amount of reading for twenty-five cents. The magazine's circulation in the 1920's was under a million and did not reach the million mark until 1937, nine years after it was bought by the McCall organization and converted to a general interest monthly.[12] Its regular cast of writers, among them Booth Tarkington, Rupert Hughes, and Robert Benchley, suggests the popular thrust that the magazine had in the 1920's: it appealed to those readers who liked the *Post*'s fiction but wanted more of it.

Between September 1925 and February 1932, *Red Book* published four Fitzgerald stories: "The Adjuster," "The Rich Boy," "The Dance," and "Six of One—." Fitzgerald, at least early in his relationship with *Red Book* (30 November 1925), felt warmly toward the magazine as one which "seems most hospitable to my serious work."[13] And, in fact, the *Red Book* stories, which pull more strongly on the lost youth subject, show the degree of control Fitzgerald had gained over this subject which, along with emotional bankruptcy, was one of his favorite serious subjects. Thus, in the sense that *Red Book* encouraged Fitzgerald to explore the lost youth theme by accepting his stories on this subject and paying him well for them, his relationship with the magazine resembles the Fitzgerald-*Metropolitan* relationship which extended from October 1921 to December 1922. The *Red Book* relationship, however, was not based on a contract, though the first *Red Book* story was apparently written expressly with that magazine in mind.[14]

In addition, the body of *Red Book* stories, particularly the careful editorial packaging of each, provides as accurate a reflection of Fitzgerald's popular image between *The Great Gatsby* and *Tender Is the Night* as can be found anywhere. The first *Red Book* story, "The Adjuster" (December 1924; *Red Book*, September 1925; $2,000; ASYM), for example, is identified in the table of contents in this way: "The famous author of 'This Side of Paradise' and 'The Great Gatsby' tells the finest story of his career."[15] And the headnote that accompanies the text of the story gives an even more flattering picture of Fitzgerald and the story:

> Following his startling first novel, "This Side of Paradise," Mr. Fitzgerald concerned himself for a few years with short stories of "the younger generation." Critics wondered if his youthful genius would survive. Then, recently was published "The Great Gatsby," one of the most important novels of the current year. Now again, in France, Mr. Fitzgerald is writing short stories, stories that may be defined, really as great. This one, for instance.[16]

This praise is excessive considering the artistic merit of "The Adjuster"; the story is decidedly not great.[17] However, the headnote reveals the change that was taking place at this time in Fitzgerald's public image. Popular audiences remembered him chiefly as the author of his first novel, *This Side of Paradise*, and as the chronicler of youth. The *Red Book* editors suggest in this headnote that this image was changing; the "new" Fitzgerald, the one now being packaged and sold to the public, was the author of an "important novel" (*The Great Gatsby*) and "great" short stories.

However, as late as 1932 *Red Book* was still trying to get mileage out of the old Fitzgerald label: it published "Six of One—," subtitled by the editors as "A story of Youth *by* F. Scott Fitzgerald who wrote 'This Side of Paradise' and 'The Great Gatsby.'"[18] Aside from the fact that "Six of One—" is not primarily a story of youth—its major statement concerns the difference between the rich and the rank and file—it is curious that an important Fitzgerald drawing card remained *This Side of Paradise*, a book separated from "Six of One—" by two other novels and twelve years. The insistence of the magazine editors in his time to keep the old Fitzgerald alive in order to sell magazines indicates the kind of pressures that contemporary audiences placed on Fitzgerald's output; the historian of youth was always in demand—a fact which may make Fitzgerald's later choice of the youthful *Post* subjects, Basil and Josephine, more understandable. In addition, the confusion in the public mind between 1925 and 1934 about the precise nature of Fitzgerald's talent is similar to the state of confusion existing today.

Closely akin to "His Russet Witch," "The Adjuster" is a story of lost youth in which Fitzgerald uses a shadowy figure, Dr. Smith,[19] to personify five crucial years in the life of Luella Hemple. During these five years, 1920-1925, Luella becomes bored with her husband and with the drudgery of being a mother, the husband has a nervous breakdown, and their two-year-old baby dies—events which occur in this order. At the end of the story Dr. Smith convinces Luella that she has been selfish in expecting the world to give her unlimited happiness. But, as she tells Dr. Smith after the death of her child, "I want the light and glitter. That's all there is in life." The omniscient old Smith replies that it is her turn "to be the center, to give others what was given to you for so long."[20] Consequently, she decides to take his advice, thus profiting from the five "lost" years, and becomes a model wife to her recuperating husband.

In this story Fitzgerald has sharpened the focus of the "His Russet Witch" idea; but instead of attempting to cover the whole life of Luella as he had recorded the life of Merlin Granger, Fitzgerald distills his idea—that life does, indeed, fly by—into a five-year period. In addition, he makes it clear almost from the beginning that Dr. Smith stands for quickly passing time, whereas the reader of "His Russet Witch" may never understand for certain what Alicia Dare represents. But the two stories contain the same essential ingredients: a character who has at one time wanted "the light and glitter" and the final acceptance on this character's part of the fact that youth is gone and he or she must make the best of it.

To these ingredients Fitzgerald adds others that he has used before and will frequently use again. The disillusionment-in-marriage theme, for example, makes its second major appearance in this *Red Book* story. There is also in "The Adjuster" a germ of the idea around which Fitzgerald will construct "Your Way and Mine": at one point in "The Adjuster" Dr. Smith warns Luella that her husband's nervous collapse has resulted from his "trying to live your kind of life"[21]—the same cause to which Fitzgerald ascribes McComas's nervous collapse in "Your Way and Mine." In "The Adjuster" Fitzgerald demonstrates his ability to integrate a number of serious topics into the framework of a single short story, a characteristic of his commercial writing that assumes importance in Fitzgerald's creative process, particularly in his use of the big magazines as a workshop, not only for his novels, but also for other stories.

"The Rich Boy" (April-August 1925; *Red Book*, January and February 1926; $3,500; *ASYM*) was featured on the cover of the magazine as "A great story of today's youth. . . ."[22] And in an editorial headnote the story is hailed, reportedly by Fitzgerald, as the best of his short stories to date:

> The author of this story believes it to be the best of the forty-three he has written. It is the first piece of work he has done since the publication of his highly praised novel, "The Great Gatsby," and will appear in book form following publication here.[23]

The story is one of Fitzgerald's most impressive achievements. It also offers an excellent opportunity for examining the integral relationship that exists between Fitzgerald's novels and his commercial short fiction. In "The Rich Boy" Fitzgerald uses many of the subjects—among them, lost youth and disillusionment in marriage—that he has used in previous stories.   In addition, he employs in "The Rich Boy" devices such as the narrator-observer point-of-view that he had successfully used in *The Great Gatsby*; moreover, he pulls from *The Great Gatsby* subjects such as the idealization of a woman who finally loses her place on a pedestal (Daisy-Paula Legendre). And finally in stories like "The Rich Boy," which embody Fitzgerald's attitudes toward a variety of his old, serious subjects, he often blends in new topics that he will later distill and treat singly in another story. The relationship between the novels and the stories, therefore, is triangular: the stories provided a workshop for the novels, which, in turn, served as a store of material that Fitzgerald could draw on for more stories.   And the process repeated itself with the minor variation of Fitzgerald's drawing material for other stories such as "Six of One—" from expansive stories like "The Rich Boy."

A measure of Fitzgerald's growing professionalism is found in his increasing use of the magazines, not just for money to live on while composing his novels, but also for the disciplined practice that these magazines afforded—a mastery of his craft that is evident in "The Rich Boy." The story's major thesis—that the rich "are different from you and me"—is presented explicitly in "The Rich Boy," and it is an idea that Fitzgerald had worked with many times before: few could have read "Winter Dreams" or *The Great Gatsby* without believing that Judy Jones and Daisy Buchanan are, to Fitzgerald, fundamentally different from the Irene Sheerers of this world. Certainly, all of Anson Hunter's ideas are predicated on the belief that he is superior to everyone else. Not only does he have wealth and social position, but he is also sensitive to those personal problems in others that he can help to solve; and he is intelligent, industrious, and well-liked by almost everyone. Thus while one may argue with Fitzgerald's thesis, few could question that his rich boy was different: that he was "cynical where others are trustful" and "soft where others are hard."[24]   To this softness and this cynicism, Fitzgerald gives Anson another quality: remarkable intuition. He knows from "hard intuition" the minute he sees Dolly, "the gypsy of the unattainable," that she was weak, an observation few would have made even after knowing her for a while. Similarly, he knows enough to counsel others in church school and in marriage, but also he knows that he would never marry, because "a happy marriage is a very rare thing."[25] There seems, in fact, to be no end to his insight. However, the narrator suggests at the beginning of the story and at the end that he knows more about Anson and his life than Anson himself does: "If I accept his [point of view] for a moment, I am lost,"[26] the narrator states in the introduction to the story; and at the end, the narrator gleans the insight that Anson was happiest when he was flanked by a woman who affirmed "that superiority that he cherished in his heart."[27] But, in fact, the narrator knows nothing about Anson that he himself did not already know. He was "superior," and he knew it, as the reader must also know after the events of the story are related.

Perhaps his only weakness, the narrator indicates, is that his life will not contain deep personal relationships; instead they will be one-sided monologues in which either Anson advises others about how to run their lives or in which another person tells Anson that he is superior. Thus, the question of whether Anson's life is emptier than Paula's, after her second "happy marriage," involves the reader's value judgement; the narrator implies that, all considered, Anson's life could have been more satisfying if he had married Paula, but he also suggests at the end that Anson would have needed more than Paula could have continued to give. Because Anson does not choose to marry Paula, he may emerge to some as an unsympathetic character. To others, he may seem a victim, one trapped by his superiority with no choice at all. If he had married Paula, she would, after all, have had only one life to sacrifice—that is, only a limited number of her "brightest, freshest, rarest hours to nurse and protect that superiority that he cherished in his heart."[28] Then she would have faded, as she did, and Anson would have needed someone else brighter and fresher. The narrator gives no solutions and the story is left open-ended.

Anson was part of the waste at the top, robbed of the chance to succeed or interact with others in any way that is meaningful and fulfilling to himself.   But through Anson's alienation, Fitzgerald bombards the *Red Book* audience with comments on American life, love, marriage, and lost youth—subjects which both flash back to earlier material and forecast things to come in his short stories and novels. In the main plot—the Anson Hunter and Paula Legendre story—the Anson and Paula love relationship is reminiscent of the Jonquil Cary and George Rollins love story in "'The Sensible Thing'" (*Liberty*, 5 July 1924). Both relationships are genuine, but there is a tragic note in the outcome of each. In addition, in the Dolly Karger subplot there is a story that resembles Dexter Green's affair with Irene Sheerer in "Winter Dreams." Both Dexter and Anson take Irene and Dolly on the rebound—Dexter from Judy, and Anson from Paula—and both Irene and

Dolly lose in their competition with the ideals, Judy and Paula. Also, as mentioned previously, the narrator-observer point of view of "The Rich Boy" links it with an earlier Fitzgerald work, *The Great Gatsby*. And finally, the comments on marriage in "The Rich Boy" remind the reader not only of earlier stories such as "One of My Oldest Friends" (*Woman's Home Companion*, September 1925) and "Not in the Guidebook" (*Woman's Home Companion*, November 1925), but also of later disillusionment-in-marriage stories like "The Rough Crossing" (*Post*, 8 June 1929). Anson counsels couples with minor marital problems such as the one Marion and Michael had in "One of My Oldest Friends," and he also leads his aunt Edna back into the fold when she is attracted to a younger man, Cary Sloane, a situation similar to Adrian Smith's attraction to the younger Betsy D'Amido in "The Rough Crossing." Certainly, the entire "the-rich-are-different" idea works its way into *Tender Is the Night* in Baby Warren's attitude. The validity of "the workshop theory"—that is, the idea that Fitzgerald used the stories both as a place to explore ideas he had worked with earlier and as a more orderly writer's notebook—is clear from "The Rich Boy." Not only are there remnants of earlier stories such as "Winter Dreams" in it, but also there are distinct hangovers such as the narrator-observer from *The Great Gatsby*. And moreover, there are in it foreshadowings of stories and the novel, *Tender Is the Night*, to come.

"The Dance" (January 1926; *Red Book*, June 1926; $2,000) has no such far-reaching applications either to Fitzgerald's other stories or to any of his novels. In a telegram, Fitzgerald rather urgently indicated his feelings about the worth of "The Dance": "DON'T TRY DANCE POST," he telegraphed Ober.[29] In a later letter he told Ober that it was "the first detective story I've ever tried [and] I'm afraid its no good."[30] Apparently *Red Book* had some misgivings about the story's worth. Unlike the other stories, which the *Red Book* editors had lauded for their merits, "The Dance" is only referred to in its headnote as a story of "a different sort": "NO recent volume there is of short stories by an American author has attracted more critical praise than that recently published by F. Scott Fitzgerald,[31] which contains the tales he has latterly written for this magazine. And now he tells another of a different sort—a drama of a country club in a small Southern city."[32] The fact that it is set in "a country-club," an attempt to capitalize on Fitzgerald's notoriety as historian of the wealthy, is of no importance except that the murder weapon in this somewhat brutal tale falls out of a golf bag near the end of the story.

The mystery centers around a murder witnessed by "The Dance's" unnamed female narrator in the small Southern town of Davis. The murder, it turns out, is perpetrated by Catherine Jones, a girl who specialized in dancing the shimmy—"then the scapegrace of jazz."[33] Catherine, during a loud dance band number, shoots a girl who has lured her fiancé into a vacant room and kissed him. And Catherine skillfully diverts the attention of would-be sleuths away from her by having her loyal maid fire a gun blast while Catherine, in full view of everyone, is doing the Charleston, "the dance" alluded to in the story's title. The narrator, however, is not fooled and solves the crime single-handedly, thus freeing the man who has been misapprehended by the police—a man whom she loves and later marries. "The Dance" stands as an example of a plan that barely made it past the drawing board—that is, it was an experiment that was only partially successful. But as such, it shows that Fitzgerald was searching for new material.

In "Six of One—" (July 1931, *Redbook*, February 1932; $3,000)[34] Fitzgerald extends his comment on the corrosive influence of wealth further than he has elsewhere in his short fiction: he suggests that wealth, when it is possessed early, ruins its possessor. The six boys who received wealth after puberty fare well: they become successful, responsible citizens, capable of both giving and receiving. By contrast, five of the six "rich boys," who possessed wealth early, fail. The first "lost interest in things" and his ambition fades; a second elopes with "an Eastern girl" and after a few years of partying every day they are divorced; the third marries a manicurist and sinks into anonymity; a fourth opens a sporting goods store and runs it with moderate success; and the fifth "went to pieces."[35] One of the six matures and becomes the astute businessman who successfully takes over the family business and remains happily married. Through Barnes, Fitzgerald comments on the experiment with a message that he would never have given in the *Post*: "Probably it proved something. . . . Only it was too bad and very American that there was all that waste at the top; and he felt that he would not live long enough to see it end."[36]

The *Red Book* and *Woman's Home Companion* years, February 1925 through May 1927, constitute what may be viewed as a profitable interlude between the publication of *The Great Gatsby* and Fitzgerald's virtual employment by the *Post* beginning in August of 1927 when he wrote serious, though characteristically weak stories. But it also marks a turning point in his magazine fiction following *The Great Gatsby*: after "The Rich Boy" there is little of Fitzgerald the stunt man and entertainer visible in the short stories. The subjects, for the most part, are serious; and characteristically they end bittersweetly. Moreover, after combining many subjects into the framework of "The Rich Boy," Fitzgerald seems to have lost the urge to "put it all into one story";

instead, he became professionally economical, dealing with one subject at a time in those stories which follow. And more often than not, the subjects and ideas dealt with after "The Rich Boy" are rough treatments of similar subjects that will be incorporated into *Tender Is the Night*. The profitable interlude, then, emerges as a recuperative time during which Fitzgerald reoriented himself as to what he had done in his previous commercial fiction; and, more importantly, he began to look toward new material that he could market in order to support himself and his dependents in this period which marks the end of his reign as the flapper's historian.

All the Sad Young Men

Immediately after the appearance of "The Rich Boy" in *Red Book*, Scribners published Fitzgerald's third short story collection, *All the Sad Young Men* (February 1926). *All the Sad Young Men* was unquestionably a critical success. Of the thirty-nine reviews located by Bryer, twenty-three are favorable, nine are mixed, and only seven are unfavorable.[37] Aside from the usual litany of words and phrases like "uneven," "popular magazine fiction," "money-making"—by now stock phrases used by unreceptive reviewers of Fitzgerald's story volumes—what finally surfaces in the reviews of *All the Sad Young Men* is a willingness to consider the artistic merit of Fitzgerald's stories. The most perceptive of the critics, those who analyzed the stories first and generalized later, applied phrases like these to Fitzgerald and the collection: "noble volume"; "Fitzgerald is brilliant!"; "never writes dully"; "a big advance over his previous stories"; "splendid pieces of work." William Rose Benét's "Art's Bread and Butter" from *Saturday Review of Literature* perhaps best stated what many of the reviewers implied: "Well Mr. Fitzgerald had his own day at being the 'boy wonder,' and now, certainly, after 'The Great Gatsby,' he must be judged entirely as a mature artist."[38] After the financial failure of *The Great Gatsby*, Fitzgerald was obviously concerned with assembling in *All the Sad Young Men* a collection that would clear his debt with Scribners; but he also wanted to follow his best book to date with a collection of artistically good stories. The stories which he finally chose for inclusion in *All the Sad Young Men*, then, reflect both of these concerns; and from Perkins's viewpoint it was remarkable "that you have been able to make them so entertaining for the crowd, when they have so much significance."[39] The collection contains nine stories which were taken from the twenty stories that had appeared in magazines between September 1922—the publication date of *Tales of the Jazz Age*—and February 1926.

Four of these—"The Rich Boy," "Winter Dreams," "Absolution," and "'The Sensible Thing'"—rank high in any list of Fitzgerald's best stories. The five remaining stories are uneven in quality and, based on a preliminary table of contents sent to Perkins, Fitzgerald selected them for one of two reasons: he thought they were artistically the best stories available for inclusion, as in the case of "The Baby Party" and "Hot & Cold Blood,"[40] or he felt that they were representative of the kind of story the public had come to associate with his name. Two of the stories—the gimmicky "Rags Martin-Jones and the Pr-nce of W-les"[41] and the success story "Gretchen's Forty Winks"[42]—can be described as "popular." It should be noted, however, that Fitzgerald was quite conscious of the fact that reviewers would be quick to criticize any story in the volume which appeared to be commercial—written expressly for the popular magazines. He included only one *Post* story, for example, because "people were so snooty about [them]."[43] And it was, perhaps, a similar consideration which led him to omit "Dice, Brassknuckles & Guitar," a story which he had planned initially to include;[44] in spite of its basic seriousness, the story relies on the improbability that such a school as Jim's could exist, and moreover, that Amanthis, as Jim first sees her, would happen to be in such good standing with the Southampton elite. In consciously omitting stories that might be considered slick, then, Fitzgerald anticipated some of the criticism that he knew reviewers would have directed toward the book; and this, no doubt, accounts partially for its critical success. But the primary reason that the book was received well is that it contained some of Fitzgerald's best writing about lost youth and disillusionment. In this sense, the collection accurately represents the work Fitzgerald had been doing in commercial magazines since the publication of *Tales of the Jazz Age*: he had been writing stories about serious subjects and publishing them in a wide variety of popular magazines. The nine stories in *All the Sad Young Men* had appeared in seven different magazines—an accurate gauge of this variety. In the eight years following the publication of *All the Sad Young Men* Fitzgerald continued to write more good, serious stories about lost youth and disillusionment, most of which clustered around *Tender Is the Night* and appeared almost exclusively in the *Saturday Evening Post*.

Post Stories: 14 March 1925 - 4 November 1933

The forty-seven stories which were published in the *Saturday Evening Post* in the 1925-1933 phase of Fitzgerald's career comprise a second stage in his relationship with that magazine—a stage marked by his virtual employment by the *Post*. Whereas in the 1919-1924 years the *Post* published only eleven of the thirty-two stories—slightly more than thirty-four percent—to appear in that period, the percentage was much higher in the 1925-1934 period: the *Post* published forty-seven of the fifty-eight Fitzgerald stories—over eighty percent—that appeared in the nine years following the publication of *The Great Gatsby*. Of Fitzgerald's association with the *Post* in 1932 and in those six preceding years, Ober stated, "virtually all of Mr. Fitzgerald's work has been done for and at the request of the *Saturday Evening Post*."[45] For his work Fitzgerald was paid sums ranging from $1,750 to $4,000 per story. A major function of the *Post*, therefore, during the composition of *Tender Is the Night* was that it served as a predictable and profitable outlet for Fitzgerald's stories and thus added a measure of financial stability to Fitzgerald's life in a time during which the Fitzgeralds were travelling back and forth between America and Europe and during which Zelda suffered two breakdowns—years characterized by anything but stability.

A second function served by the *Post* in the 1925-1933 period was that of providing a writer's workshop for *Tender Is the Night*. But, as suggested earlier, Fitzgerald gained the *Post* as a workshop for *Tender Is the Night* by no accident. He had demonstrated in other magazines that he could be something more than an historian of youth and the wealthy—a position he had occupied during his early *Post* years. In the second *Post* stage he enjoyed a much greater latitude to experiment. And within the framework of this new freedom he began to work with subjects, settings, and characters that he would incorporate into *Tender Is the Night*. Therefore, this second stage in the symbiotic Fitzgerald-*Post* relationship provides an excellent opportunity for examining the ways that Fitzgerald found of resolving the dichotomy between being both a professional writer and a literary artist—that is, how he succeeded in maintaining a popular following during the composition of his what is arguably his best, if most "unpopular" novel.

The forty-seven *Post* stories of the 1925-1933 period fall into three distinct groups or categories: (1) the *Tender Is the Night* cluster stories, which because of characters, settings, and subjects are clearly associated with that novel; (2) the Basil Duke Lee and Josephine Perry stories, in which Fitzgerald again taps the vein of his early youth material but now from the skillfully controlled viewpoint of one who is less blinded than the author of *This Side of Paradise* by the glamour of his subject and thus more sensitive to the humor and pathos of adolescence; and (3) the Early Material stories, which because of their treatment of previously explored subjects are more closely akin to early stories than to the material that Fitzgerald would incorporate into *Tender Is the Night*.

Tender Is the Night Cluster Stories

The largest and in many ways the most important group of Fitzgerald's *Post* stories is the *Tender Is the Night* cluster group. During the long nine-year composition period of this novel Fitzgerald used the pages of the *Post* as a laboratory in which to test various ingredients that he would include in the novel. For that reason many of the stories which lie between *The Great Gatsby* and 1934 bear the distinctive stamp of *Tender Is the Night*. In order that the major similarities between each story and the novel can be shown, the cluster stories have been divided by subjects into the following groups:[46] (a) the European setting stories, which resemble the novel primarily because of their locale; (b) the character study stories, in which Fitzgerald works with the development of characters and relationships—primarily the Dick-Nicole-Rosemary triangle—that will finally appear in *Tender Is the Night*; (c) the general cluster stories, each of which has some noteworthy ingredient which links it to the novel and which is not covered in the previous groups.

European Setting

An important question that one might ask in reading through *Tender Is the Night* cluster stories is how they managed to get into the *Post*. This question is particularly appropriate regarding the group of stories with European settings and characters which "will appear shady, to say the least, to American readers" in Thomas B. Costain's words.[47] There are five of these stories whose major link to the novel lies in their common settings: "Love in the Night," "A Penny Spent," "Majesty," "The Bridal Party," and "The Hotel Child."[48] In the first of these, "Love in the Night" (November 1924; *Post*, 14 March 1925; $1,750), is Fitzgerald's earliest treatment of the Riviera setting which provides the scenic backdrop for most of *Tender Is the Night*. In the story seventeen-year-old Val Rostoff, half American and half Russian, boards the wrong yacht in the dark Cannes harbor and finds the girl he will later marry. Invited to attend a party aboard the *Minnehaha*, Val hires a small boat to take him there so that he can meet his parents at the party. He happens, instead, upon the *Privateer*, a boat which is anchored next to the *Minnehaha*. On board the *Privateer*, Val meets a beautiful seventeen-year-old girl whose sixty-year-old husband has left her alone for the night. Val, who refuses to give his name, and the girl fall immediately in love; the husband returns, however, and Val leaves this girl whom he imagines he will never see again. After eight years—a period during which the war is fought, Val loses his money, and the mystery girl's husband dies—Val and the girl are reunited. They marry, go to New York to live, and return once a year on a mid-April night to the dark Cannes harbor where they first met.

Of the European setting stories, this one stands out, in spite of its locale, as being a "typical" *Post* story. It has the standard ingredients of young love, wealth, and adventure that earmarked Fitzgerald's early *Post* stories such as "The Offshore Pirate." And in these elements lies the primary entertainment value of "Love in the Night." But within the framework of this heavily plotted, highly improbable narrative there are ingredients that are not characteristic of Fitzgerald's earlier *Post* fiction. One of the most obvious of these is Val's flirtation with the young girl; she is, after all, married during the blossoming of her love for Val. Never before in Fitzgerald's *Post* stories had such a relationship seemingly been sanctioned, however unrealistic the girl's first marriage may have been. The more significant break with his earlier material, however, lies in Fitzgerald's choice of setting itself. At a time when popular American magazines were leery about publishing the work of expatriates—*Red Book* spoke with disdain about the "so-called European 'taint'"[49]—it is noteworthy that Fitzgerald was able to publish his European stories in the middle American mouthpiece, the *Post*. As a pilot story "Love in the Night" offers suggestions as to how he managed it. The story is primarily a love story—a wish-fulfillment, escape story—and it is an American story; the girl is American, Val is half American, and they choose to settle in America. To *Post* readers it was, no doubt, of minor interest that the story depended for its mood on the Riviera moon, as opposed to the Florida moon of "The Offshore Pirate."

In "Love in the Night," though, the careful description is the "something extra" that Fitzgerald gave popular readers; in terms of the story's workshop value the setting is also of major signficance, as it marks an early stage in the development of the *Tender Is the Night* Riviera setting—specifically that of the T. F. Golding yacht episode, during which Nicole meets Tommy Barban for the first time in five years. At least logistically the *Privateer*'s position corresponds to that of the Golding yacht. Important also to this study is the position of "Love in the Night" as a first: in it Fitzgerald uses one of the slickest plots in his repertoire to counterbalance would-be complaints that his work had a "European taint." And by doing this he made a first step in establishing the *Post* as his workshop for *Tender Is the Night*.

In "A Penny Spent" (July 1925; *Post*, 10 October 1925; $2,000), Fitzgerald carries his readers from France to Italy to America, though not as close to the precise setting of *Tender Is the Night* as he had done in "Love in the Night." In "A Penny Spent" Corcoran, the main character, has both a real knowledge of Europe and a flair for spending money. Since he is out of money when the story begins, he gladly accepts the opportunity to serve as a tourguide for the wife and daughter of Julius Bushmill, a vacationing American millionaire whom he meets in Paris. When the daughter Hallie complains to Corcoran that she is having no fun he begins to stage elaborate parties for her amusement, most of which are as incredible as Toby Moreland's piracy in "The Offshore Pirate" and all of which are enormously expensive for Bushmill. By the time Nosby, Hallie's fiancé, arrives to join her as he had planned, he is too late: Hallie has already fallen in love with Corcoran, who at the end of the story marries Hallie and becomes the leader of Bushmill's purchasing department. And according to Bushmill, at the end of this heavily plotted success story, "the young idiot really has a talent for spending money."[50]

Through Corcoran, who decides to return to America, Fitzgerald manages to make "A Penny Spent" an American story. Indeed, the story revolves around the idea that Bushmill's Ohio-earned money can buy for his daughter the company of European nobility, which with Corcoran's ingenuity it does. Because of her father's hard work and subsequent accumulation of money, she has her choice of both worlds, American and European; and in the bargain she gets Corcoran, who essentially chooses the life of the American businessman over that of the expatriate. The story, therefore, is an affirmation of the American Dream: that money, earned through hard work, will gain for one anything he wants, even the company of European royalty—an idea which reinforced the convictions of the *Post* audience. In the process Fitzgerald established himself as a competent tourguide, one who allowed his readers to enjoy the European countryside and yet made them happy, as were the Bushmills, to return to their homeland.

In "Majesty" (May 1929; *Post*, 13 July 1929; $3,500; *TAR*), Fitzgerald breaks the tradition of "Love in the Night" and "A Penny Spent," the heroes and heroines of which finally opt for the good

American life. "Majesty's" Emily Castleton, "one of America's perfect types" has the opportunity to marry one of the wealthiest, most eligible bachelors in the country, but she chooses instead to marry the prince of a little South European country, Czjeck-Hansa. The story begins after Emily's family moves from Harrisburg to New York, where she attends Miss Thatcher's school, makes her debut, and finally goes on to do "various fashionable things" abroad. At the age of twenty-four, however, she returns to America and becomes engaged to William Brevoort Blair, a wealthy, eligible Newport bachelor. True to her unconventional character, Emily leaves Brevoort standing at the altar and goes immediately back to Europe. But Brevoort, not one to withstand public humiliation for long, that night marries Emily's cousin Olive, who is happy to have him even on a quick rebound. After two years Emily's father calls Olive and Brevoort into the library and asks that they go to Europe to rescue Emily, who is now engaged to a "dissipated ne'er-do-well from nowhere named Petrocobesco."[51] When the two ambassadors arrive in Czjeck-Hansa they find that Emily is, in fact, scheduled to marry Petrocobesco, a man who has just been named king of the little European country which consists of only two towns. Emily rejects all pleas to return to America and settles into her new role as queen of Czjeck-Hansa.

Fitzgerald's substantial break with the tradition of his other European stories comes in a kind of epilogue to the story. On a return visit to England, Olive, Brevoort, and their young daughter watch a procession which consists of Queen Emily and the Queen of England. In response to the child's query as to whether "Aunt Emily" was a princess before she was a queen, Olive replies, "No, dear; she was an American girl and then she got to be a queen."[52] Fitzgerald's comment then follows in a exchange between Brevoort and his daughter. He asks if she had rather marry him—an allusion to his rejection by Emily—or become a queen. "'Marry you,' she said politely, but without conviction."[53] And Olive, too, seems to envy Emily's position as she views Emily "with helpless adoration."[54] Thus Fitzgerald formulates a new version of the American Dream: that a girl whose father has made a great deal of money may grow up to be the queen of a small European country and live happily ever after.

In many ways it is puzzling why the *Post* jumped at this story: Costain accepted it the first day it was offered by Ober.[55] The answer, it seems, lies in Fitzgerald's growing knowledge of the workings of the middle-American mind. He introduces the story with a note calculated to make the story acceptable to *Post* readers: "The extraordinary thing is not that people in a lifetime turn out worse or better than we had prophesied; in America that is to be expected. The extraordinary thing is how people keep up their levels, fulfill their promises, seem actually buoyed up by an inevitable destiny of their own."[56]   And so in two sentences Fitzgerald manages to laud typically American individualism and excuse Emily as an individual who was "blatantly and successfully showy to the end."[57] The implication is that individualism itself is good: while some individuals, like Emily whose non-conformity leads her to reject America, may become eccentric oddballs, there is never any doubt in the reader's mind that American life is much more comfortable and nicer than Emily's European one. In fact, in the way Fitzgerald describes Emily's early life with Petrocobesco, "Majesty" is anti-European, as are most of Fitzgerald's *Post* stories set abroad. Emily's adventures, therefore, entertain because Fitzgerald answers in advance what might have been a predictable *Post* query about the story: "How could she!" Emily's choice becomes an alternate American Dream that will be courted by Baby Warren and followed by Mary North Minghetti in *Tender Is the Night*.[58]

"The Bridal Party" (May 1930; *Post*, 9 August 1930; $4,000) has major links to the novel. The story is set in Paris which associates it loosely with the Paris section of *Tender Is the Night*, where Abe North was given a sendoff to America by Dick, Nicole, and Rosemary. "The Bridal Party" revolves around the frustration experienced by Michael Curly, whose inheritance comes too late to enable him to marry Caroline Dandy. She has chosen, instead of Curly, a successful American stockbroker who gives elaborate parties at the Ritz—the setting of Abe North's impersonation of General Pershing in *Tender Is the Night*.

The story, however, is an American story in every sense other than its Paris setting. Rutherford Hamilton, Caroline's fiancé, has made his money by shrewd dealings through the New York stock exchange; and when he loses it all shortly before the wedding takes place, he is offered a $50,000 a year job by a big American businessman simply because "He happens to have it—that young man."[59] And even according to Curly, who is miraculously cured at the end of the story of his love for Caroline, the extravagant parties and the wedding were typically American: "Generous and fresh and free; a sort of Virginia-plantation hospitality. . . ."[60]

"The Hotel Child" (November 1930; *Post*, 31 January 1931; $4,000) does not sparkle with American manners and customs as did "The Bridal Party," for example; and because of its dominant European color and its "shady" characters it "presented [for the *Post*] a few editorial problems. . . ."[61] The setting of "The Hotel Child" is Switzerland—the

Hotel des Trois Mondes in a little "corner of Europe [that] does not draw people; rather, it accepts them without too many inconvenient questions—live and let live."[62]   Fifi Schwartz, an eighteen-year-old "exquisitely, radiantly beautiful" girl, is the only noteworthy American in the story; and like "Majesty" which revolved around Emily's adventures with European royalty, "The Hotel Child" is the story of Fifi's experience with the similarly decadent aristocrats who wandered around in Europe after the war trying to exploit their now-worthless titles for food and lodging.

The plot of the story is incidental to the local color that it provides. Fifi, as the center-stage character, walks around the inner circle of bogus aristocrats and moral invalids and is impressed by them, although they frown upon her because she dresses flamboyantly. Finally she is wooed by Count Stanislas Borowki, who was "hooked firmly to the end of a line older than the crown of St. Stephen."[63] The affair dies quickly, however, when Borowki steals $200 from Fifi's mother to buy an engagement present for Fifi. Subsequently, he is jailed and Fifi is waiting only for his trial before she returns to America.

But Fifi, though she is beautiful, lacks the charm and grace of most eighteen-year-old Fitzgerald heroines—she is not an Emily Castleton, for instance. Rather, she is an outlandish caricature of the "American dream girl," in Borowki's ironic words.[64] Because Fifi is a nouveau riche stereotype, she would confirm the *Post* audience's preconceptions about her inability to distinguish real aristocrats from the scores of unscrupulous, titled men and women who surround her.[65] Fifi's major function in this story is that of a vehicle through which Fitzgerald creates the mood of decadence and immorality, which saturates the walk-on characters such as Lady Caroline Sibley-Biers in *Tender Is the Night*.

Indeed, "The Hotel Child" serves as one of the most useful of the European stories for examining Fitzgerald's method of using the *Post* as a laboratory for the novel. He employs the character of Lady Caroline, for instance, for verisimilitude as part of the local scenery in *Tender Is the Night* rather than as an individual who significantly advances the story line. The clan of which she is a part is fully developed in "The Hotel Child"—and the members of the group were those who "did fine embroidery or took cocaine in closed apartments and meanwhile laid claim to European thrones."[66] The specific prototype for Lady Caroline is "The Hotel Child's" Lady Capps-Karr who, like Lady Caroline, mutters from time to time "a chep's a chep and a chum's a chum."[67]

This group of European setting stories is important in examining the ways Fitzgerald came to use the *Post* as a workshop for the setting of *Tender Is the Night*. The Cannes harbor, a hotel in Switzerland, and the Paris Ritz would seem to be remote from the experience or even the imagination of the average middle American reader. Fitzgerald, however, managed to make the setting acceptable by using a variety of techniques. In two of these five stories, "Love in the Night" and "The Bridal Party," the settings are incidental to the plots of the stories. It could matter little to most popular readers of the time that the *Privateer* was anchored in the Cannes harbor as opposed to the New York harbor, just as it, no doubt, made very little difference that the wedding of Caroline Dandy and Rutherford Hamilton occurred in Paris as opposed to New York, for example. The important feature of both stories is that they are finally American business and success stories with romantic love at the core. This is what made them *Post* stories. The European settings were luxuries that Fitzgerald could afford because the stories were first of all romantic and American.

Similarly, "A Penny Spent" and "Majesty" are also middle American romances. Although each plot depends on its European setting, each story confirms the popular bias that the American dollar will buy anything. In the last of these stories, "The Hotel Child," Fitzgerald uses the Swiss setting to give the *Post* audience a fundamental course in social history, a chronicle of the decadent European nobility.

The "European taint" is absent from the stories in this group because Fitzgerald remained, himself, untainted. Like Dick Diver, Fitzgerald could participate in the local scenery of Europe and he could describe it intimately; but also like Diver, his allegiance was finally to America. That this "Americanness" seeped through the European settings—a facet of Fitzgerald's "double vision"—made him an acceptable interpreter of the European experience for the millions of *Post* readers.

Character Study

The character study cluster stories are even closer to the novel than the European setting stories. In them Fitzgerald builds the major characters—Dick, Nicole, and Rosemary—in *Tender Is the Night*. The characters walk on stage in these stories, they interact, and then they disappear until Fitzgerald reconstructs them in a later story or finally in the novel. For this reason the *Post* character studies can be viewed as dress rehearsals for *Tender Is the Night*. There are eight of these stories in which the development of the major characters of the novel can be followed: "Jacob's Ladder" (1927; Dick, Rosemary); "Magnetism" (1928; Dick, Nicole, Rosemary); "The Rough Crossing" (1929; Dick, Nicole, Rosemary); "The Swimmers" (1929; Dick, Nicole); "Two Wrongs" (1930; Dick, Nicole, Rosemary); "One Trip Abroad" (1930; Dick, Nicole); "Indecision" (1931; Rosemary); "A New Leaf" (1931; Dick).

"Jacob's Ladder" (June 1927; *Post*, 20 August 1927; $3,000) is the first story in which major characters who appear later in the novel make their first appearance. The stages in the relationship between Jenny Prince and Jacob Booth in "Jacob's Ladder" roughly parallel the development of the Dick-Rosemary relationship in the novel. Jacob's initial interest in Jenny, evidenced in his securing for her an audition for a movie, is paternal, just as Dick's early concern that Rosemary not get sunburned during her first day on the beach is fatherly. And further, Jacob reprimands Jenny for drinking, just as Dick expresses concern over Rosemary's champagne drinking during the celebration of her eighteenth birthday. Jenny not only appreciates Jacob's fatherly attention but also soon reacts to it by getting a crush on him, a reaction similar to Rosemary's.

In a second stage of the Jacob-Jenny relationship Jacob falls in love with Jenny, but by this time she is no longer romantically interested in him. Instead, she finds excitement in her leading man, Raffino, who corresponds to Nicotera in *Tender Is the Night*. Jacob, like Dick, becomes extremely jealous of this other interest. As the story ends, Jacob is unable to recognize that his infatuation with Jenny is not genuine love, whereas Dick eventually recognizes that his feelings for Rosemary were such an infatuation. And Jacob is left to worship her image on the screen, as many other movie fans do, in the "fast-throbbing darkness"[68] of the theater.

"Jacob's Ladder" is not only the first story in which Fitzgerald works with characters that will appear in the novel; it is also the first Fitzgerald *Post* story that does not pretend to offer a happy solution to the main character's problem. Earlier, it is true that Fitzgerald had published stories with bittersweet endings like "John Jackson's Arcady" in the *Post*. But the unhappy vein that Fitzgerald taps beginning with "Jacob's Ladder" marks a new stage in Fitzgerald's development as a popular magazine writer. The *Post* reported that "they like[d] the story tremendously, and [were] going to be very much disappointed if [Fitzgerald didn't] do a lot more for them just as good."[69]

To Fitzgerald this praise was, no doubt, construed as an invitation to write more sad, perhaps sentimental, stories, a cue which he followed to the degree that the character study stories are composed of increasingly lamentable situations. True, early Fitzgerald stories had been sentimental. But in the *Post* stories prior to "Jacob's Ladder" the prevailing emotion—and the one with which the reader was finally left—was happiness, the happiness that one usually could feel after he found that John Jackson's optimism finally eclipsed his cynicism. At the end of "Jacob's Ladder" the sentimentality is quite different: the reader is encouraged to cry along with Jacob and luxuriate in his misery which, from an intellectual viewpoint, is disproportionate to the misery warranted by his situation.[70] His "love" for Jenny is founded on the shaky foundation of her pretty eyes, and it flowered only in the presence of her rejection of him. The basis for his attachment to her is simply not documented well enough for it to qualify as a substantial love relationship. Unlike Dick's infatuation with Rosemary, which is presented as a symptom of Dick's decline and thus assumes a tragic dignity, Jacob's feelings for Jenny begin and end with self-pity. "Jacob's Ladder," therefore, does not, as it may seem to do at first glance, indicate that the *Post* had radically altered its editorial policy regarding Fitzgerald at that point in accepting this story with an unhappy ending; what the editors had done, in effect, was to approve the replacement of one kind of sentimentality—the virtue-is-always-rewarded variety in "The Third Casket," for example—for another which, as in "Jacob's Ladder," invites sympathy for the hero's sad plight. Fitzgerald quickly learned that the characters he was grooming for serious, even tragic, roles could be temporarily placed in such sentimental situations as that of "Jacob's Ladder," and he capitalized on this fact, although to a lesser degree than in "Jacob's Ladder," in the next character study story, "Magnetism."

In "Magnetism" (December 1927; *Post*, 3 March 1928; $3,500) Fitzgerald broadens the scope of the character study he had begun in "Jacob's Ladder" and introduces an early version of the Dick-Nicole-Rosemary triangle. A thirty-year-old movie star, George Hannaford, shares many of Diver's qualities: George has the kind of personal magnetism that draws women of all ages to him. One of them is the Rosemary-like, eighteen-year-old starlet, Helen Avery, whose attraction to George jeopardizes his happy marriage to a Nicole counterpart, Kay. The relationship between George and Helen does not develop beyond the stage of open mutual admiration, but while it is going on, Arthur Busch, an old admirer of Kay's, takes advantage of George's flirtation with Helen and tries to convince Kay that she should leave George for him. An encounter follows similar to the final Dick-Nicole-Barban scene in which Dick gracefully gives Nicole her freedom. In

"Magnetism," however, George refuses "to be mixed up in [Arthur and Kay's] emotions."[71]   Unlike Nicole, Kay does not leave her husband, and after the short Helen-George interlude, Kay and George resume their rare, happy Hollywood marriage.

Among other things, George's charm links him to Dick Diver. As his secretary tells him, "You can't control charm. You've got to . . . go through life attaching people to you that you don't want."[72] Moreover, the similarities between Kay and George's relationship to Dick and Nicole's are underlined by Kay's statement which was incorporated directly into *Tender Is the Night*: "but promise me you'll remember. . . . I'll be different, but somewhere lost inside of me there'll always be the person I am tonight."[73]   And Helen—at eighteen "a dark, pretty girl with a figure that would be full-blown sooner than she wished"[74]—is an early, authentic Rosemary.

But Fitzgerald subordinated the importance of this love triangle to a blackmail plot which furnishes the main story line for "Magnetism." The plot involves George and his secretary, who has been in love with George since she first saw him.   She has him unsuspectingly sign documents which she has composed and which falsely incriminate George.   After a half-hearted attempt to use them for blackmail purposes, the secretary Margaret destroys the letters because she is still infatuated with him and realizes that she has no desire to hurt him. True to his essentially "good" character, George refuses to report Margaret to the studio, thus allowing her to keep her job; and everything, George's marriage included, returns to normal at the end.

After developing George's character and the quality of his charm through his encounters with Kay, Helen, and his maid Delores, Fitzgerald cashes in on the sympathy the reader will have for Margaret, who is so taken by his attractiveness that she will even attempt blackmail just to gain his attention.   It is the sympathy for Margaret and the added affirmation of the essential goodness of the most glamorous people like George that make "Magnetism" a successful popular story.   Noteworthy is the fact that George's charm was potentially self-destructive, as was Dick's, but at this stage in the development of Dick's character—at least in the stories—Fitzgerald only shows how this quality may adversely affect others. It is not until Dick Ragland's suicide in "A New Leaf" (1931) that Fitzgerald begins to examine charm as a self-destructive force. In "Magnetism" Fitzgerald was laying the groundwork for a character decline that grew out of an excess of "goodness." However, such an idea contradicts the popular bias that virtue is rewarded. Thus Fitzgerald stops short of George's potential decline and leaves him at the height of his success, having at that point hurt only Kay and Margaret, the story's sentimentalized heroine whose unrequited love for George had driven her to attempt suicide. Fitzgerald has taken from his *Tender Is the Night* material that part which was predictably saleable; or at the time of "Magnetism" he might well have been formulating in an early stage the concept of emotional bankruptcy, which is the logical conclusion to George Hannaford's situation.

In the six stories of this group which follow, Fitzgerald shifts the focus of his attention from one character to the next, he makes alterations in the characters already introduced, and he begins to scruntinize love triangles like the Dick-Nicole-Rosemary triangle. But there is a quality about this group of stories which marks them as different from any of the other *Post* stories: they are, by no means, frivolous like "The Camel's Back"; nor are they simply "unhappy" stories which are consciously sentimentalized like "Jacob's Ladder." They are instead bleak, somber stories in which Fitzgerald seems, at first glance, to disregard the fact that he is writing for an audience that likes to have its biases reinforced rather than challenged.

Like "Magnetism," "The Rough Crossing" (March 1929; *Post*, 8 June 1929; $3,500) develops further the Dick-Nicole-Rosemary triangle. This story, though, is closer in many respects to the novel than any previous one, and it is properly viewed as a companion piece to "One Trip Abroad" (1930), the "miniature *Tender Is the Night*."[75] Adrian and Eva Smith at the beginning of "The Rough Crossing" have happily escaped from the United States and are en route with their children to France. Shortly after sailing, Adrian meets the eighteen-year-old Betsy D'Amido who, by her own account, "fell in love with you [Adrian] the first time I saw you."[76] Eva becomes insanely jealous and during "the wildest hurricane on the North Atlantic in ten years" she becomes irrational. She then runs around the boat deck for an hour, among other things, cursing the nurse who was sent to put her to bed. But after they arrive in France, both Eva and Adrian look back on the adventure as a nightmare that involved a side of them that they neither understand nor want to think about again. As Adrian says, "It was two other people. . . . There are so many Smiths in this world."[77]

If this were a happy ending, the *Post*'s acceptance of "The Rough Crossing" would be understandable. It does not seem, though, that Fitzgerald intended to pass it off as such even to the most casual reader. Adrian and Eva are restless people who are discontent with America and with themselves. Adrian's first comment when the boat leaves the American dock is "We've escaped." Eva's first observation about the boat is that she likes it better than the *Majestic* or the

Aquitania, a remark Fitzgerald points out as "unfaithful to the ships that had served their honeymoon."[78] Moreover, Adrian begins looking for attractive girls almost before the trip has begun and quickly finds one with whom he can spend much of his time aboard the ship. They are set up in the beginning of the story, therefore, as people who are chronically dissatisfied with America and with their marriage. In their mockery of America itself and of one of its most prized institutions, the Smiths could scarcely have been sympathetic characters to *Post* readers. When they finally step onto French soil, then, it is unlikely that American readers would rejoice with them in apparently being able to leave their bad selves in America or on board the ship. It is more likely that they would be viewed as still dissatisfied, deluded people who are, for the moment, as deceived about the quality of their present happiness as they were earlier deceived in believing that the trip to Europe would solve the problem of their basic dissatisfaction with everything.

If the average *Post* reader accepted the ending as happy, he would be sanctioning the expatriate act by recognizing it as a miraculous cure-all, which is unlikely.[79] The response from *Post* readers was, no doubt, that the Smiths got what was coming to them: more dissatisfaction. A rule of thumb concerning *Post* fiction—and there are few contradictions in Fitzgerald's *Post* work—is that the stories cannot contradict the middle-American value system. For Fitzgerald to have asserted that the expatriate Smiths lived happily ever after in France would have been to fool no one, especially the readers of the *Post*.

In "The Swimmers" (July-August 1929; *Post*, 19 October 1929; $4,000), an important cluster story which is Fitzgerald's Pledge of Allegiance to America, Fitzgerald carefully wins the reader's sympathy for the Dick Diver-like Henry Clay Marston while he systematically destroys all confidence in Marston's French wife Choupette. It is not enough that Choupette brings on Marston's nervous collapse by having an affair, which she describes as an "indiscretion"; she proceeds, after they come to America, to have another affair during which she threatens to expose Marston's psychiatric history unless he grants her a divorce and custody of the children. The last laugh is on Choupette, though, who is forced to sign away custody of the children to Marston before he will agree to swim away from her and her Barban-type lover to seek help for their adrift boat.

"The Swimmers" is interesting on several major counts. It is a gimmicky story in its contrived ending, at which point Marston is able to retrieve the bogus psychiatric record that Choupette's lover Wiese had obtained through bribery to incriminate him. Among other unlikelihoods contained in this ending, it is incredible that Wiese's engine would have failed at a place so close to the cross-current which, as only Marston among the group knew, would finally have carried the boat safely into Peyton Harbor; because he has this knowledge Marston can confidently demand Wiese's sworn statement before he will swim to the lighthouse for help.   In addition to the farfetched ending which links the story with such other *Post* stories as "The Popular Girl," a second noteworthy ingredient of "The Swimmers" is its intensely patriotic message.   As in "The Rough Crossing," Fitzgerald plays on the anti-expatriate sentiment of his readers.   Marston is a Virginian who is contrasted to the immoral, insensitive French wife Choupette.   And Marston, though he is returning to France at the end of the story, is at heart a true American, as revealed by his final monologue: "France was a land, England was a people, but America having about it still that quality of an idea, was harder to utter—it was the graves at Shiloh and the tired drawn, nervous faces of its great men. . . . It was a willingness of the heart."[80]

Therefore, because the story succeeds as good escape literature, highly melodramatic with its trick ending, and because its patriotic sentiment was certainly in line with the biases of *Post* readers, Fitzgerald was able to fashion in between a realistic picture of expatriation: what it meant to leave America and what it meant to return after having lived abroad.   The idea of Europe projected in "The Swimmers" is a somber one.   It becomes a place in which "the lost generation" must wander around aimlessly; and those like Marston who seem destined to exile there are shown as unfortunate people biding their time until their generation is gone.   The mood that results from this image, of course, would have been too gloomy for *Post* readers if Fitzgerald had not consciously entertained in "The Swimmers" with such devices as the trick ending and if he had not heightened his protagonist's feelings that in America things cannot remain bad for very long.   As Marston indicates, "it seemed to him that the men coming on . . . were better. . . . The best of America was the best of the world."[81]   "The Swimmers," with its blend of despair, hope, and patriotism, illustrates as well as any story how Fitzgerald was able to use the *Post* as a workshop for his novel.   In it he accentuates those things present in nearly all of the European cluster stories which made them saleable to the *Post* while at the same time suitable as experiments for his serious *Tender Is the Night* material.

In "Two Wrongs" (October-November 1929; *Post*, 18 January 1930; $4,000; *TAR*) Fitzgerald again cultivates sympathy for a Dick Diver character, Bill McChesney.   Pictured at first as rude, callous, indifferent to the feelings of others, Bill experiences a series of misfortunes beginning with the stillbirth of his child, which he might have prevented if he had not been out drinking, and ending with the collapse of his left lung, which came from his disregard for his health. In the end he must leave his wife and go alone to Denver where the reader assumes he will probably die. His wife decides to stay behind with their only son and pursue her dancing career. Bill's last thought in the story is that "Emmy would come at the end, no matter what she was doing or how good an engagement she had."[82] This extreme self-pity links Bill with Jacob Booth ("Jacob's Ladder"). But Bill is granted an insight denied Jacob at the end: that he was receiving an appropriate penalty for his wrongdoing, a judgment that would have, at once, tallied with the *Post* audience's and elicited its sentiment.

The "miniature of *Tender Is the Night*," "One Trip Abroad" (August 1930; *Post*, 11 October 1930; $4,000), illustrates well the close relationship which often exists between the stories and the novels. The emotional bankruptcy idea at the core of Dick Diver's decline, which is also at the center of "One Trip Abroad," is the most significant link between the story and the novel. But other details underline the closeness: the trip to North Africa and the T. F. Golding Yacht episode, for example.

Read with *Tender Is the Night* in mind, "One Trip Abroad" is a study of the depletion of emotional resources—that is, emotional bankruptcy—which results from Nicole and Nelson Kelly's inclination, early in the story, to make themselves available to almost everyone with whom they come into contact. The snobbish Mileses, an American couple who have been in Europe for fifteen years and who are dissipated when the Kellys meet them, forecast what the reader is to expect of the Kellys if they remain in the international set for a comparable period of time. Originally very naive, the Kellys, with the inspiration of the Mileses and the help of Nelson's newly inherited half-million dollars, begin a downhill plummet characterized by snobbishness, heavy drinking, and marital infidelity. They arrive finally in Switzerland having been depleted, physically and emotionally. At the beginning of what seems a recuperative period, Nicole finally realizes that a couple whom they have seen from time to time and who now appear quite worn out are, in fact, their ghostly counterparts; and the story closes with her shriek of horror: "They're us! Don't you see?"[83]

The fact of the Kellys' emotional bankruptcy is lamentable; but for most readers, the *Post* audience included, the Kellys' stature is, at no point in their lives, comparable to the stature of Dick Diver: Nelson after a few years as a fur dealer in Alaska aspires to be a great painter, though his talent is apparently negligible; Nicole wants to be a singer, but tries only half-heartedly. Consequently, their descent lacks the dimension of tragedy. And the average *Post* reader may not even have felt sympathy for the Kellys in their misfortune. Fitzgerald seems, in fact, to have written the story in such a way that the emotional bankruptcy idea is of relatively minor significance and the Kellys may be legitimately viewed as antagonists to the bulk of middle Americans. Their story is one not merely of emotional depletion that could occur anywhere; it is, rather, a chronicle of progressive estrangement from America. They are, before they meet the Mileses, proud of the Benjamin Franklin education that they have gotten from their tours, and they are certainly not snobs. They are, in fact, prevented from fully enjoying the kind of non-touristy sort of living the Mileses would have them enjoy because they are "at once too old and too young, and too American."[84] Their education, then, takes the form of a cram course in snobbery and debauchery: "But you Americans," they are told, "you're having a rotten time. If you want to wear the green hat or the crushed hat, or whatever it is, you always have to get a little tipsy."[85] And when they finally succeed in becoming Europeanized they wind up in a Swiss sanitarium: the predictable wages of sin, *Post* style, for an American expatriate couple.

Unlike the other character study stories, "Indecision" (December 1930; *Post*, 21 February 1931; $4,000) is a light, comical story. In it, a Rosemary Hoyt type, Rosemary Merriweather, is one of the two girls pursued by Tommy McLane, the story's indecisive, self-centered hero. Tommy's inability to decide whether he will allow Rosemary or Emily, an older divorcée, to be his companion during his ten-day vacation in Switzerland provides the humor which is the backbone of this story. Fitzgerald's intention is to amuse the reader with Tommy's egocentric reflections on the state of his own desirability; when he finally decides that he will ask Rosemary to marry him, he only regrets that Emily is not present so that he can again compare the two girls.

Tommy's "indecision" over Rosemary and Emily is a burlesque of Dick Diver's inability to distinguish, at one point in the novel, between infatuation and love in his relationship with Rosemary Hoyt. Fitzgerald, however, allows Dick not only to finally make the distinction, but also to view it as a symptom of his emotional bankruptcy. Tommy, on the other hand, remains ignorant of his motivations and one feels that he will never be able to see objectively his embarrassingly laughable egocentricity. Tommy's relation to Dick, then, is a rather superficial one.[86] Rosemary Merriweather, though, has qualities which link her more definitely with Rosemary Hoyt: aside from having the same first name, she is eighteen, very attractive, and infatuated with an older man. But in this story Fitzgerald does not attempt to develop her character. She is, instead, presented merely as a pretty ornament, a vehicle without which Tommy's indecisiveness would not have been bought by the *Post* readers. "Indecision's" comic relief, though, is unique in the group of character study stories. After it, Fitzgerald returns to the somber mood which characterizes the group as a whole.

The bleak picture with which Fitzgerald leaves the reader in "One Trip Abroad" is paralleled only in the suicide of Dick Ragland in the final character study, "A New Leaf" (April 1931; *Post*, 4 July 1931; $4,000). Just as George Hannaford ("Magnetism") is a Dick Diver type at the high point of his life, Dick Ragland is a study of a man with great charm, like Diver and Hannaford at the lowest possible point. Ragland has good looks, money, charm, and a terrible reputation which he has earned from his drunken escapades. Julia Ross, a good Samaritan by nature and a girl devoted to Ragland because he moved her "chemically," tries to rescue him from his inevitable descent into alcoholism. The reader learns—and Julia is told by her one-time boyfriend Phil, but does not believe—that Dick's predicament is hopeless, his decline irreversible: "Sometimes they dry up or even flow into a parallel channel, but I've never known anybody to change."[87] After trying very hard to alter the course of his life in order that he may have Julia as the prize, Dick apparently realizes, as did Phil, that there was no hope. As a solution he drowns himself in the Atlantic, a gesture that indicates to Julia that "he broke rather than bent."[88] But Phil and the reader know, though Julia never learns the truth, that Dick has not been able to avoid liquor; he had not changed as she will always believe he had. Dick's suicide is understandable and is, in fact, only a degree more drastic than the fate that Fitzgerald prescribed for Dick Diver in upper New York state at the end of *Tender Is the Night*. The suicide, however, is decidedly not *Post*y. The philosophy expressed by Phil, that once a person reaches a certain emotional low point there can be no return, is deterministic. Few of the millions of *Post* readers would have chosen to curl up with this story on a Thursday night, a fact supported by the words of warning Fitzgerald received through Ober from the editors: "The *Post* are taking FLIGHT AND PURSUIT but they want me to tell you that your last three stories ["Flight and Pursuit," "A New Leaf," and "Indecision"] have not been up to the best you can do."[89] The *Post* then, and not Fitzgerald, signalled an end to the somber stories that served as a laboratory for the character studies that worked their way into *Tender Is the Night*. Perhaps the only thing that is surprising about their decision is that they allowed Fitzgerald to carry his prototype, Dick Ragland, to the bottom of the parabola—a distance that he was unwilling to carry Dick Diver, perhaps because of his "A New Leaf" experiment.

General Cluster Stories

There is a final group of novel-related stories whose association with the novel is less direct: "The Love Boat" (1927), "At Your Age" (1929), "Babylon Revisited" (1931), and "On Schedule" (1932). All except "Babylon Revisited" share the ingredients of an older man pursuing a young girl in hopes of recapturing the past.

Bill Frothington in "The Love Boat" (August 1927; *Post*, 8 October 1927; $3,500) returns after a number of years to the town where he had attended a high school dance and looks nostalgically for Mae Purley, a girl whom he had met when he crashed a high school party on a boat. According to Bill, Mae had become "the symbol of his youth." When he finds that she is now happily married and that she is no longer the pretty, young girl he remembered, he goes uninvited to a high school dance which, coincidentally, is like the one at which he and Mae had first met. And again by coincidence, Bill makes innocent advances toward a young girl named May who is much like Mae Purley was years ago. Then after an attempt to show the high school boys that he can fight as well as any of them, Bill is thrown into the river, a kind of baptism that leads him to the realization that his youth is gone: "At my age you can't fight against what you know you are."[90]

Fifty-year-old Tom Squires of "At Your Age" (June 1929; *Post*, 17 August 1929; $4,000), though he is older than Bill Frothington, also pursues a young girl, Annie Lorry. But Tom's pursuit is successful and Annie, despite protests from her mother, dates him seriously. On one occasion, however, Annie is several hours late for her date with Tom because she had gone riding with a boy her own age. Finally convinced that he is, in fact, too old for her, Tom leaves her house "with the courteous bow of another generation." In Fitzgerald's words, "he had lost the battle against youth and spring, and with his grief paid the penalty for age's unforgivable sin—refusing to die."[91]

In "On Schedule" (December 1932; *Post*, 18 March 1933, $3,000) René du Cary, a widower with a teenage daughter, pursues his lost youth as it is embodied in the pretty, nineteen-year-old Becky Snyder. After rescuing her from the hands of a drunken date, René falls in love with Becky, but the plans for their marriage must be postponed for months in order that a clause in the will of René's dead wife be satisfied. Becky turns out to be not only a good companion for René and his daughter, but also an excellent janitor who fires the furnace just in time to save the laboratory experiment which is an obsession with René. Ironically, her appearance not "on schedule" and her subsequent kindling of the fire with René's appointment schedule sheet cause René to announce their engagement immediately.

These lost youth stories, therefore, are characterized by older men trying to recapture the past, which is in each case symbolized by a young girl. The general application of their quest to *Tender Is the Night* is clear. Dick's affection for Rosemary is anchored primarily in his wish to be young again and in his realization, illustrated in the surfboard episode, that his strength and timing are not the same as they once were. It is possible that Fitzgerald, in these stories, was working with the motivation for Dick's infatuation with Rosemary in the novel. However, his treatment of the lost youth idea in the stories is quite different from his handling of this subject in *Tender Is the Night*. In the first two stories Fitzgerald makes the subject a very sentimental one. Bill Frothington, unlike Dick Diver, seems incapable of giving in any relationship because of his obsession with having lost his youth. And while one is apt to view Bill's plight at the end as sad, it is not of the dimension of Diver's tragedy. Unlike Dick, who gave everything to Nicole, Bill was willing to give his wife nothing. Thus, for *Post* readers Bill's potentially tragic predicament, similar to Jacob Booth's, calls for tears. Tom Squires in "At Your Age" is also a character designed to win the sympathy of the *Post* audience. When he murmurs near the end of the story, "it's a darn pity . . . A darn pity," the *Post* audience, as Fitzgerald well knew, was likely to agree. And they might even suffer with Tom in the miserable script he has dictated for his life: he had "those three months [with Annie]—he had them forever."[92] Tom and, in some ways, Bill Frothington are grown old before their time and through them Fitzgerald gave many *Post* readers an opportunity to vicariously share their sadness. With René du Cary, whose problem is like Bill and Tom's—that is, they are all growing older—Fitzgerald simply reverses the coin and allows René, in marrying Becky, a reprieve, a wish fulfillment device which Fitzgerald had used in "The Third Casket," for example.

The lost youth subject lends itself to sentimental treatment, and "The Love Boat," "At Your Age," and "On Schedule" are indeed three of the weakest, most sentimental stories in the canon. They do not, however, necessarily indicate a lack of skill on Fitzgerald's part. A good way to measure Fitzgerald's skill as a professional craftsman, in fact, is to compare his treatment of the lost youth idea in the stories with that of the novel. The stages of Dick Diver's infatuation with Rosemary are carefully documented in *Tender Is the Night*. The reader is asked only to observe and draw his own conclusions as to the dimensions of the tragedy, one of which must be that the affair is a symptom in a complex process of deterioration. By contrast, the reader of the stories is presented primarily with the symptom itself and is nudged or pushed by Fitzgerald to react in a prescribed way. The stories, specifically the three in this group, confirm the preconceptions of the *Post* readers: that sad situations merit sympathy ("Jacob's Ladder" and "At Your Age"); and that an individual, if he tries, can conquer almost anything, even occasionally lost youth ("On Schedule"). That Fitzgerald was able to treat the lost youth subject in a way suitable both to popular readers of the stories and to literary critics of the novel is a gauge of his versatility as a writer, without which he could not have made the money to allow him to complete *Tender Is the Night*.

"Babylon Revisited" (December 1930; *Post*, 21 February 1931; \$4,000; *TAR*)[93] is unique in the Fitzgerald canon. In it Fitzgerald not only manages to create a mood that will inform *Tender Is the Night*,[94] but also he composes one of his most brilliant stories, which was a first-rate, popular magazine piece as well. Few would argue about the story's artistic merit. In Charlie Wales, Fitzgerald creates a character whose future, in spite of his heroic struggle, is prescribed by his imprudent past. He is destined to be haunted by reminders of his early life embodied by Lorraine and Duncan; to be judged for them by the Marions of the present who, like Charlie's conscience personified, are disgusted by his past and demand punishment; and to be denied, for his penance, any right to fill the emptiness of his life with Honoria, the only meaningful thing left. Fitzgerald fashions Charlie as a sensitive channel through which the reader can simultaneously view the Paris as it existed for expatriate wanderers before the Depression and the now-dimmed Paris to which Charlie returns. The contrast is masterfully handled in that the course of Charlie's emotional life closely parallels the changing mood of the city—from a kind of unreal euphoria to a mood of loss and melancholy. The contrast at once heightens the reader's sense of Charlie's loneliness in a ghost town of bad memories and foreshadows his empty-handed return to Prague. All of Charlie's present misery has resulted, in Fitzgerald's precise summary, from his "selling short" in the boom—an allusion to the loss of his wife Helen. Charlie, though, refuses to be driven back to alcohol, even in the face of his loss of Honoria. Although he might easily have done so, Fitzgerald avoids drawing the reader into a sentimental trap of identification with Charlie's plight, the responsibility for and consequences of which must finally be borne by Charlie. As he later did in Dick Diver's case, Fitzgerald has shown how one—here, Charlie—works his way into an existence with nothing at the core and how he has managed to dissipate, "to make nothing out of something," and thus prescribed for himself a future without direction, whether it is spent in Prague, Babylon, or upstate New York. In this mood of Charlie's isolation lies the kinship between the story and *Tender Is the Night*.

The highest price that Fitzgerald received for any magazine story was $4,000; "Babylon Revisited" was one of the stories that earned this sum. It is important, therefore, to examine those features of the story that allowed it to be both a popular "best seller" and a masterpiece.[95] One may be sure that most *Post* readers missed many of the subtle touches that have since been analyzed by critics. The popular thrust of "Babylon Revisited" is a dual one in which Fitzgerald plays on what were apt to be the readers' ambivalent feelings toward Charlie. On the one hand, Charlie is an expatriate; however, American audiences may have been skeptical about his resolution to remain abroad. It would have been logical for readers of the *Post* to ask why Charlie insisted on returning to a bar in Paris if he was determined to stick to his resolution that liquor would never again play an important role in his life. And why did he not go first to see his daughter? Therefore, when Charlie finally arrives at the home of the Peters, they are likely to be favored in the contest, to the degree that a contest is already in motion for the custody of Honoria. Moreover, the Peters' living room when Charlie arrives is pictured as "warm and comfortably American"—another mark in the Peters' favor as far as *Post* audiences were concerned. At that point Fitzgerald reverses the tide of sympathy against Marion Peters in favor of Charlie. Marion, now in the past tense, "had once possessed a fresh American loveliness."[96] And Charlie shows the reader that he would, in fact, be an excellent father to Honoria if given the chance: his warmth toward her in the restaurant scene is so genuine that it is bound to be moving to any audience except the most cynical. The conflict of the story, therefore, revolves around the contest staged between the sincere, well-intentioned father Charlie and the sister-in-law Marion, who is determined that Honoria will not leave with her father unless he has completely changed. But no sooner have the allegiances been aligned than the reader is reminded by the intrusion of Lorraine and Duncan, and by Marion's over-reaction to it, that Charlie had once sinned and still has part of the consequences left to pay. In this way Fitzgerald is able to prepare the reader for an unhappy ending. And whereas a careful reader might have remembered that if Charlie waits much longer he will "lose Honoria's childhood" and "his chance for a home,"[97] most readers would feel that Charlie has a second chance coming and that he will not remain "so alone" for much longer.

The story is successful on three major counts: it served as a workshop in which Fitzgerald shaped the mood of *Tender Is the Night*; it succeeds on a purely entertaining level in the sense that few readers could fail to become intrigued by the struggle against unfair odds of a well-intentioned father for the affection of his daughter; and it succeeds on the mythic level, suggested in the title, as a story in which all ingredients conspire to lead one to Charlie's inevitable exile—a permanent isolation from the city that has fallen in the absence of a now-reformed sinner, while carrying with it not only the bad but also the good which Charlie has come to salvage. Thus "Babylon Revisited" stands as a monument to Fitzgerald's talent then of pleasing the popular readers of his time and the "schoolmasters of ever after."

Two stories that followed are closely related to *Tender Is the Night* and were both rejected by the *Post*. The first of these, "On Your Own" (1931; *Esquire*, 30 January 1979), written shortly after "Babylon Revisited" and prompted by Fitzgerald's return from Europe for his father's funeral, contains a graveyard scene in which Evelyn Lovejoy bids farewell to "all my fathers" in much the same way that Dick Diver will do in the novel. Evelyn's attack on Americans, and especially on the American upper class, however, is so strong that it offends her suitor, George Ives, and his mother. The tone of her comments makes the story itself seem a criticism of American values and thus probably accounted for the story's unacceptability to the *Post* and half a dozen other popular magazines to which Fitzgerald tried to sell it.

The second cluster story that was also a *Post* reject is "Crazy Sunday" (January 1932; *American Mercury*, October 1932; $200; *TAR*), cited by Fitzgerald as a story which he stripped for *Tender Is the Night*.[98] This story is unique in strongly anticipating the two novels, *Tender Is the Night* and *The Last Tycoon*, which follow it.   Like "Babylon Revisited," "Crazy Sunday" resembles *Tender Is the Night* in the mood the story creates—a mood that depends in both stories as well as the novel on irreversible losses suffered by the major characters in each. The Miles Calman-Stella-Joel Coles relationship from which this mood is generated in "Crazy Sunday" is in some respects similar to the Nicole-Dick-Rosemary relationship in the novel, though the sexes are reversed in the novel counterparts. Stella is attracted to Joel, who is an intruder in Stella and Miles's marriage—a role similar to

Rosemary's in the novel. Clearly, though, Stella is no Dick Diver, and the specific parallels between the story and the novel are less important than the general feeling which surrounds both strained marriages and their tragic aftermaths. In its particulars, the story shares several features with *The Last Tycoon*. Miles Calman, the successful Hollywood producer whose mother "always expected a lot from Miles," is an early version of Monroe Stahr. His wife Stella, as was Minna Davis, is one of the brightest stars in Hollywood. But perhaps most important, the personal void that Joel feels when he learns that Miles has been killed captures the sense of loss that will accompany Stahr's death.

The marketing problem Fitzgerald had with "Crazy Sunday" has interesting implications in the course that Fitzgerald's short story career took from 1932 until his death. Until the time that Fitzgerald tried to sell "Crazy Sunday," his luck in disposing of the serious stories which anticipate *Tender Is the Night* had been good: the *Post* had bought all eighteen of the stories which have significant parallels with the novel. "Crazy Sunday" is a better story than any of the cluster stories except "Babylon Revisited"; Fitzgerald recognized it as such as he indicated to Ober: "I'm not sorry I went to Hollywood in November 1931 because I've got a fine story about Hollywood which will be along in several days."[99] The *Post* declined the story because "although it was beautifully written and a very accurate picture of Hollywood . . . it didn't get anywhere or prove anything." Harry Burton, editor of Hearst's *Cosmopolitan*, rejected the story because "Hearst's policy man said they wouldn't dare use the story as they were afraid it might offend the moving picture people with whom they are affiliated." And *Collier's*, a potential buyer, was ruled out as a market because "it would hurt Mr. Lorimer's feelings to see a story of Fitzgerald's in Collier's."[100] When Fitzgerald submitted "Crazy Sunday" he was only a year away from completing *Tender Is the Night* and, thus, could scarcely afford to pursue a subject that seemed patently tabooed by popular magazines since he was depending on selling stories to pay his bills. In the case of most of his *Tender Is the Night* material he had been able to dress it for the slick magazines largely by making it patriotic; Hollywood manufactured the dreams of middle America and Fitzgerald would have entertained few people by exposing the empty core beneath the tinsel of this institution. In abandoning his Hollywood material, therefore, he took what must have appeared as the only alternative that seemed compatible with the successful completion of *Tender Is the Night*. His reluctance, discussed below, to attempt to return to the popular magazines as a possible workshop for *The Last Tycoon* is easier to understand in light of the unanimous rejection of his "Crazy Sunday" subject matter by editors of the slicks—a rejection which, after the popular failure of *Tender Is the Night*, may account for the fact that he did not seriously return to the Hollywood material until he began *The Last Tycoon*, which was separated from "Crazy Sunday" by eight years. In the case of that novel he attempted only twice, in "Last Kiss" and "Discard," to test his material first in the popular magazines. Based on his experience in attempting to market "Crazy Sunday," he would, no doubt, have felt that any time spent doing this would have been wasted, which, if his lack of success in selling "Last Kiss" and "Discard" is an indicator, was a correct impression.

Several general observations which establish the position of the *Tender Is the Night* cluster stories in the Fitzgerald canon can be made. First, as a group, the stories are of an even, high quality when compared with any other group of Fitzgerald's stories. With the exception of "Indecision," whose association with the novel is less direct than any other cluster story, all of these stories deal with serious subjects of more than topical interest, a quality almost dictated by the nature of the *Tender Is the Night* material which informs them.

But in addition to being good art works, the cluster stories are important as a laboratory in which Fitzgerald experimented with settings, characters, and themes that were used in *Tender Is the Night*. Every locale that was used in the novel first appeared in a *Post* story; the three central characters, Dick, Nicole, and Rosemary, as well as numerous minor characters like Lady Sibley-Biers and Tommy Barban, are explored in the *Post* cluster stories; "the mood of loss and regret [which] informs much of the novel"[101] is established in the *Post*, most notably in "Babylon Revisited"; and the theme of emotional bankruptcy which is at the heart of *Tender Is the Night* evolves from the Dick Diver character study stories. The nature of the *Post* as a workshop for the novel, therefore, is clear: it paid Fitzgerald well for his stories while he experimented with various ingredients that would go in the novel.[102] In its capacity as a workshop the *Post* also imposed a discipline on Fitzgerald during the composition of the book; it gave him the incentive, primarily financial, to keep writing during a time in the Fitzgeralds' lives marked by disorganization and tragedy.

And finally, the cluster stories mark a new stage in Fitzgerald's career as a popular magazine short story writer. In them Fitzgerald found ways of making entertaining those things which were ordinarily tabooed by *Post* editors: alcoholism and suicide ("A New Leaf"); marital infidelity ("The Swimmers"); expatriatism ("Majesty"); disillusionment ("The Love Boat"); and dissipation ("One Trip

Abroad"), to name a few. Occasionally, as in "Jacob's Ladder," Fitzgerald popularizes his material and makes a potentially tragic situation simply a melodramatic one, thus relying on the audience's sentimental response for the entertainment value of the story. But more often he was able to tailor these subjects for popular readers by playing on the anti-expatriate sentiment of many middle Americans; "The Rough Crossing" is a case in point. In other instances he played on the strong nationalistic spirit of the *Post* readers in order to create antagonists, on the one hand, like Choupette Marston whom the audience could feel justified in disliking, and on the other, to create sympathetic characters like Hallie Bushmill and Corcoran, who are more sympathetic after they have travelled abroad and chosen to return home.

For the most part, therefore, the cluster stories managed to be *Post* stories because Fitzgerald externalized the source of conflict and placed the burden for it on predictable biases of the average middle American. He created antagonists, primarily expatriates and foreigners, rather than protagonists in the stories so that their sad situations confirmed the belief of *Post* readers that the rejection of America, or the unwillingness to accept it, often results in misery and unhappiness. The market value of the *Tender Is the Night* cluster stories was of a negative sort which relied on the fact that an expatriate's tragedy was in many cases a *Post* reader's entertainment. Viewed in this light the "unhappy ending" stories, which seem to indicate a radical departure in the *Post*'s editorial policy regarding Fitzgerald, appear less radical.

Adolescence Stories

There are two major groups of stories in the 1925-1934 phase of Fitzgerald's career: the group of serious, somber stories discussed above which are directly associated with *Tender Is the Night* and the group of stories dealing with adolescence, the Basil-Josephine stories and their companions. The *Post* stories published from 1925 through 1931, with four exceptions, "The Last of the Belles" (1929), "Between Three and Four" (1931), "A Change of Class" (1931), and "A Freeze-Out" (1931), fall distinctly into one or the other of the two groups. Any examination of Fitzgerald's reputation between the publication of *The Great Gatsby* and that of *Tender Is the Night* must take into consideration, not only the tremendous difference in kind between the cluster stories and the adolescence stories, but also that they existed together simultaneously in the same magazine, all earning similar sums for Fitzgerald. The cluster stories, bleak as they often are, contrast sharply with the adolescence stories, the most distinguishing feature of which is comic irony. The effect on Fitzgerald's contemporary reputation of the extreme swings in mood between the cluster stories and the adolescence stories may have been to confuse popular audiences as to the nature of his talent. Nevertheless, there is evidence to suggest that Fitzgerald might well have calculated this effect with his vogue in mind. He expressed concern to Ober that if the Basil stories were published as a book, he "might as well get tickets for Hollywood immediately,"[103] indicating that he felt these stories would perhaps be criticized as commercial and flashy. The adolescence stories understandably, then, come in segments preceding heavy concentrations of the cluster stories in the *Post*: the Basil stories, for instance, precede the unbroken run of novel-related stories, including "The Rough Crossing," "Majesty," "At Your Age," "The Swimmers," and "Two Wrongs." Fitzgerald's intention, perhaps, was to play the extremes against each other and thus maintain a reputation as an entertainer, since this was how he earned his keep, and as a serious artist—an impression that he must have relayed with such cluster stories as "Babylon Revisited" and "One Trip Abroad." But whether his intention in returning to the youthful Basil and Josephine was to draw on material that kept his identity with youth alive in the popular mind, to explore this early material with the idea of drawing on it for a novel, or simply to begin with a series that would be profitable, the effect was a combination of these three things.

The Basil and Josephine stories appear to have grown, at least partly, out of specific experiments with the subject of adolescence conducted in the *Post* between 1926 and early 1928. Seeds of both series are found in four stories of those years: "Presumption" (1926), "The Adolescent Marriage" (1926), "A Short Trip Home" (1927), and "The Bowl" (1928). Fitzgerald's tendency in 1924 and 1925 had been to work away from the stories of youth on which his early popular reputation was founded. Only one story in those two years, "Rags Martin-Jones and the Pr-nce of W-les" (*McCall's*, 1924), had been "a typical Fitzgerald story about youth." As indicated above he had, instead, been concerned in those years with the subjects of success and marriage. The stories which anticipate the Basil and Josephine series represent Fitzgerald's attempts to reestablish his touch with that early material and to formulate a strategy for writing stories about it.

One of the early stories in this group, "The Adolescent Marriage," is viewed through the eyes of Chauncey Garnett, a sixty-eight-year-old architect who is trying to regain an appropriate perspective on youth—that period "between adolescence and disillusion." He remarks that, "From where he stood, this youngest generation was something infinitely distant, and perceived through the large end of a telescope."[104] This statement applies also to Fitzgerald, whose main difficulties, illustrated in the adolescence stories leading up to the Basil and Josephine series, were in gaining sharp focus on his subjects and of deciding what stance—sympathetic or ironic—to take toward this rediscovered vein of material.

The story of the group most typical in that it clearly suggests these problems of focus is the first story, "Presumption" (November 1925; *Post*, 9 January 1926; $2,500). Potentially a funny story, "Presumption" begins with the agonized attempts of young San Juan Chandler to treat an outstanding pimple with black salve. His efforts to make himself as attractive as possible are aimed at gaining the approval of the rich, beautiful Noel Garneau, whom Juan had met on a Montana dude ranch. The first half of the story deals with Juan's visit to his aunt's hometown, where Noel also lives, and with his futile, frustrating attempts to make Noel love him. Fitzgerald maintains a consistently detached view of Juan in the first part of the story, and Juan's presumption in pursuing a girl so much richer than himself becomes as painful for the reader as his bout with acne is laughable. But in the last part of the story Fitzgerald gives in to an overwhelming sympathy for Juan, who although he is twenty could easily pass for fifteen, and allows him, somewhat mysteriously, to make the fortune which prepares him to rescue Noel from a bad engagement to another man.

In the first half of the story, therefore, Fitzgerald blends humor with pathos and stands in approximately the same position toward Juan that he will later assume in relation to Basil. Had he concluded the story after that first half, "Presumption" would rank with the Basil stories in terms of its artistic merit and its quality of entertainment. Instead, however, Fitzgerald abandons his ironic stance in the second half and presents his subject in much the same light that he had earlier presented Amory Blaine—a character whose awkward moments do not always seem to be recognized as such by Fitzgerald. But "Presumption," pulled apart at the center as it is, illustrates well the difficulty that Fitzgerald had in coming to terms with the material that he would handle skillfully in the Basil and Josephine stories. It remained for him merely to experiment with a predominately sentimental view of his adolescent creations in three more stories before he decided to adopt the comically ironic, though essentially serious, attitude that characterizes his viewpoint in the Basil and Josephine stories.

The three stories which follow "Presumption"—"The Adolescent Marriage," "A Short Trip Home," and "The Bowl"—show Fitzgerald as reluctant to abandon the romantic view of youth that had marked his early popular fiction. "The Adolescent Marriage" (December 1926; *Post*, 6 March 1926; $2,500) is the story of two immature young people[105] who rush into marriage against everyone's advice and file for a divorce, again against everyone's advice, three weeks later, after a dispute over a hat the sixteen-year-old wife had bought. They are reconciled at the end and live in a dreamhouse designed by the husband, an architect: Fitzgerald's way of saying that young love can conquer anything, even immaturity.

Similarly, Fitzgerald's attitude toward his young subjects reflected in "A Short Trip Home" (October 1927; *Post*, 17 December 1927; $3,500; *TAR*) is essentially romantic, unlike his later attitude toward Josephine. In the story Fitzgerald speaks without irony through the first-person narrator, Eddie Stinson, and recreates an atmosphere of involvement with his young subjects that he had not achieved since "Dice, Brassknuckles & Guitar" (1923). "A Short Trip Home" is an affirmation of the basic innocence of young American girls as embodied in Ellen Baker, a debutante whose goodness is threatened by the shady gangland figure Joe Varland. Symbolic of the evil which corrupts innocence, Varland becomes a force which Eddie must help Ellen overcome. Eddie, in going with her on the trip back East, helps Ellen resist the evil force until the mystical Varland, who has taken a short trip home to St. Paul, vanishes forever as the train goes through Pittsburgh. And Eddie is around not only for the remainder of the trip to comfort Ellen, but also for the rest of her life if she ever needs him. As Eddie summarizes it, "I'll be there—I'll always be there."[106]   "A Short Trip Home" with its happy resolution of a serious situation represents a retreat both in subject matter—youth—and in treatment to such earlier stories as "The Popular Girl" in which Fitzgerald shows a young girl who attempts to rely on her own resources but must finally be saved in the nick of time by a man. The message is a clear one: that women are fragile and should be watched over by men who abide by the chivalric code—a message that echoes through the canon from offshore pirate Toby Moreland's successful attempt to save Ardita from a life of boredom to the tragic consequences suffered by the too-independent Pamela Knighton in "Last Kiss," a woman who refuses to recognize that she needed the help of a man and dies in the process. As an affirmation of a belief in chivalry, "A Short Trip Home" is relatively successful compared to earlier stories such as "Dice, Brassknuckles & Guitar" (*Hearst's*, May 1923) in which Fitzgerald treats the same idea. Its weakness arises primarily from the haziness of the events which surround Varland's death.

In "The Bowl" (November 1927; *Post*, 21 January 1928; $3,500) Fitzgerald uses a first person narrator, Jeff, in much the same way he had used Eddie in "A Short Trip Home." As Eddie was involved in the life of Ellen, the central character in "A Short Trip Home," so does Jeff have an interest in the life of his Princeton roommate Dolly Harlan. Although he is a natural athlete and was a good football player at St. Regis, Dolly does not want to play football for Princeton because he has come to detest the routine of practice and "the apprehension of disaster" that he felt before a game was over. He plays, however, out of a sense of obligation to his classmates until the beautiful and callous Vienna Thorne convinces him that he should not play. Though her disapproval of the game has resulted from the fact that her brother was killed playing football, the reader is led to believe through Jeff that her violent objections to Dolly's playing are as selfish as most of her other actions. Dolly finally refuses to accept Vienna's mandate when he plays in the Yale Bowl, and he loses Vienna in the process. But he gains something much better: Daisy Cary, a beautiful movie star, who believes, as Dolly does, that one should fulfill one's moral obligations. As in "A Short Trip Home" Fitzgerald in "The Bowl" subscribes to the idea that destructive forces, like those embodied by Joe Varland and Vienna Thorne, will threaten to corrupt the innocence of essentially good young people—Ellen and Dolly, for example. However, good forces can overcome destructive ones, as Ellen is saved with Eddie's help and as Dolly is finally saved by his unwillingness to reject his principles. In "The Bowl," especially, Fitzgerald's message is a very American one: that happiness and success are the result of hard work, performed regardless of whether a person is sick or well. Both Dolly and Daisy subscribe to this belief in the story, and they—not Vienna and her urbane suitors—are the happy people in "The Bowl."

These stories, though they have weaknesses—all are improbable, for example—should properly be viewed in the context of their function in the body of Fitzgerald's work. They are, first, moneymakers which, in these cases, depend on the happy resolution of essentially sad situations for their entertainment value. As such they convey the moral that youth and love can conquer anything. In this group Fitzgerald "rediscovered" the subject of youth, and by experimenting in the framework of that subject with aesthetic distance he found the potential for both pathos and humor in the subject of adolescence, a discovery which led directly into a series of stories which are outstanding artistically as well as financially rewarding: the Basil Duke Lee series.

Basil Duke Lee: 28 April 1928 - 27 April 1929

While there is no evidence in Fitzgerald's correspondence with Ober to indicate why Fitzgerald turned when he did to the Basil series, the most obvious reason is money.[107] Just as Mary Roberts Rinehart's Babs series and Booth Tarkington's juvenile stories became popular moneymakers for their authors, Fitzgerald, no doubt, considered that his store of adolescent experiences was similarly marketable. The idea of putting them into a series was one that would have appeared to Fitzgerald as a profitable and predictable way of appealing to *Post* audiences who had a strong appetite for series as illustrated, for example, by the success of Norman Reilly Raine's Tugboat Annie stories. In this sense, then, the stories are patently commercial.

But more than this, the Basil stories are artistically good stories which indicate a facet of Fitzgerald's talent visible in only a few stories which precede them. In the sense that they are autobiographical, the stories represent no radical departure from Fitzgerald's habit of converting episodes of his life into marketable fiction; "'The Sensible Thing,'" for example, is one of numerous autobiographical stories. Nor does the difference lie simply in the fact that the series is retrospective: *This Side of Paradise* pulls heavily on Fitzgerald's adolescence. The quality of the Basil stories which sets them apart from anything before or after them is the degree of control over his material, the quality of the objectivity which Fitzgerald exercises over his material in these retrospective stories. Basil, by nature almost identical to Amory Blaine, is a sensitive and ambitious romantic hero who succeeds artistically because Fitzgerald in 1928 was able to view Basil much less seriously than he had viewed Amory Blaine eight years earlier. In addition to the artistic merit which derives from Fitzgerald's ironic stance toward Basil, much of the entertainment value of the series for its middle American audience depends on Fitzgerald's detached viewpoint. If he had presented Basil in a totally sympathetic light, he would have lost a large part of his audience who, because they were not like Basil, could not have accepted him as a figure with whom they could identify. Basil, after all, is not just an average member of the American middle class: he has more than an average amount of sensitivity, intelligence, and ambition. Most *Post* readers, therefore, would have related to the general sphere of Basil's experiences while they would often have viewed his individual attitudes toward these experiences as overly serious. Thus Fitzgerald in standing back from his subject allies himself with his audience and presents Basil's story as the often-humorous, occasionally serious adventure of a romantic hero who, if he "embodies the insecure American middle class," as has been suggested,[108] does so with a flair that would, more often than not, amuse the average *Post* reader rather than call his attention to a class insecurity that he may or may not have been aware of.

The chief difficulty Fitzgerald appears to have had with making the series authentic was that of giving his youthful subjects an age appropriate to their actions—a difficulty foreshadowed, among other places, in the pre-Basil story "Presumption," in which twenty-year-old San Juan Chandler has humorous qualities that one would find more amusing in a sixteen-year-old.   And this problem of assigning appropriate ages to his characters carries over into the Basil story "That Kind of Party" (c. May 1927; *Princeton University Library Chronicle*, Summer 1951).[109]   In this story Fitzgerald is still in the process of sharpening the focus of the telescope whose small end is aimed toward Basil (called Terence R. Tipton in the manuscript). Whereas San Juan Chandler in "Presumption" had acted too young for his age, Terence and his ten and eleven-year-old companions in "That Kind of Party" appear to be older than they are.   Terence, after masterminding a party at which the amusement will be kissing, is stopped short of executing his plan. But he is rewarded when Dolly, who admires his boldness in the matter, invites him to dinner thus granting him an hour with her that makes all of his efforts worthwhile. After rejecting the story, the *Ladies' Home Journal* editor advised Ober that parents did not "like to think of children ten years old being so much interested in sex." And Ober, in turn, advised Fitzgerald that he might easily add a couple of years to the ages of the children, but that he should, by all means, "make the children more attractive."[110] The eight Basil stories accepted by and published in the *Post* suggest that Fitzgerald was prompted, no doubt partly by the *Ladies' Home Journal*'s rejection and by Ober's suggestion, to carefully scrutinize the picture he had begun to form of his young subject so that Basil could be tailored for a popular audience. Whatever the reason, the Basil of the eight *Post* stories is so clearly and systematically defined through the varied experiences of his growth, the episodes can accurately be described as forming a novelette of growth.

In "The Scandal Detectives" (March 1928; *Post*, 28 April 1928; $3,500; *TAR*), the first story of the *Post* series, Basil, after having lost to Hubert Blair a battle in the contest for Imogene Bissel's affection, comes up with a scheme to scare the wits out of Hubert and his parents. With the help of best friend Ripley Buckner and another companion Bill Kampf, Basil plans to bind up Hubert just as he leaves his home on the way to a Basil- planned rendezvous with Imogene and stuff him into a trashcan in the Blairs' backyard. The plan fails when Hubert decides to chase the disguised scandal detectives rather than allow them to pursue him. But the incident, related in exaggerated form by Hubert to his parents, convinces the Blairs that if he is to go to visit Imogene, Hubert must be accompanied by his father. Shortly after they arrive at the Bissels' house, Basil, Ripley, and Bill also show up with stories that they too have been chased by "toughs" just as Hubert has. An impromptu party is arranged by Mrs. Bissel, who rises to the occasion even though she suspects that the whole business was somehow arranged as an improper social overture by Mrs. Blair. By the party's end everyone—Basil, Ripley, and Bill included—has been genuinely convinced that there actually are toughs in the neighborhood, and they are thus afraid to walk home alone. Hubert's father subsequently sends Mrs. Blair and Hubert to the seashore for the summer.

In the middle of this funny story, there are serious moments. After the initial contest and the temporary loss of Imogene, Basil "was alone with himself"[111]—a feeling that he recalled after the chase episode as a "moral" loneliness which had come from a fleeting realization that he really did not want to hurt Hubert Blair; that he "liked him as well as any boy he knew."[112] And, in fact, Basil is alone with his romantic visions, unable to share the feelings even with Ripley, much less with his mother's generation between whom the "gap was infinite and unbridgeable."[113] As Basil knows finally, and as the reader is shown, part of his motive grows from the wound his pride has received when Imogene's friend Margaret tells him that "Hubert Blair is the nicest boy in town and you're the most conceited"[114]—the first of many steps in Basil's moral education.

Thus through the action in the first story Fitzgerald reveals Basil's basic character: he is a romantic; he is sensitive to everything around him; and he is ingenious. Moreover, Fitzgerald sets up the elements which will, in one form or another, appear in all of the stories: a beautiful girl, usually rich (Imogene); an arch rival (Hubert); and an experience like the Basil-Imogene-Hubert encounter designed by Fitzgerald to trigger in Basil a reaction from which he can learn something about himself and to trigger in the audience a response of laughter that is mingled with the realization that Basil will grow morally in the next episode.

"A Night at the Fair" (May 1928; *Post*, 21 July 1928; $3,500) advances Basil's education a step further. His first night at the fair turns into a nightmare of humiliation and rejection when he is laughed at for being the only boy in his group with short pants on. Even Basil's old friend Ripley, whom he had always led, turns away from Basil and toward Elwood Leaming's more grown-up world of pick-up girls. Suddenly Basil realizes, as he tells his mother, that he would rather be dead than live through another day without long pants. When the long pants he orders finally arrive just in time for Basil to attend the fair with Elwood and Ripley, he finds that the pants do not solve all of his problems: he is stuck with an ugly sister of Elwood's date whom he finally gets rid of by giving her to Ripley. With some delight, then, he accepts rich Gladys Van Schellinger's invitation to sit in her parents' box at the fair only to find that she wants to use him to introduce her to his rival from Scandal Detective days, Hubert Blair.

Thus in this episode Basil is initiated into the sphere of unfamiliar girls who, unlike the girls he has grown up with, roam around unchaperoned at the fair. And he barely escapes spending a miserable evening with one of these girls by retreating into the secure upper-class world of the Van Schellingers'. But as he stands on the corner of his street where the Van Schellingers' chauffeur has left him at the end of the story, he has learned a lesson: long pants, while they may be a ticket into a more grown-up world that from a distance looks better than his own, do not necessarily make his existence in the world to which he already belongs any more comfortable. Therefore, in advancing Basil's story another step Fitzgerald brings Basil from his short-pants isolation back into the brotherhood of his exploring peers only to have him choose to retreat into the security of a familiar world. But left alone at the end to reflect on his situation, Basil comes back full circle into isolation; this time an isolation which results from Gladys's rejection of him in favor of Hubert Blair. At the end as he gazes thoughtfully at the Van Schellingers' limousine, the reader can be sure that Basil's two nights at the fair have been as educational to the supersensitive Basil as they have been entertaining to the audience—a typical instance in which Basil takes himself more seriously than does Fitzgerald or the audience.

In "The Freshest Boy" (April 1928; *Post*, 28 July 1928; $3,500; *TAR*) it becomes clear that Fitzgerald is selecting the specific episodes from Basil's life with a clearcut purpose: to underline the fact that his hero's education is an intensely personal, moral one which has little to do with formal education or adult instruction. Fitzgerald's choice in "The Freshest Boy" of St. Regis preparatory school as the setting for what is perhaps Basil's most valuable lesson is artfully ironic. In this academic environment Basil's maturation proceeds at a rate that is inversely proportional to his mastery of the subject matter he is supposed to be learning. It is only because of his poor academic performance that he gains an audience with the headmaster—a man who had ignored Basil until he is confronted with Basil's physical presence and who then only comments on his social maladjustment. But this man passes up the opportunity to help Basil, now known to his classmates as "Bossy," out of his role as the school scapegoat. Similarly a football coach, Mr. Rooney, on a trip with Basil to New York only tries half-heartedly to help him "g'wise to yourself."[115] While Basil is attending a show, Rooney goes off to get drunk. Thus, Basil bears the full burden of responsibility for extricating himself from his miserable social situation at St. Regis. His realization that he must face and change the reality of his plight rather than escape to Europe with his mother, then, becomes a milestone in Basil's maturation process. And the success that he enjoys in finally being accepted by his classmates also provides the happy ending which makes this story a good *Post* piece as well as a "minor classic of prep-school life."[116]

In the five stories which follow, Basil, who now has the dual success of his own self-acceptance and the acceptance of his St. Regis classmates, proceeds to learn some finer points about the adult world of which he has just become a member. In "He Thinks He's Wonderful" (July 1928; *Post*, 29 September 1928; $3,500; *TAR*) the cocky Basil boasts his way out of favor with his once-admiring friends and he gets the reputation, as he is told by Margaret Torrance, of thinking he is wonderful. But Basil does not fully learn how offensive his conceit is to others until, by virtue of his boasting, he loses an opportunity to vacation with the desirable Minnie Bibble of New Orleans. After this episode Basil begins with modesty to redeem himself with his old friends.

In "The Captured Shadow" (September 1928; *Post*, 29 December 1928; $3,500; *TAR*) Basil's desire to have Evelyn Beebe perform in his play leads him to knowingly allow Evelyn's brother Ham to catch the mumps, thus prohibiting Evelyn's family from leaving town during the time of the rehearsals. But Basil's great success with the play is blurred by his tearful realization that through his own selfish act he had not only robbed the Beebe family of a vacation but also in the process had made it impossible for the contagious Ham Beebe to see the play: "That poor kid with the mumps. . . . He had to stay home and all the other little kids were there. . . ."[117]

In "The Perfect Life" (October 1928; *Post*, 5 January 1929; $3,500; *TAR*) Basil accepts the invitation of St. Regis alumnus John Granby to lead an exemplary life for his classmates to emulate. And so, for a time Basil becomes self-righteous to the point of being offensive to his classmates; but he gives up his perfect life in order both to gain the affection of Jobena Dorsey and to keep her from eloping with Skiddy De Vinci. The lesson he learns is that extreme piety often offends others and, in the alienation which results, one loses all of his potential as a leader.

Again in "Forging Ahead" (January 1929; *Post*, 30 March 1929; $3,500) Basil, because there seems to be no alternative, attempts to face the problems of the world alone. When Basil finds that his mother might not be financially able to send him to Yale as she had promised, he resolves ambitiously, after reading an Horatio Alger story, to work his way through. An unpleasant part of the job that Basil gets for this purpose requires him to escort his unpopular cousin Rhoda Sinclair to all of the summer dances. But just as his duty demands that he forfeit an opportunity to see visiting Minnie Bibble, the Lee family fortune changes for the better and Basil is able to resign his job as Rhoda's companion—a conclusion that is the most contrived one in the series.

In "Basil and Cleopatra" (February 1929; *Post*, 27 April 1929; $3,500) there is no last-minute intervention to secure Minnie for Basil. Instead, she is lost to Littleboy LeMoyne Caruthers. And Basil's old girlfriend, now confidante, Jobena Dorsey convinces Basil that if Minnie is no longer "crazy" about him there is nothing that he can do. Thus, Fitzgerald in the last story of the series begins to strip Basil of the extreme romanticism that is his most distinguishing feature. Basil's story, therefore, ends with what the reader must assume to be the beginning of the final part of his education: a systematic dissolution of his romantic illusions, which are the only things left standing between Basil and maturity.

It is clear, then, that the Basil stories have a structural unity which derives, in part, from the progression of steps in his education. In each episode Basil learns something that will enable him to function better in an adult world. The continuity of these stories plus the sustained ironic viewpoint, which allows the reader at all times to know more about Basil than he knows about himself, conspire to make these stories a unified artwork when viewed together. But *Post* readers were, no doubt, less impressed by those features of the stories which bind them together than they were by other features which indicate that Fitzgerald wrote the Basil stories with his audience clearly in mind. The episodic nature of the narrative which allows the various segments of the story to stand alone makes Basil's story more readable than a novel to a large middle-American audience. And the idea itself behind the series—that is, the self-education of a resourceful boy—has mass appeal: that a young American boy left to his own resources can overcome almost any obstacle confirms the popular bias that personal initiative is a key to success of any kind. Moreover, the stories invite audience participation and identification, if not with Basil himself, then with the general sphere of his experiences. Each of the episodes contains at least one of the ingredients common to virtually everyone's childhood: an arch rival like Hubert Blair ("The Scandal Detectives"); a first initiation into the adult world like Basil's brief participation in the lifestyle of Elwood Leaming ("A Night at the Fair"); a choice which marks the beginning of independence similar to Basil's decision not to run away with his mother from his problems ("The Freshest Boy"); a phase of conceit and a realization such as Basil's that it is better to demonstrate good qualities rather than verbalize them ("He Thinks He's Wonderful"); a time when moral considerations are sacrificed to selfish whims as when Basil forgets his scruples in allowing Ham Beebe to catch the mumps ("The Captured Shadow"); a resolution to be more nearly perfect which is often followed by a realization like Basil's that perfection can lead to personal isolation ("The Perfect Life"); a moment of extreme disappointment similar to that when Basil learns that it may not be possible for him to attend Yale ("Forging Ahead"); and the loss of one's first love as Basil lost Minnie ("Basil and Cleopatra"). Each of these serious topics, however, is framed with humor and often entertains largely because of the comic relief. Basil's first year at St. Regis, for example, is quite lonely and sad, but perhaps more memorable than his isolation are Basil's reflections on the Harrison Fisher color reproductions that he had ordered: "After a few minutes, he found that he was looking oftenest at Dora and Babette and, to a lesser extent, at Gretchen, though the latter's Dutch cap seemed unromantic and precluded the element of mystery."[118] Therefore, the particular flavor of the Basil stories which renders them first-rate entertainment results from Fitzgerald's blending of the serious and the trivial, the sad and humorous. And so, while Fitzgerald was depending on the Basil stories for all of his income in 1928, his audience was depending on Fitzgerald to satisfy their curiosity. This is reflected in Ober's remark to Fitzgerald that "I shall never be satisfied until I hear more about Basil, and I think everyone who reads the stories feels the same way."[119]

During the time that the Basil stories were appearing in the *Post*, Fitzgerald published only one story in another magazine: "Outside the Cabinet-Maker's" (*Century*, December, 1928; $150), which was rejected by every magazine to which Ober submitted it before it was sold to *Century*.[120] The story consists of two short scenes which are developed primarily through dialogue. The father invents a story for his little girl while they are outside the cabinetmaker's shop waiting for the mother to return.   The world that the father invents is peopled by Fairy Princesses and Ogres, which according to the father live across the street from the cabinetmaker's shop.   The man tries to enter the make-believe world with his daughter but finds that he cannot enjoy it with her.   When the mother returns, the three leave together, each retreating into his own dreamworld: the mother remembers that she was poor as a child and never had the kind of doll's house that the cabinetmaker is now building; the father recalls that he almost made a million dollars at one time; and the daughter continues to think about the fantasy world her father has created.   The story, brief and developed through dialogue, foreshadows the *Esquire* stories which have these same qualities.   Also noteworthy is the fact that "Outside the Cabinet-Maker's" reflects Fitzgerald's feeling at this time that once the ability to see life through the eyes of a child is lost, it is gone forever.   The objective view that Fitzgerald takes of Josephine in the stories which follow indicate that Fitzgerald was finding it easier, perhaps, to view youth from outside rather than to view the world through the eyes of youth.   However, Fitzgerald, unlike the father in "Outside the Cabinet-Maker's," had certainly not lost forever this ability, as Cecelia Brady's believable and romantic descriptions in *The Last Tycoon* point out.

Josephine Perry: 5 April 1930 - 15 August 1931

After "Basil and Cleopatra" (27 April 1929), which followed "Outside the Cabinet-Maker's," Fitzgerald dropped the Basil series for no apparent reason and began a group of serious *Tender Is the Night* cluster stories including "The Rough Crossing" (8 June 1929), "Majesty" (13 July 1929), "At Your Age" (17 August 1929), "The Swimmers" (19 October 1929) and "Two Wrongs" (18 January 1930). With the second of these stories the *Post* began paying Fitzgerald $4,000 per story, the highest price that he would receive for a single story in his lifetime. It is noteworthy that the increase in price immediately followed the eight Basil stories and indicates, as Ober had suggested, their immense popular appeal. It is unlikely that the five somber *Tender Is the Night* cluster stories which followed the Basil group generated as much popular interest.   While the two most serious ones, "The Rough Crossing" and "The Swimmers," depend finally for their popular success on the patriotic sentiment of the *Post* audience, the stories are too bleak to have the kind of mass appeal that would make them top-price commercial pieces. It was, no doubt, with this in mind that Fitzgerald turned back to the popular formula—a series about adolescence—that had worked well a year earlier. Thus, the Josephine Perry stories seem to have blossomed from necessity: that is, from Fitzgerald's need to play the extremes—his very serious *Tender Is the Night* cluster stories and the much lighter adolescence pieces—against each other in order to maintain his posture as a popular entertainer.

In spite of the superficial similarities between the Basil and Josephine groups—both are series about adolescence—Josephine is not a female Basil, nor is the entertainment value of the series the same. Whereas Basil's middle-class background invited and allowed the *Post* audience to share in the sphere of his personal experience, Josephine's family is upper class, "Chicago society, and almost very rich":[121] her experience is bound to differ from that of most *Post* readers. Moreover, although Basil regarded himself more seriously than any popular reader was apt to have regarded him, he was sensitive to the feelings of others, ambitious, and ready to learn from his experience—qualities on which *Post* readers placed a high premium. By contrast, Josephine is insensitive, snobbish, and rude—characteristics which went counter to the value systems of most *Post* readers. In short, Basil is in Amory Blaine's direct line of descent and is thus entertaining, understandable, and tolerable as an incurable romantic in the process of almost being cured; on the other hand, Josephine, who in John Boynton Bailey's words ("A Snobbish Story") will "be married to some boy from Yale or Harvard with a couple of hundred neckties and . . . get to be a dumbbell like the rest,"[122] is in many ways an adolescent Daisy Buchanan.[123] In constructing Josephine's character as he does, Fitzgerald invites the audience to react toward her in a prescribed manner: after being entertained by her latest predicament, most *Post* readers would want to spank her. That is, they would have felt as her parents often did after the current crisis was over: "angry. . . as with a child who has toddled under the galloping horses."[124] Therefore, whereas the movement of the Basil series was toward maturity, Josephine's open rebellion against societal rules and her reckless emotional spending lead her at sixteen into emptiness and apathy—a fact, no doubt, undisturbing to most *Post* readers who would have viewed Josephine as essentially trivial, a spoiled rich girl who merited the punishment she received. And it is precisely because he fashions Josephine as he does—nearly as unsympathetic as the Smiths ("The Rough Crossing")—that Fitzgerald is able to experiment with the serious subject of emotional bankruptcy, toward which Josephine progressively heads in the five stories of the series. In each case the stories entertain primarily because one is bound to wonder where Josephine's rebellion will lead her next. But Fitzgerald, true to the dictates of middle American morality, never rewards Josephine for her misconduct; and ultimately he punishes her with irreversible emotional depletion.

In Josephine's first two adventures she is neither rewarded nor punished for the basic character traits Fitzgerald establishes in these two stories. In "First Blood" (January 1930; *Post*, 5 April 1930; $4,000, *TAR*) Josephine's flirtation leads her into a short-lived affair with twenty-two-year-old Anthony Harker, a boyfriend of Josephine's older sister Constance. Although Josephine invites and encourages Harker's affection she is neither prepared nor willing for him to reciprocate by falling hopelessly in love with her. Fitzgerald comments ironically that no one, not even her sister, could blame the sixteen-year-old Josephine for Harker's foolish pursuit of her: "If a man of twenty-two should so debase himself as to pay frantic court to a girl of sixteen against the wishes of her parents and herself, there was only one answer—he was a person who shouldn't be received by decent people."[125]   But as Fitzgerald realizes, the audience, who knows precisely how scheming Josephine has actually been, is apt to feel otherwise. A girl who has called her mother a "darn fool" and masterminded every encounter with a man whom she rejects after working diligently to ensnare is apt to invite little sympathy from an audience that believes in young love and the need to honor one's mother and father. But they would, no doubt, be curious to see how she will finally outsmart herself and be appropriately punished.

In "A Nice Quiet Place" (March 1930; *Post*, 31 May 1930; $4,000; *TAR*) Fitzgerald continues to round out the picture of Josephine's character that he had begun in "First Blood." After being forced by her parents to spend the summer at an out-of-the-way place up in Michigan, Josephine later, in a characteristic act, retaliates. On the evening of Constance's wedding Josephine succeeds in luring the prospective groom into an embrace, and his acquiescence almost causes a postponement of the wedding. For her part in the affair Josephine is supposedly sent back into exile, to Michigan. But unknown to Josephine's parents, Sonny Dorrance, a Harvard man who has tried to conceal his identity from everyone, including Josephine, is also there "keeping off his admirers."[126] The reader is left to assume that he will probably be Josephine's next victim.

After merely entertaining the audience in the first two stories with Josephine's antics and, in the process, delineating her character, Fitzgerald is ready in the final three episodes to present her with the consequences of her irresponsibility. As the woman in "A Woman with a Past" (June 1930; *Post*, 6 September 1930; $4,000; *TAR*) at seventeen—that is, as one who had the reputation of being a speed—"she was blasé and bored with falling in love," which seemed to "[have] happened once too often."[127] And as a forecast of things to come she reveals to her old friend Ed Bement a symptom of her approaching emotional bankruptcy: "For months I've felt as if I were a hundred years old and I'm just seventeen. . . ."[128] Therefore, when "the first mature thought that she had ever had in her life"—that some men are made to have fun with and some made to be married to—crosses her mind it is almost too late: her first failure to win a man she wanted, in this case Dudley Knowlton, is the first installment of her punishment, which by this time she is almost too numb to feel.

In "A Snobbish Story" (September 1930; *Post*, 29 November 1930; $4,000), instead of building a future based on the insight gained in "A Woman with a Past" thus redeeming herself with the *Post* audience, Josephine decides finally to live her life as wildly and as fully as she can. After excusing herself from her regular annual vaudeville number with Travis de Coppet in favor of the prospect of starring in a serious play written by socialistic John Boynton Bailey, Josephine regrets isolating herself from her ritzy Lake Forest companions; and she gives up any notion she had previously had to make a commitment to any future ideal such as social equality. When she hears the applause for de Coppet's new dance partner performing in what used to be her part, Josephine dedicates herself totally to the present. She decides "[t]hat any value she might have was in the immediate, shimmering present—and thus thinking, she threw in her lot with the rich and powerful of this world forever."[129]

After casting her lot as decisively as she does in "A Snobbish Story," it becomes clear that Josephine's adventures can go in only one direction—toward an epilogue, "Emotional Bankruptcy" (June 1931; *Post*, 15 August 1931; $4,000), in which Josephine, quite predictably in terms of the *Post*'s laws of crime and punishment, does not live happily ever after. She is, in fact, confronted with two alternatives, both of which Fitzgerald has prepared the reader for. On the one hand, she can continue to live in the present and enjoy herself fully as she had decided to do in "A Snobbish Story"; or she can look for a man to marry and plan to settle down, a possibility that she had earlier considered in "A Woman with a Past." But neither alternative is viable in Josephine's bankrupt state. She finds her Princeton weekend and its once-upon-a-time glamour dull. According to her friend Lillian, Josephine has "been around too much."[130] And Josephine finds the men "not like they used to be."[131] Thus, precisely when it becomes clear that Josephine's only hope now lies in finding the perfect man to marry, he, in fact, appears. But when they kiss she feels like laughing, an incongruous reaction which indicates that Josephine's emotional bankruptcy is complete. In Fitzgerald's words, "One cannot both spend and have";[132] and because Josephine's life has been a spending spree, she must now be denied what she had in "A Woman with a Past" considered as a last resort—the prospect of a comfortable marriage such as the one Dudley Knowlton's fiancée, Adele Craw, could expect.

One of the most obvious questions that arises concerning the Josephine stories is how Fitzgerald managed to fashion a popular series around a topic as grave as emotional bankruptcy. The subject does, after all, play a central role in the last three Josephine stories and gives direction to the whole series. The answer lies in Fitzgerald's choice of an inconsequential person with whom to couple this malady. It is likely that *Post* readers took Josephine at face value, essentially trivial, and thus saw her emotional depletion as of little consequence—not to be taken seriously. Even so, the fact that there were consequences suggests the underlying principle to which even the bleakest *Tender Is the Night* cluster stories adhered: wrongdoing could not go unpunished in the pages of the *Post* regardless of the stature of the heroine or the amusement which accrued in her misconduct. As Josephine said, "I'm just paying for things,"[133] which, in the eyes of *Post* readers, she certainly was.

Early Material and the Beginning of the *Post* Decline

Historically, "Emotional Bankruptcy" marks the beginning of the downward course in Fitzgerald's career as a *Post* writer—a phase of his career characterized by the depletion of his material for *Post* stories. After "Emotional Bankruptcy," the *Post* continued for nine more months (five more stories) to pay Fitzgerald his top price of $4,000 per story, but in mid-1932 the *Post* prices began to drop to $3,500 and then $2,500 per story—a result not only of the weaker stories he was submitting but also of the Depression. In the period marked at one end by the publication of *The Great Gatsby* and at the other by the last Josephine story, Fitzgerald had drawn the material for his *Post* fiction almost exclusively from two sources: from the *Tender Is the Night* material which he was then in the process of shaping into a book and from his adolescence—the Basil-Josephine stories and those four adolescence stories which precede them. In the *Post* stories which follow "Emotional Bankruptcy" Fitzgerald primarily resurrects material that had worked before with *Post* audiences; therefore, many of the stories in this last *Post* phase bear comparison with specific early stories.   But the simple truth is that even though Fitzgerald was working with material that he knew best—his material—the stories are weaker in almost every respect than the earlier stories dealing with the same subjects. From a critical standpoint most of them, because they contain too many characters, too much implausibility, and too much unrelated action, come across as blurred and disjointed. And from the standpoint of popular taste the stories are infrequently as entertaining as earlier Fitzgerald stories on similar subjects, a fact pointed out most sharply by Fitzgerald's decline in popularity with *Post* editors. There can be no question about the basic truth that Fitzgerald, somewhere in the period bounded by "Emotional Bankruptcy" (15 August 1931) and the publication of *Tender Is the Night* (April 1934), lost the knack for pleasing the *Post* readers, which later steered him in the direction of the much less profitable *Esquire*, scarcely a direction that he would have consciously chosen.

Numerous possibilities for the *Post* decline present themselves. A first possibility that must be dismissed is the idea that Fitzgerald's craftsmanship was at a low ebb: the *Post* decline coincides with the composition of his most ambitious novel. Another possible reason for the *Post*'s coolness toward Fitzgerald's stories in the years immediately preceding *Tender Is the Night* could have been the shift in editorial policy which followed George Horace Lorimer's 1932 "promotion" into semi-retirement.[134] According to Graeme Lorimer, however, the *Post* did not alter its policy regarding Fitzgerald's stories after his father's promotion. Instead, he suggests that the editorial staff would have welcomed as many Fitzgerald stories as they could have gotten if the stories had been of the same quality as Fitzgerald's earlier stories written for the magazine.[135] It is true, though, that beginning in 1937, when Wesley Winans Stout became editor of the *Post*, Fitzgerald was unable to please Stout because of what Fitzgerald called the new editor's preference for "escape stories about the brave frontiersmen . . . or fishing or football captains."[136] But as DeVoto points out, the most popular subject for magazine fiction was "what the editors call 'young love'"; the second was "the story of personal risk in a good cause"; the third was one which gave "an inside view of some unfamiliar but interesting occupation"; and fourth "young married stuff."[137] The first of these—young love—Fitzgerald worked with in several stories of the *Post* decline: "A Freeze-Out," "One Interne," and "The Family Bus," to name three. The second, the personal risk story, he attempts in "More than Just a House." The third story type, an inside view into an interesting occupation, Fitzgerald experiments with in "I Got Shoes." The fourth, "young married stuff," Fitzgerald had worked with in "The Adolescent Marriage." A logical conclusion, therefore, is Fitzgerald was not out of touch with the preferences of the *Post* audience. Instead, in attempting to find a way to give a new slant to material that he had used often before, Fitzgerald began moralizing, and he began padding to make his subjects fit the 6,000-word *Post* requirements. Both of these practices led him to violate the most important rule of popular magazine fiction that, above all, it should entertain. Each of the stories of his *Post* decline illustrates the fact that Fitzgerald, if he had not lost sight of this rule, found it increasingly difficult to maintain a high level of interest for a space of 6,000 words. He simply did not at that time have enough material.

"The Last of the Belles" (November 1928; *Post*, 2 March 1929; $3,500, *TAR*), which appeared chronologically near the end of the Basil series and which preceded the last group of *Tender Is the Night* cluster stories, indicates Fitzgerald's attempt to pick up strands from his old *Post* repertoire even before he had exhausted either his new *Tender Is the Night* subject matter or his then successful adolescence material. In this sense, therefore, the story anticipates that looking backward quality which characterizes most of the *Post* stories which follow "Emotional Bankruptcy"; it also indicates Fitzgerald's awareness at that point that he was running out of material for commercial fiction. "The Last of the Belles" is the last story in the Tarleton, Georgia, series.[138] Whereas Fitzgerald had already spotlighted Sally Carrol Happer and Nancy Lamar—two of the "only three girls" in Tarleton, in "The Last of the Belles" he is concerned, among other things, with the past and future of the remaining one, Ailie Calhoun. The story is a nostalgic one in which Andy, the first person narrator, looks back ten years to the enchanted time of 1919 when he was stationed in Tarleton and was, for a time, Ailie's companion and confidant. After detailing the events of 1919, including the suicide of one of Ailie's rejected suitors, Andy brings the reader up to the present and his decision to return to Tarleton to recapture Ailie and the past. But Fitzgerald does not give in to what must have been a temptation to unite Ailie and Andy. Instead, after he proposes to Ailie, Andy finds that she is engaged to marry a man from Savannah. He is, therefore, forced to return to the North realizing that "in another month Ailie would be gone and the South would be empty for me forever."[139] Andy is the sympathetic core of the story, and his return trip to Tarleton is a romantic journey prompted by Andy's idealization of Ailie.[140] When he returned to Tarleton and began to feel a sense of dissatisfaction, he "realized what was the matter, what had always been the matter—I was deeply and incurably in love with her."[141]   His empty-handed return north, then, directs the audience's reaction to the story. As a story about romantic love, however, "The Last of the Belles" is less successful than many other Fitzgerald stories that fall into this category—"'The Sensible Thing,'" for instance. The primary reason for this is that Andy, whose story this finally is, lacks the drive and intensity of other Fitzgerald men in love. Even back in 1919 he lacked the perseverance necessary to get a kiss from Ailie whom he very much wanted to kiss. Similarly, he does not have the initiative necessary to dissuade Ailie from carrying through with a marriage that both he and she know is not firmly grounded in love. Indeed, the story lacks the sparkle characteristic of many early Fitzgerald stories, not because the heroine is less desirable than her antecedents like Sally Carrol or because the plot of the story fails to provide the hero with ample opportunity to succeed. Rather, the weakness lies in Andy's relative lack of the competitive drive to win when he tries to pursue an ideal, though, too, in this case the ideal Ailie has an antipathy toward smart men. But in some respects Andy's attitude suggests that Fitzgerald was attempting in his commercial fiction to retreat from disenchantment and once again make the romantic quest credible.

"Between Three and Four" (June 1931; *Post*, 5 September 1931; $4,000), the first story to appear after "Emotional Bankruptcy" (1931), relies on the atmosphere of the Depression. In the story Fitzgerald develops the audience's sympathy for Sarah Belknap Summer, a forty-year-old woman who has been fired by a one-time suitor Howard Butler. Butler's suicide at the end, prompted partly by the belief that he has driven Sarah to leap nine floors to her death, is presented as just punishment for a man who has maliciously prevented Sarah from getting a job. But as in most stories after "Emotional Bankruptcy," Fitzgerald in "Between Three and Four" leans on material that he had used earlier. The situation in this story is reminiscent of "Hot & Cold Blood" in which Fitzgerald sets up James Coatesworth for the guilt he would have felt, similar to Butler's, if he had allowed old Bronson to die after refusing to lend him money. The major difference lies in Fitzgerald's opting in "Hot & Cold Blood" for a happy ending in which Coatesworth and Bronson live happily ever after instead of the bleak conclusion, more suitable to the Depression era, of Sarah's salvation at the expense of vengeful Butler's life—an ending which would have tallied with the *Post* audience's sense of what Butler deserved.

Similarly, "A Change of Class" (July 1931; *Post*, 26 September 1931; $4,000) is a Depression story which, rather than pointing to a casualty of this period, demonstrates that Earl is actually much happier as a good, successful barber than he ever could have been in the monied world to which he gained entrance through a good stock market tip. And though there are no specific parallels to this story in Fitzgerald's earlier short fiction, Earl's story is an overnight success story like "The Third Casket." Fitzgerald's view of monetary success in "A Change of Class," however, more closely parallels his feelings about the corrosive influence of wealth examined in *The Great Gatsby* and would, therefore, have been more appealing than a happy, standard rags-to-riches story to a Depression-ridden American public.

In "A Freeze-Out" (September 1931; *Post*, 19 December 1931; $4,000) Fitzgerald attempts to take the formula of his earlier romantic love stories and add another ingredient, an explicit attack on the erosion of sacred American virtues. Forrest Winslow, a pillar of Minneapolis society, stubbornly refuses to admit his attraction to the "lovely and expensive" Alida Rikker because her father was once engaged in a shady business deal and spent several months in prison. But Forrest, to the chagrin of his hypocritical, socialite parents, decides after judging Alida on her own merits—not according to the misdeeds of her father—to marry her. His decision is made easier by the encouragement of his old pioneer-stock great-grandmother who represents the once-good American value system which has now become corrupt. The hypocrisy-of-the-rich idea is made strongly when in a characteristic, self-serving act Forrest's father decides at the last minute to attend the wedding because, in his words, "They'll say I'm an old grouch and drop me out of the picture entirely."[142]

Alida, unlike most rich, beautiful Fitzgerald heroines, is totally sympathetic, and the story is at least partially successful as a story of young love in Fitzgerald's early manner. It is also successful, in part, as a criticism of upper class hypocrisy as embodied in Pierce and Charlotte Winslow. The two elements, however, vying for central attention as they do, diminish the overall effect of the story. Forrest, in order to be a believable convert to open-mindedness, must first be presented as ultra-conservative; and he is. But for such a man to get drunk and lead off Chauncey Rikker's ball as a prelude to swearing undying affection for Alida involves a character change that must have led *Post* readers to wonder how this frog was changed, even by liquor, into such a prince. On the one hand, the old Forrest is more reserved than the unspeakable egg; the new Forrest behaves like Perry Parkhurst ("The Camel's Back") in hot pursuit of Betty Medill's hand. The point is this: Fitzgerald projects the idea in his later *Post* stories dealing with romantic love that the love itself is not sufficient to inspire great enthusiasm in his heroes; there must be a greater moral at stake, such as the principle of fairness Forrest adheres to in pursuing Alida.

In the case of "Diagnosis" (October 1931; *Post*, 20 February 1932; $4,000), Fitzgerald so complicates the love affair between Sara Etherington and Charlie Clayhorne that their final coming together at the end is anti-climatic. Sara returns from Europe to find her fiancé Charlie suffering from emotional bankruptcy, which he attributes to the Depression. She arranges a meeting for him with Marston Raines, a character reminiscent of (though less shadowy than) Dr. Smith in "The Adjuster," which prompts Charlie to make a pilgrimage to his home in Alabama. The story then veers off into an elaborate subplot involving Charlie's father's will, his brother, and $10,000. Charlie returns to New York, apparently cured and ready to marry Sara. The many twists and turns of the plot make the reunion seem contrived and leave the reader caring very little about their future. As in "The Last of the Belles" and "A Freeze Out," the qualifying conditions that are imposed on the main characters detract from the spontaneity of the basic love plot. The result of such complications and heavy plotting is that the later Fitzgerald *Post* stories about romantic love lack the sparkle that had characterized early ones such as "The Offshore Pirate," and in the process, from the standpoint of the popular reader, the emotional payoff may well have been buried too deeply somewhere in the middle of the story's cross-purposes. As Bruccoli observes in his headnote to "Diagnosis" in *Price*, the *Post* positioned the story fourth in the issue, farther back than he had been since 1920, indicating that his popularity with readers was slipping.

In "Flight and Pursuit" (April 1931; *Post*, 14 May 1932; $4,000) Fitzgerald sets up a situation which, at an earlier time in his career, he might have fashioned into a story about the romantic rescue of a beautiful young girl by an infatuated suitor who refused to give up his pursuit, as in "The Popular Girl," for example. The elements for such a story are certainly there. Caroline Martin, a Virginia thoroughbred, reacts to the disappointment of wealthy Sidney Lehaye's apparent rejection of her by eloping with George Corcoran, "a trivial young lieutenant from Ohio."[143] But Fitzgerald has Caroline linger in the misery of her unhappy marriage for so long and so firmly grounds the motivation for her eventual rescue by Lehaye in such extreme guilt that the final reunion of the one-time young lovers becomes a dubious romantic achievement. As in "The Last of the Belles" where Andy has been blasé in both his early and late attempts to win Ailie whom he professed to love, so in "Flight and Pursuit" does Lahaye lack the personal incentive, or he is too much paralyzed by guilt, to pursue

Caroline with the degree of enthusiasm that would make his love of her more believable. In this story as clearly as any other, Fitzgerald's difficulties in turning out the kind of popular fiction that he had written earlier are apparent. Romantic love, of course, had been the subject on which his early popular reputation had been founded; and guilt and remorse had figured importantly into more recent stories like "Babylon Revisited." When Fitzgerald attempts to bring together these elements as in "Flight and Pursuit," however, he is less successful in creating either a believable love story or a meaningful atonement. Thus, the amusement value of "Flight and Pursuit" like that of "A Freeze-Out" is undercut by the coupling of two elements—in the case of "Flight and Pursuit," romantic love and guilt—which in the popular mind are essentially incompatible.

From a popular standpoint Fitzgerald's problem in "Family in the Wind" (April 1932; *Post*, 4 June 1932; $3,500; *TAR*) is how to take Forrest Janney, a now-cynical surgeon with an alcohol problem and "cirrhosis of the emotions"[144] from point A—his semi-retirement from life—to a final destination acceptable to *Post* readers, and that destination turns out to be the rather predictable return of Dr. Janney to his profession. However, in the process of resolving the situation, Fitzgerald dilutes the main plot line with a number of ingredients which are tangential to the popular readers' primary interest: how Janney will confirm their belief in the ultimate integrity of medical men. Janney's return is actually precipitated by his desire to become a good substitute father for young Helen Kilrain, whose real father has been killed by a tornado. But Fitzgerald introduces subordinate plots which have little to do with the nature or resolution of Janney's problem and which, in themselves, yield too little entertainment to merit inclusion in the story. For example, the separate drama of Janney's love for a seventeen-year-old girl, who does not make an appearance in the story, and Janney's lingering hatred of a nephew, who apparently had a hand in her death, is not explored and has little bearing on the main story line. That readers were, no doubt, misled into expecting more from the Janney-Mary subplot is suggested by the *Post* illustrator's preoccupation with the pair: of the two quarter-page illustrations, one is devoted to depicting the two in a drugstore encounter which does not occur in the story, and a cameo picture of Mary Decker graces the story's first page. In addition, Fitzgerald, in a figurative sense, promises the reader vicarious pleasure in the conflict between Janney and his no-good nephew, Pinky, but does not pursue the idea: Janney, after endless begging from his brother's family, performs an operation to remove a bullet from the nephew's head; but by the time the boy finally dies, the reader has, no doubt, forgotten how much face Janney would have saved if Pinky had lived.

This is not to suggest, however, that there is too much action in "Family in the Wind," or in any of the stories written in Fitzgerald's *Post* decline, for that matter. Certainly, earlier stories such as "The Offshore Pirate" were complicated and full of action. The fact is that in most of the earlier stories Fitzgerald had led the reader through mazes of details which bore directly on, and thus reinforced, the predictable outcome. But in the later *Post* stories—"Family in the Wind" is one of the best examples—he diffuses the reader's interest by involving him in the many unrelated events of the subordinate plots and thus diminishes the impact that a much simpler story might have had.

The seven stories which appeared in the *Post* between "Family in the Wind" and the publication of *Tender Is the Night*[145] have this feature in common: all of the stories pull heavily on the subject matter of earlier Fitzgerald stories such as success, unhappy marriage, and romantic love, all of which have antecedents in Fitzgerald's pre-*Gatsby* popular fiction. But more important than this, all of the stories, with the possible exception of "One Interne" and "The Family Bus," violate a cardinal rule of popular magazine fiction: according to DeVoto slick fiction "uses any theme primarily as material for the creation and resolution of a situation."[146] In most of these later *Post* stories the reverse is more often true: the plots become the vehicles for various themes. In short, they become slick parables whose messages often interfere with that primary object of any popular magazine story: to amuse its readers.

In "The Rubber Check" (May 1932; *Post*, 6 August 1932; $3,000) Fitzgerald shows that the wealthy are not only capable of being insensitive and superficial; they also expect those who are not wealthy to live by rules that they are not willing to observe themselves. Val Schuyler's social life is wrecked because Mrs. Charles Martin Templeton will not allow those in her social circle to forget that Val wrote a bad check. By the time word travels from Philadelphia, where the Templetons live, to New York, which is Val's home, his check cashing experience has been tremendously exaggerated and the mothers of leading debutantes soon forbid their daughters to dance with Val. Ironically though, the social set from which Val is being excluded is made up of people who have left bad checks "all over New York."[147] And the Mortmains, who represent the glamour that Val has always associated with wealth, have not really had a fortune for quite some time. As Ellen Mortmain, a Judy Jones-type heroine whom Val has nearly worshipped, reveals, "It seems we've been in the red for years, but the market floated us."[148] The purpose of the story, then, is to suggest that wealth may insulate its possessors against the kind of criticism that was directed at the middle-class Val. However, the vehicle of the message—the story of Val Schuyler's check-cashing experience—is much less entertaining than many other Fitzgerald stories dealing with the corrosive influence of wealth—"Dice, Brassknuckles & Guitar" or "Winter Dreams," for example. Because Val is such an unsympathetic character, his story is as often irritating as it is entertaining. Unlike Dexter Green ("Winter Dreams"), who is admirable because he works hard, or Jim Powell ("Dice, Brassknuckles & Guitar"), who is admirable because he is morally superior to the members of Southhampton society, Val is an often-obnoxious social climber. At the end of the story *Post* readers may well have been glad that such a pretentious person as he finally found his place in a cabbage patch planting cabbages for Mr. Charles Martin Templeton. Fitzgerald obviously intended that his social criticism be double-edged: that is, that ambitious social climbers like Val be castigated along with the Mortmains and the Templetons. The amusement value for popular readers of the story, though, is diminished by what appears to be the story's first purpose: to convey a serious message.

"What a Handsome Pair!" (April 1932; *Post*, 27 August 1932; $2,500) pits the happy marriage of musician Teddy Van Beck and his "peasant" wife against the miserably competitive marriage of "the handsome pair," Helen and Stuart Oldhorne, in order to support one of Teddy's "favorite themes": "People tried to make marriages cooperative and they've ended by becoming competitive. Impossible situation. . . . A man ought to marry somebody who'll be grateful, like Betty here."[149] Curiously enough, Betty has already demonstrated her gratitude by allowing, even slightly encouraging, Teddy to run around with other women while she is at home caring for sick children. But their kind of marriage, says Fitzgerald, will last because it is founded on the mutual appreciation of very different kinds of talent: Teddy's revolves around piano playing; Betty's around child-rearing and housekeeping. By contrast, a marriage like the Oldhornes, in which the partners share common interests, is doomed to fail because of the inevitable competition that will finally work its way into every area of the relationship; and this is true, the story implies, even when the foundation for such a marriage is romantic love like Stuart's and Helen's. Moreover, by depicting a practical marriage that lasts like Van Beck's, Fitzgerald seems to sanction an open relationship in which the male is free to pursue romantic interests outside marriage.

Certainly many of the *Post* readers must have felt that these conclusions were outrageous, flying as they do in the face of middle-class morality, but the Van Becks and the Oldhornes were perhaps exempt from middle-class standards because both lived in marginal worlds (the Van Becks in the musician's world and the Oldhornes in the sportsman's world). Even in the marginal worlds, however, no one seems rewarded for infidelity: Teddy's flirtation with Helen Oldhorne comes to nothing, and Helen, for her mild infidelity, seems to receive nothing but misery. The rewards, meager though they are, go to the patient and longsuffering in the story: Betty, who will do anything to make Teddy happy, is rewarded with peace of mind; and Stuart, who is more than understanding of Helen's unpleasantness, maintains his self respect.

There is no such moral in "One Interne" (August 1932; *Post*, 5 November 1932; $3,500; *TAR*), a story whose purpose is solely to entertain. The tale concerns the love affair of Dr. William Tulliver V, with himself and then with a pretty anesthetist, Thea Singleton. And in some ways "One Interne," at least in its intent, approaches Fitzgerald's early romantic stories which existed only for the amusement of their readers. Fitzgerald's attention, however, moves progressively away from the central affair between Tulliver and Thea; and instead one is left primarily with a thorough knowledge of Bill's trials as a novice diagnostician, information that would be very interesting to a second-year medical student. Consequently, Thea Singleton's personality, which has as much promise as any recent Fitzgerald heroine's, remains unexplored as she finally must retreat "back into her own mystery,"[150] in part perhaps to escape the less-than-endearing egocentricity that is Tulliver's most notable quality. In Thea, as in Ailie Calhoun ("The Last of the Belles"), Fitzgerald creates an intriguing woman; but in both stories he shifts his focus, for one reason or another, from the promising love affairs that would have best shown them off for what they are—potential old-style Fitzgerald heroines from whom no one stole the center stage.

Despite several implausibilities in its plot, "More than Just a House" (April 1933; *Post*, 24 June 1933; $3,000) is perhaps the best of the thirteen *Post* stories that lie between "Emotional Bankruptcy" and *Tender Is the Night*. From the initial situation in which twenty-six-year-old Lew Lowrie rescues Amanda Gunther from the path of an oncoming train, Fitzgerald skillfully uses the old Maryland house in which the Gunthers live as the embodiment of primary virtues of the American past. Because Lew was the son of a gardener who tended an estate similar to the Gunther's, Lew feels an immediate warmth for this house which, on one level, represents his personal past and, on another, stands for the past heritage which Lew among all Americans shares. In a manner reminiscent of "The Fall of the House of Usher" Fitzgerald indicates that the decay of the house parallels the fall of the Gunther family. The oldest daughter Amanda leaves the house to live with her husband in New York on Park Avenue and dies in childbirth; Jean, the middle daughter, begins drinking and finally moves to China with her husband. Only the youngest girl Bess, early in the story a self-proclaimed Cinderella, stays with the house and the virtues of hard work and simplicity that it represents. For her reward she wins Lew, who after many years has become wealthy and gladly rescues her from the poverty she now lives in. With their marriage "The purpose of the house was achieved—finished and folded—it was an effort toward some commonweal, an effort difficult to estimate. . . ."[151] Fitzgerald's point is that there are things in the grand American past which, even to a man who deals primarily in futures as does Lew, are indispensable; and in the act of salvaging that past, represented by Bess who had maintained her ties with tradition by remaining in the Gunther house, lies Lew's hope in the present. The story has connections to "Winter Dreams" and *The Great Gatsby*: Lew, like Dexter Green and like Gatsby, is a social climber who has come under the spell of the upper class. The story's deeper tie with *Gatsby*, however, lies in its message that people who have had advantages (like the Carraways in the novel and the Gunters in the story) have certain responsibilities. This point is implied in Nick's father's advice to him in the first chapter of the novel and is stated explicitly to Amanda by her mother when she tries to get Amanda to be courteous to Lew. As is true of most of the previous stories of Fitzgerald's *Post* decline, he is obviously concerned in "More than Just a House" with relaying a serious message—in this case, one about social responsibility. In this story, though, the combination of love and success, which from a popular standpoint provides the backbone of Lew's adventure, sufficiently veils the deeper message of this story for those readers—and this would apply generally to *Post* readers—who could better leave social criticism than take it.

"I Got Shoes" (July 1933; *Post*, 23 September 1933; $2,500), like "More than Just a House," deals with success in the present which has blossomed from a deprived past. Less subtle in relaying his message in "I Got Shoes," Fitzgerald uses a device unique in his short fiction: the parable within a parable. Nell Margery's story, as it is relayed to reporter Johanna Battles, convinces the reader that she might, indeed, have a good reason grounded in her past for saving shoes. But the larger message that Nell learns from recounting her own story about blisters—and this is also the larger moral for the reader—is that obsessions such as Nell's may interfere with one's chances of forming meaningful relationships in the present. Therefore, her final decision to give away her old shoes is a symbolic rejection of those things in the past that interfere with the present, an act similar to the one expected from Lew Lowrie when he will probably discard the old Gunther house after salvaging Bess. Nell Margery's story, though she gets her man after the self-revelation, lacks the intrigue of Lew's adventure. That *Post* editors had misgivings about the story's amusement value is suggested by the low $2,500 fee that they paid Fitzgerald for it—the lowest point to which Fitzgerald's *Post* price dropped.

In "The Family Bus" (September 1933; *Post*, 4 November 1933; $3,000), the final story to appear before *Tender Is the Night*, Fitzgerald's hero, Dick Henderson, endures the personal tragedy of losing his brother and, not many years afterward, his family fortune. But while he is working downward on a social scale notched by money, a childhood girlfriend whose father was once an employee of Dick's father is working her way up with the help of her father's newly acquired fortune. The strong childhood bond, which serves as Fitzgerald's reminder that there can be good hangovers from the past as well as bad ones like Nell Margery's, remains intact in spite of the dissimilarities in their early social backgrounds or the differences in their present financial situations, now ironically reversed from the beginning of the story. Through their final happy ride in "the family bus," an emblem of their shared pasts, Fitzgerald suggests that money need not make so much difference after all. But whether the new-rich Jan Mel-Loper will ever need or attempt to buy a hard-working American mechanic, which is what Dick now is, is not a question that Fitzgerald chooses to answer in this story which combines those well-worn subjects of young love and success.

5

The *Esquire* Period
(1934-1940)

Fitzgerald delivered the *Tender Is the Night* manuscript to Scribners in October 1933. The first installment of the serialization appeared in *Scribner's Magazine* in January 1934, and the book was published in April 1934. The natural sense of relief that Fitzgerald would have felt at the end of the novel's nine-year composition period, however, was marred by the popular and critical failure of the book.[1] Thus, instead of relaxing at the end of this major creative strain Fitzgerald was immediately forced to get back to the business of supporting himself with magazine work. In an 8 December 1934 letter to Ober he recreates his physical, emotional, and financial state as he returned to his commercial fiction:

> With yours and Max's help and some assistance from mother the thing was accomplished but at the end it left me in the black hole of Calcutta, mentally exhausted, and perhaps, morally exhausted. There seemed no time or space for recuperation. . . . The necessary "filling up" that a writer should be able to do after great struggles was impossible. No sooner did I finish the last galley on the last version of the last proof of the book proof of "Tender is the Night" than it was necessary to sit down and write a *Post* story.[2]

Any examination of those stories which came out of the final phase of Fitzgerald's career—1934 until his death on 21 December 1940—must, therefore, take into account these facets of the aftermath of *Tender Is the Night*: that Fitzgerald was understandably let down by the coolness of the novel's critical reception; that his popular image, indexed both by the poor public reception of the novel and his price cut by the *Post*, was at an all-time low;[3] and that Fitzgerald had no "filling up" time after completing the novel and, thus, approached the idea of writing commercial fiction with an understandable lack of enthusiasm.

Perhaps more than in any other period in Fitzgerald's life the downward direction that his literary career took from 1934 until his death was dictated by the magazine-reading public which determined whether or not Fitzgerald could stay in business as a writer. An overview of the period indicates the alternatives open to Fitzgerald—none of them particularly good—and the ones he finally chose in order to continue making a living after the publication of his most unpopular novel. After writing "The Family Bus" in September 1933[4] Fitzgerald stopped working on his commercial fiction in order to see *Tender Is the Night* through its serial publication and into book form. Less than a month after the April first-printing of the novel Fitzgerald returned to the business of earning a living: in April he wrote the first story of *The Count of Darkness* series, four medieval stories whose main character Philippe was based on Hemingway and which were apparently first intended for the *Post*;[5] and he wrote a *Post* story, "No Flowers" in May 1934.[6] In 1935, because Fitzgerald needed money badly he began submitting stories to *Esquire*, whose publisher Arnold Gingrich was a fan of Fitzgerald's and who would pay Fitzgerald a quick but low $200-$300 per story. But it is noteworthy that even through the last years of his life, during which most of his stories appeared in *Esquire*, Fitzgerald never stopped trying to write stories that would be suitable for the *Post*. In fact, not only did *Esquire* publish stories that were written for the *Post*, but also, every story written after the publication of *Tender Is the Night*, excluding those stories written expressly for *Esquire*, was written with the *Post* in mind.

The stories of Fitzgerald's final phase, therefore, fall into four distinct groups, the boundaries of which are determined both by Fitzgerald's aim in various stories to please specific audiences and by his inability on several occasions to do so. The groups are these: (a) the *Post* stories, written according to Fitzgerald's conception of what would still please readers of the *Post* and published in that magazine; (b) the *Post* rejects, written with the *Post* in mind but finally published in various other magazines after being turned down by the *Post*; (c) the four stories of *The Count of Darkness* series, begun as a serious novelette but continued as an apparent attempt to exploit the cheap, serial-novel market; and (d) the *Esquire* stories, generally written in sparse prose, which show Fitzgerald experimenting with his prose style as he attempted to make cash quickly by exploring one of the few avenues left open to him at that time.

Losing the *Post*: 21 July 1934 - 6 March 1937

As indicated in the previous chapter Fitzgerald's declining popularity with the *Post* did not occur overnight and it was firmly grounded in the 1932-1933 stories which, by comparison with Fitzgerald's earlier *Post* stories, have low entertainment value. Between 21 July 1934 and 6 March 1937 the *Post* published its final seven Fitzgerald stories. These stories, like most of the 1932-1933 stories, are weak for many of the same reasons as the *Post* stories which immediately preceded them. Thus on the basis of the quality alone of the final seven stories it is understandable that Fitzgerald lost favor with his largest audience. But because Fitzgerald's relationship with the *Post* is of central importance in his career as a professional writer and because Fitzgerald continued until his death to try to write more *Post* stories, it is important to examine the inner workings of the relationship between Fitzgerald and the *Post* editors who finally made the decision to put him out of circulation for their readers.

To survey briefly, the most accurate reflector of Fitzgerald's solid relationship with the *Post* during the late twenties and early thirties is Ober's sworn statement to the Internal Revenue Service; in it he is able to certify that Fitzgerald was "virtually an employee" of the magazine in 1929 and 1930, and thus, not a free-lance writer.[7] And as late as February 1932 Ober suggested that it would hurt Lorimer's feelings if Fitzgerald published a story in *Collier's* because, according to Thomas B. Costain,[8] ". . . Mr. Lorimer likes to feel that there were certain writers that the Post readers would look for and expect to find in the Post, not in Collier's and that you were one of those few authors."[9] Then by April 1933, although Fitzgerald was concerned about his future with the magazine in the presence of some *Post* editorial changes,[10] Ober was able to assure Fitzgerald that "we are both in a particularly good position with all the editors of the Post. . . . If we keep on as we have been going I think everything will be all right no matter what happens at the Post."[11]

However, things did not continue to go as they had in the past, and most of the fault seems to have been Fitzgerald's. Shortly before the publication of *Tender Is the Night* Fitzgerald began sending stories which because of both their content and physical appearance[12] gave the correct impression to the *Post* that he needed money quickly. This, according to Ober, had adverse psychological effects on the editors.[13] After the publication of *Tender Is the Night* Fitzgerald, by contacting the magazines directly rather than through Ober, heightened those feelings *Post* editors might have had about Fitzgerald's need to receive immediate decisions on his submitted stories.[14] Whatever weaknesses any particular *Post* submission might have had, therefore, were compounded by Fitzgerald's insistence on having it accepted or rejected quickly. Certainly then, Fitzgerald's bad public relations work with the *Post* must have figured into the final termination of the relationship.

But even if Fitzgerald's personal relations with *Post* editors had been perfect, it is doubtful that the magazine would have accepted many more stories after *Tender Is the Night* than the seven they finally published. His commercial efforts after the publication of the novel simply underline the fact heavily foreshadowed in the stories between "Emotional Bankruptcy" and 1934 that Fitzgerald had lost the knack of pleasing the millions of middle Americans who constituted the *Post* audience; and whether consciously or unconsciously, he had done this primarily by subordinating his effort to entertain to the effort to teach—a violation of the first rule of popular magazine fiction.

With "No Flowers" (May 1934; *Post*, 21 July 1934; $3,000) Fitzgerald returns to his very early college material. But unlike such a story as "Benediction" (*Smart Set* February, 1920), which revolves almost solely around the central character Lois, the focus of "No Flowers" changes back and forth between Marjorie, a young girl who grows up to attend college proms in the "tin age" thirties, and her mother Amanda, who was young in "a sort of golden age"—the twenties. Marjorie's era, Fitzgerald suggests, is better. Her escort, Billy Johns, is poor but he has the kind of ambition and the value system that will someday make him successful: he is working his way through college knowing that he will have a bright future later working with an uncle who has an "Horatio Alger complex." His uncle feels that Billy, after supporting himself in college, will have earned the right to a position with him. Billy can then pursue Marjorie seriously. In contrasting the "tin age" and the "golden age" Fitzgerald uses a bouquet of flowers to underline the differences: the bouquet discarded by Marjorie's mother back in the Golden Age was, unknown to her, held together by a diamond ring that would have been her engagement present had she not coyly substituted an identical corsage from another suitor; Marjorie's escort, on the other hand, could afford "no flowers," much less a ring to hold them together. But his moral fiber is shown to be better than that of any of those suitors who had surrounded Amanda.

However, flowers and the absence of flowers, symbolizing as they do the differences in the two ages, fail to sufficiently unify the very different stories of Amanda and Marjorie. Subsequently, the reader is apt to see a blur amidst the didacticism and ask finally if either story is worth the effort. Although Fitzgerald clearly demonstrates in "No

Flowers" that he is able to step back and objectively observe the college proms which he once revered, he does not infuse enough glamour into Amanda's story to generate the reader's identification with it. Instead, by concentrating on the "golden age" he robs himself of the space needed to document the hope that lay in the "tin age"—a hope that would logically have been the payoff for most *Post* readers in the Thirties.

"New Types" (July 1934; *Post* 22 September 1934; $3,000) is similar to "No Flowers" in expressing Fitzgerald's faith in college-age Americans who have grown up during the Depression. Paula Jorgensen, the story's heroine and a female counterpart to industrious Billy Johns of "No Flowers," is a hard-working New York City model who was forced to earn a living early in life when her father died leaving the family only enough money to pay for his funeral. She has become a very practical, ambitious young woman who is described by one of her rivals as "the tall indifferent type."[15] But to Leslie Dixon, a thirty-three year old man from whose viewpoint the story is told, Paula's practicality is admirable, and her seeming indifference is attractive. One of the story's most striking features is, in fact, Fitzgerald's effective use of Dixon to introduce and remain sympathetic to Paula, who may have offended many *Post* readers with her extreme ambition before finally redeeming herself near the end of the story. When the reader first sees Paula she is visiting a stingy aunt who has refused to help Paula's family financially and is, in Paula's words, "the most obnoxious person."[16] In view of remarks like this, reminiscent of Ardita Farnham's disrespectful comments to her uncle in "The Offshore Pirate," *Post* readers would have viewed Paula as impertinent; though the aunt may have bad qualities, she is nevertheless an older person who, in the eyes of the audience, would have deserved being treated with respect. Dixon remains loyal to Paula, however, until he finds that she has locked her aunt, whom she believes to be dead, in an upstairs room while she attends a dance arranged in her honor by the aunt. The reader also knows, though Dixon does not, that Paula, in one of the most bizarre scenes in Fitzgerald's *Post* fiction, has spoken at length to what she believes to be the aunt's corpse; and in the conversation she has reprimanded the corpse for having been stingy when it was alive. Shortly after the corpse scene, though, Fitzgerald wins the audience's sympathy for Paula while, at the same time, reestablishing Dixon's admiration for her: the aunt was not really dead; and Paula allowed the dance, at which she modeled and was photographed, to go on in order to make the money necessary to pay for her European nobleman-husband's operation. When the operation is unsuccessful and her husband dies, Paula is free to marry Dixon. The story's message is geared to the tastes of the *Post* audience: Americans, particularly young Americans, have the ability to triumph over unfortunate circumstances, as Paula was able to earn a living when her father died. Moreover, the ending of the story, in addition to being simply a happy one in which two people in love are united, is patriotic. In the death of Paula's European husband and the triumph of Dixon, Fitzgerald asserts his faith in America: "the cloth of a great race cannot be made out of the frayed lint of tired princes. . . ."[17]

The story is not finally, however, a successful *Post* story in spite of its patriotic message and the heavy plotting which often makes a slick story successful. Paula, though she is ultimately presented as an admirable character, is not, in the process, also likeable: many readers may have understood her reasons for talking to her aunt's corpse and also have sympathized with her nearly desperate attempt to make money for her husband's operation; but few would agree with Dixon that she is lovable. In "New Types," as in many of the previous stories which mark his declining popularity with *Post* readers, Fitzgerald subordinates the amusement value of the story to its didactic purpose. And while part of Fitzgerald's appeal to popular readers had always rested to some degree on his moralizing, it was not until the stories of the *Post* decline, during which his material was depleted, that his characters and situations became more important as vehicles of a message than as ingredients of stories which would simply have amused *Post* readers.

Of the four stories about young people in the medical profession which Fitzgerald published in the *Post*, "Her Last Case" (August 1934; *Post*, 3 November 1934; $3,000) is the most successful.[18] Ben Dragonet, the central character in the story who is viewed through the eyes of nurse Bette Weaver, is as convincing as any male character that Fitzgerald had created since Lew Lowrie of "More Than Just a House" (*Post*, 24 June 1933)—the story which "Her Last Case" most closely resembles. Dragonet, similar to the Gunthers of "More Than Just a House," is a prisoner of the past symbolized in both stories by Southern mansions. Dragonet succeeds in escaping the Confederate ghosts which haunt him and will presumably marry Bette, who has given up her doctor-fiancé in order to be free for Dragonet.

The story succeeds, not because Fitzgerald is learning the trick of turning out doctor-nurse stories, but because he is able to transcend the usual limitations of romantic stories about the medical profession. Dragonet is an early, optimistic "alcoholic case" ("An Alcoholic Case," *Esquire*, February 1937); and both stories are effective because

Fitzgerald could place himself in the position of men who, like Dragonet, have experienced a "lesion of vitality."[19]

The less serious "Zone of Accident" (Fall 1932-May 1935; *Post*, 13 July 1935; $3,000) is a companion story to "One Interne" and points out a last identifiable trend in Fitzgerald's *Post* fiction: a tendency to pick up a thread which offered even the slightest hope for a series from his earlier and, at least partially, more successful attempts with the magazine. William Tulliver IV[20] makes a second appearance in "Zone of Accident," but now he is cured of his love for Thea Singleton and caught in a dilemma as to which of two girls he will love. The conflict arises from the fact that his new girlfriend Loretta is an actress and thus in the hospital resorts to such theatrical stunts as rubbing her thermometer in order to seem sicker than she actually is. Tulliver disapproves of her theatrics, but he finally settles for Loretta and lets his discarded beauty queen Amy go to Hollywood. Of the exchange of Amy for Loretta, Fitzgerald moralizes through Tulliver, "The movies give and the movies take away. . . ."[21]

Like "Zone of Accident" the Gwen stories, of which "Too Cute for Words" (December 1935; *Post*, 18 April 1936; $3,000) is the first installment, indicate Fitzgerald's attempt to create a new series fashioned after earlier *Post* work. The concept on which the Gwen stories rest comes directly from the Josephine Perry series and, as such, Ober felt—and the *Post* supported his feeling—that Fitzgerald could, perhaps, turn them into a successful commercial venture: "The *Post* like the character of Gwen very much indeed and they would like for you to go ahead and do another story in the series. I think from the way they spoke they would like to have a series the way they had the Basil stories and the Josephine stories."[22] The series, however, was short-lived and the *Post* bought only two of the three stories—"Too Cute for Words" and "Inside the House" (April 1936; *Post*, 13 June 1936; $3,000).[23]

Ironically, the series was weakened by a fact that would seem to have made it stronger than the Basil and Josephine groups: growing as they did from Fitzgerald's "desire to write about children of Scotty's age,"[24] the Gwen stories would have been, it appears, much closer to him than the Basil and Josephine material from which Fitzgerald had been twenty years removed. But whereas Fitzgerald had maintained primarily an objective position toward both Basil and Josephine, his stance toward Gwen is paternal and thus very subjective. Bryan Bowers is a doting father whose view of his daughter's actions is colored by the awareness that Gwen is the only tangible link to his dead wife. Consequently, he is very much involved in and approving of

Gwen's every action. In this fact lies the main weakness of the short series both from a critical and popular standpoint: the stories are as much Bryan's as they are Gwen's—a fact which suggests the blurred view that the audience receives.

As was the case in "No Flowers," both of the *Post* Gwen stories suffer from Fitzgerald's use of two protagonists; both Gwen and her father alternately occupy the spotlight at irregular intervals and thus neither succeeds in directing the reader, as protagonists in   slick magazine fiction typically do, into a prescribed reaction to his individual plight. In "Too Cute for Words" the purpose that the prom finally serves is simply to bring Bryan and Gwen together in a nostalgic Harvard setting so that he might mildly reprove her for being there. But neither the thirteen-year-old Gwen nor her long-since graduated father belong at a prom for debutantes and college men.   Their encounter and joke over Gwen's favorite word "cute" are finally uninteresting. Similarly, in "Inside the House" Bryan and Gwen vie for central attention. Gwen's two friends assume importance as vehicles through which Bryan demonstrates his erudition; and her defiance in going to the movies against Bryan's order becomes significant, not primarily because the theater caves in, but because Gwen missed the opportunity that Bryan could have provided her to meet her idol Peppy Valance. Like "Too Cute for Words," then, "Inside the House" is as much Bryan's story as it is Gwen's. Resting as they both do on themes of slight significance—"Too Cute for Words" on a private family joke and "Inside the House" on a case where father did know best—the stories lack the intensity that they would have had if Fitzgerald had clearly indicated to the audience precisely in whom they should invest their sympathy. In the Josephine Perry stories, Fitzgerald intentionally made his heroine unsympathetic to the *Post*'s readers. Gwen, on the other hand, was not unsympathetic in spite of Bryan's, or Fitzgerald's, determination for didactic reasons to magnify her misdemeanors. But if the Gwen stories fail to entertain largely because of their lack of objectivity it is noteworthy that biographically they point to the strength of his relationship with his daughter: it was, perhaps, one of the few relationships to succeed in resisting Fitzgerald's double vision.

Fitzgerald's tenure with the *Post* ends with "'Trouble'" (June 1936; *Post*, 6 March 1937; $2,000), a story which embodies all the ploys, gimmicks, strategies, and weaknesses evident, to some degree, in every *Post* story after *Tender Is the Night*. The story is a direct descendent of an earlier Fitzgerald *Post* experiment: the aborted Dr. William Tulliver series.[25] Like the Tulliver stories, "'Trouble'" is a story about the medical profession; but in it Fitzgerald presents his story from the feminine viewpoint of a nurse "Trouble," whose real name, Glenola McClurg, indicates the lack of sparkle in her life. Just as Tulliver was a fine young doctor, so "Trouble" is an excellent young nurse. Designed as it was to be a series pilot[26] there is room in "Trouble's" character for endless adventures—none of which Fitzgerald is able to sufficiently explore—such as her falling into the arms of Dr. Dick Wheelock at the annual hospital turtle race. The reader, however, can be sure that her allegiance will always be to her profession—a weakness of the story in that it precludes the kind of suspense typical of earlier Fitzgerald stories such as "Myra Meets His Family" or "The Offshore Pirate" in which the reader can rightfully expect anything from the Fitzgerald heroine. Moreover, "Trouble," again as is characteristic of the post-*Tender Is the Night* protagonists, shares the limelight with "formidable" hospital hero, Dr. Wheelock, who represents to her the ultimate in glamour—a dubious sparkle that may have led readers to wish, for the sake of amusement, that she had cast her lot with the alcoholic, but rich, Fred Winslow. As the story stands, however, the "Trouble"-Winslow subplot crowds the story and diverts the reader's attention from the story's central issue: an exploration of the romantic and familiar doctor-nurse symbiosis. "'Trouble,'" then, provides a study in miniature of those qualities which marked Fitzgerald's decline with the *Post*: it grew out of an earlier *Post* experiment, the Dr. William Tulliver stories; it was begun with the idea of a "nurse series" in mind; its main love plot, the "Trouble"-Wheelock story, is blurred by the involved story of "Trouble's" entanglement with Winslow; and it ends with the moral that devoted nurses must stay in the hospital in order to "bloom"—"a flower beside the bed of man's distress."[27]

Adelaide Neall, a *Post* editor, was encouraged by "'Trouble,'" seeing in it an indication that Fitzgerald "can still write the simple love story."[28] Understandably, Ober passed this encouragement along to Fitzgerald, but Miss Neall's diagnosis was wrong: "'Trouble'" is not a simple love story except in terms of "Trouble's" love for the hospital and all it stands for. In fact, one of the primary reasons that Fitzgerald's stories ceased to be *Post* stories was precisely because he had lost the knack of writing a simple love story—something that, although it might have surprised many editors, Fitzgerald had not tried since perhaps "The Popular Girl" (1921). Over and over the *Post* stories following "Emotional Bankruptcy" (*Post*, 15 August 1931), and even the earlier love stories surrounding *Tender Is the Night*, suggest that for purposes of his short stories the pursuit of love as an end in itself was gone; there must be other reasons such as guilt ("Flight and

Pursuit"), practicality ("What a Handsome Pair!"), or a greater good ("'Trouble'").

The last *Post* stories suggest that Fitzgerald ultimately was not made of the stuff that it took to write cheap magazine fiction. It is noteworthy that Fitzgerald had not written a *Post* formula story, in the sense that he had written a "love story" or a "success story," since "John Jackson's Arcady" (*Post*, 26 July 1924). And while he had written his popular stories with his public in mind, taking care not to go against the grain of middle American morality, he had at no time written stories that were simply dictated by a precise formula; more often the *Post* stories in particular were published in spite of the fact that they violated the *Post* formula, as the *Tender Is the Night* cluster stories, for example, clearly indicate. When his *Tender Is the Night* experiences ran out, Fitzgerald was simply unable to infuse an enthusiasm which he did not feel into his commercial fiction—that is, to write "pattern stories." Those qualities so clearly evident in the *Post* stories which lie between "Emotional Bankruptcy" and "'Trouble'" document the fact that Fitzgerald's store of material was depleted and that although he had "tried not once but twenty times,"[29] he could not write "the simple love story" that Miss Neall suggested the *Post* wanted. Ironically, the end of Fitzgerald's relationship with the *Post* is clouded by what appears to be a misapprehension on the part of *Post* editors and the public alike as to what Fitzgerald had been publishing in that magazine after *The Great Gatsby*. O. O. McIntyre indicates in 1936 what the magazines and their readers expected from Fitzgerald at that time:

> . . . editors continue to want stories of flask gin and courteous collegiates preceding ladies through windshields on midnight joy rides. The public has acquired this Fitzgerald taste, too. But Fitzgerald has taken an elderly and naturally serious turn. Mellowed is the term. He wants to write mellowy, too. And if they won't let him he won't write at all. So there.[30]

The irony is this: Fitzgerald had not written the kind of story McIntyre describes since 1921. He had left the subject of the gin-drinking collegiate by his own choice in the early twenties and turned to more serious, novel-related subjects which had dominated his commercial fiction in the late twenties and early thirties. The stories of these years had been easily forgotten if McIntyre's remarks accurately mirrored popular opinion. The primary fact, though, that McIntyre and the readers of the *Post* who stopped seeing Fitzgerald's name in the magazine were not apt to know, is that Fitzgerald would have done almost anything in 1936 to get back into the *Post* stable. But when he tried to write "pattern stories" for the *Post*, as he told Ober, "the pen just goes dead on me"[31]—in retrospect, perhaps, one of the best gauges of the quality of his artistic conscience. What he seems to have lost, as indexed by the termination of his relationship with the *Post*, was not the knack for turning out by formula quick moneymakers—a knack that he never had; instead he simply had never learned the skill of composing a story without material, about absolutely nothing at all.

The *Post* Rejects

Seven of the stories which Fitzgerald wrote expressly for the *Post* between February 1935 and August 1936 but which were rejected by that magazine point out even more emphatically the symptoms, already examined, of Fitzgerald's "lost knack" for writing mass-appeal stories for popular magazines. In each of these stories with the exception of "Lo, the Poor Peacock!" and the Gwen story, "Strange Sanctuary," Fitzgerald attempts to revive his 1920's heroine; but for various reasons he does not succeed—though he comes close in "The Intimate Strangers"—in giving her the kind of vitality that he had given such earlier characters as Ardita Farnham and Betty Medill.

In "The Passionate Eskimo" (February 1935; *Liberty*, 8 June 1935; $1,500)[32] Fitzgerald introduces Edith Cary, who has many of the qualities of the 1920 Fitzgerald heroine: "—a ripley blond who, had it been necessary, could have posed for any of those exquisite creatures in the advertisements."[33] But Edith is buried in the improbable and uninteresting story of an Eskimo's trip to the Chicago World's Fair, a trip dominated by the Eskimo Pan-e-troon's awkward attempts to understand why his forty-seven cents will buy so few souvenirs. When, midway through the story, Fitzgerald finally introduces Edith through Pan-e-troon's eyes, she is unable to give a sense of direction or any real sparkle to what has essentially become a rambling, though occasionally humorous, adventure tale. The story suggests that Fitzgerald, in attempting to retrieve his knack for writing popular magazine fiction, was willing to explore the avenue of comedy; and "The Passionate Eskimo" stands with "The Camel's Back" as one of the very few Fitzgerald stories outside of the later *Esquire* group whose thrust is primarily comic. Fitzgerald is less successful in the former, however, because his subject, Pan-e-troon, is as pathetic as he is funny. And, in fact, he is finally a relatively serious character who, back in Lapland, remains devoted to his picture of Edith, "a princess of the fabled trading post in the far away."[34]

"Lo, the Poor Peacock!" (February 1935; *Esquire*, September 1971), particularly by contrast to the excellent "Babylon Revisited" whose mood it attempts to recapture, illustrates how little of Fitzgerald's magic is to be found in the *Post* rejects that Fitzgerald wrote in 1935 and 1936. At the center of "Lo, the Poor Peacock!" is a relationship strikingly similar to Charlie and Honoria Wales's relationship in "Babylon Revisited." The girl has been brought up in France and is precocious; the father is a businessman whose luck changes; and father and daughter have a close relationship, in the absence of an adult female (in "Lo" the wife is terminally ill in a hospital), more like husband and wife than father and daughter. The similarities between the two stories, however, do not go much beneath the surface. The French phrases in "Lo, the Poor Peacock!"—which, unlike "Babylon Revisited," is set in the United States—sound hollow and pretentious. The change in luck at the end of the story is based on unbelievable coincidence—the whim of a Pan-Am-Tex official, a preposterous apology of a school principal, and the recollection of a sausage recipe by the terminally ill wife. When Jason (the father) and Jo (the daughter) experience a rebirth of optimism in April at the end of the story, the reader must feel that it is contrived—which is, no doubt, part of the reason that the story was rejected both by the *Post* and *Ladies' Home Journal*, not to be published until 1971 in *Esquire*.

"The Intimate Strangers" (February-March 1935; *McCall's*, June 1935; $3,000), a story which Fitzgerald considered to be one of the three best stories rejected by the *Post*,[35] indicates a more obvious attempt on Fitzgerald's part to revive his heroine and, in this case, a much more successful one than in "The Passionate Eskimo." The young, pretty Sara of "The Intimate Strangers," although she is the wife of a French nobleman and the mother of two children, is impulsive enough to run away for a week with the musical and athletic Killian; and, moreover, she is brazen enough to return home as if nothing happened. What follows is a series of implausible circumstances which enable Sara and Killian to be married: Sara's husband dies at an opportune time and the young woman whom Killian had married, seemingly on a rebound from Sara, also conveniently dies. But in spite of the improbabilities on which the love story turns, Fitzgerald manages to give Sara a charm which links her with several of his earlier, desirable heroines. She is, in fact, a composite of several *Post* women: in her impulsiveness she is like an Ardita Farnham; and in the mystique which comes from her early marriage into the French nobility she resembles the unnamed young girl whom Val Rostoff ("Love in the Night") encountered in the Cannes Harbor and later married. And significantly, Fitzgerald presents Sara in a sympathetic light, avoiding the opportunity of rendering her in her indiscreetness as a Choupette

Marsten ("The Swimmers"). Fitzgerald comes closer in "The Intimate Strangers" than he had come since the *Tender Is the Night* cluster story "Majesty" (Emily Castleton) to resurrecting the heroine that had much earlier been his trademark.

In spite of the strengths of "The Intimate Strangers," however, the *Post*'s censorship rules dictated that the story be rejected: Sara's adultery could never have been rewarded in the *Post*, and her marriage to Killian, though it is haunted at times by the ghost of his first wife, is sufficiently happy to constitute a reward.   Even so, the story approaches, more nearly than any story that follows it, the romantic mood which had earmarked so many of Fitzgerald's *Post* stories in the twenties.   That *McCall's* was willing to pay $3,000—Fitzgerald's regular *Post* price at this time—points clearly to the fact that Fitzgerald's heroine was still in demand; but in 1935 this was a demand that Fitzgerald was unable consistently to supply.

In the remaining four *Post* rejections which follow "The Intimate Strangers," Fitzgerald's attempts to write entertaining stories in his early *Post* manner are much less successful.   In "Fate in Her Hands" (*American Magazine*, April 1936)[36] Fitzgerald uses a kind-hearted fortune-teller's ominous prediction to hold the reader's interest in Carol, a heroine who has very little sparkle of her own.   At nineteen Carol is told by the fortune-teller that she will marry within a month, gain notoriety within three years, and experience a "black accident" in six years.   Carol's superstitious nature leads her to actively avoid situations which might cause her to fulfill the fortune-teller's prophecy; but the first two parts of the prediction go according to schedule, though from the reader's viewpoint the sequence of events which leads up to both are farfetched and ludicrous.   Carol impulsively marries her fiancé's best friend ten minutes before her planned marriage is to occur and just in time to make the fortune-teller's first prediction come true. Three years later she tries so hard to avoid any kind of publicity that, in hiding out from the press, she is thought to have been kidnapped, thus gaining the notoriety that was the second part of the prophecy.   In the sixth year she does everything possible to keep the black accident from occurring and finally concludes that "I've been a nut."[37]

As the story closes she has only six hours to wait until the fortune-teller is proved to have been wrong in her prediction, at which point the reader will, of course, remember the fortune-teller's comforting admission to Carol that she was not always right in her predictions. The main weakness of the story, as the summary indicates, lies in Fitzgerald's reliance on improbability, a fact which Carol acknowledges: "I wonder what would be the mathematical probabilities of these two cards turning up one after the other,"[38] she asks about two cards which she received from a penny machine and which supported the fortune-teller's predictions. But in addition to the improbabilities in the story, the other major weakness results from Fitzgerald's seeming lack of enthusiasm for his characters, a characteristic of every story rejected by the *Post* between 1935 and 1937 with the possible exception of "The Intimate Strangers."

"Image on the Heart" (September 1935; *McCall's*, April 1936; $1,250)[39] has at its core a love triangle reminiscent of the Dick-Nicole-Barban triangle, but the heroine Tudy is too meek to voice any real objections to the jealous rages of her lover Tom; and, in addition, she is too acquiescent to admit the attraction she obviously feels for Riccard, the French aviator who pursues her and who is, in fact, the only character that gives the story a measure of glamour.

"Strange Sanctuary" (c. December 1935; *Liberty*, 9 December 1939; $250), the third Gwen story,[40] suffers from the two very different purposes that Fitzgerald was attempting to accomplish: the story is, first, a narrative which describes the understandable feeling of isolation experienced by a motherless thirteen-year-old child Dolly whose father must travel for his health; but it is also a mystery story—a tale about the apprehension of two burglars—into the middle of which Dolly is almost pasted as a figure in a collage. Consequently, the contrivance that Fitzgerald must employ to bring Dolly into the lives of the story's burglary team diminishes the effectiveness the story might have had if Fitzgerald had concentrated on either Dolly or the burglars—a problem which marks not only the Gwen stories, but other *Post* stories such as "No Flowers." "The End of Hate" (c. August 1936; *Collier's*, 22 June 1940, $250)[41] also suffers from the split focus which results when Fitzgerald combines the story of heroine Josie Pilgrim's obsessive love for thumbless Tib Dulaney and the story of Dulaney's hate for Josie's brother, who is to blame for the fact that Dulaney's thumbs were amputated. Curiously, Josie, in standing between Tib and her brother, blocks the punishment of her unlikable brother, and thus she stands in the way of poetic justice. In the process she is inviting the audience to ask what she could possibly find so romantically alluring about this man with no thumbs.

The catalogue of faults itself which must necessarily accompany any discussion of the 1935-1936 *Post* rejections—the fact that they have such faults accounts for their appearance in other magazines—is less significant here than the insights that these stories provide into Fitzgerald's creative processes and also into the state of his reputation during this very low point in his career. These stories reveal that

Fitzgerald, when his *Post* acceptances were becoming rare, attempted to resurrect his heroine: Edith Cary ("The Passionate Eskimo"), Sara ("The Intimate Strangers"), Carol ("Fate in her Hands"), Tudy ("Image on the Heart"), and Josie Pilgrim ("The End of Hate"). And moreover, these stories indicate that in such a slump as Fitzgerald found himself in 1935 and 1936 he instinctively returned to stories about romantic love: "The Intimate Strangers" and "Image on the Heart," for example. But the *Post* rejections also underline the fact that Fitzgerald was finding it increasingly difficult to invent new situations in which to place his revived heroines, no better example of which exists than the preposterous Eskimo narrative which frames Edith Cary's characterization.

The Philippe Stories: October 1934 - November 1941

A good indicator of just how far Fitzgerald was willing to go after the failure of *Tender Is the Night* in order to please the public that he had, from all indications, lost is the baffling and atypical "Philippe" stories that he began almost immediately after the publication of *Tender Is the Night*. The four stories of the series, which were published in *Redbook*, grew out of a plan to write a novel, *The Count of Darkness*. He was initially quite serious about his plan for this novel, and he had high hopes for it. When he had finished the first installment of the series he wrote to Perkins that he thought it was good. And after he had gotten three episodes into the story he reminded Perkins that the series was "more than a string of episodes."[42] After the fourth episode was written he told Perkins that he had outlined the novel in detail: it was "tentatively called 'Philippe, Count of Darkness' and would run to about some 90,000 words."[43] Even as late as January 1939 Fitzgerald hung onto the idea that he would turn his Philippe material into a novel because "Philippe interests me."[44] His serious intention for the picture of Philippe that he planned to paint is revealed in his notebooks: "Just as Stendahl's portrait of a Byronic man made *Le Rouge et le Noir*, so couldn't my portrait of Ernest as Philippe make the real modern man?"[45] A noteworthy point about Fitzgerald's enthusiasm for his subject, however, is that most of his comments concern the novel that would grow out of his idea—not the series itself, which was not nearly so ambitious as the plan for the novel as he had outlined it for Perkins.[46]

The most logical conclusion that may be drawn about the series in light of Fitzgerald's original plan and the fragments of that plan which survive in the four *Redbook* stories is one similar to Edmund

Wilson's, expressed in his introduction to the "Note-Books" section of *The Crack-Up*: that Fitzgerald was compelled by the popular fiction market "to depart from his original conception."[47] In short, it became Fitzgerald's version of the cheap, serial novel which was traditionally the most profitable source of income for full-time slick magazine fiction writers.[48]

"In the Darkest Hour" (April 1934; *Redbook*, October 1934; $1,250) reflects both Fitzgerald's initial intention to write a serious series and also his apparent realization somewhere in the middle of this first installment that it had, in fact, already become a melodrama. Philippe's first appearance as a legitimate heir to a kingdom in France that had been taken by the Northmen is set against Fitzgerald's convincing picture of the desolate French countryside in 872. By coupling his account of Philippe's exile in Spain with a detailed historical account of the state of affairs in France during the Dark Ages, Fitzgerald prepares the backdrop against which Philippe might have grown into a formidable leader whose motivations for assuming leadership are honorable and crystal clear. The plausibility of Philippe's character and of the narrative, though, lasts only as long as Fitzgerald is able to keep Philippe isolated from other people. In search of a language through which he can communicate with strangers he meets, Philippe settles on a substandard, slangy English which in the later stories becomes laughable and unbelievable. When Philippe asks if "Many people live hereabouts," a stranger replies: "Used to be a right smart lot of them. But since them yellow devils come through, and them red-headed heathen from the north, it sort of thinned us out a little."[49] Then having made Philippe, by virtue of his dialect, a contemporary man, Fitzgerald uses him to arouse every conceivable emotion in the reader. Philippe, after a confrontation with his new arch rival, organizes a band of men and slaughters the first intruders who come into his kingdom. When the massacre is complete Philippe becomes a dreamer who envisions the building of his future fort and bridge. At the end of the installment he is approached by a pretty young girl who throws herself at his feet to be taken in by her new hero.

In "The Count of Darkness" (October 1934; *Redbook*, June 1935; $1,500)—promised by the editors to "even more significantly [illuminate] recent events in Europe"—Fitzgerald works openly through Philippe to arouse feelings of horror, pity, and jubilation in the audience. Having now, seven years later, established a kingdom, Philippe is a count, and as such demands that his woman, Letgarde, call him "Sire" instead of "Darling." His reason: "There's no bedroom talk floating around this precinct!"[50]   Shortly thereafter he tenderly holds the head of the drowned Letgarde. Before this he had split a man's head with an ax—a man who had not told him Letgarde was dead. Then in a moment of deep sorrow he selects a young orphan to be his adopted daughter, a monument to Letgarde's memory. Each emotion-charged event in the story, in fact, is juxtaposed against another, producing rapid and extreme swings in the mood of the audience—an emotional bombardment characteristic of melodrama in general and typical of this series in particular.   In "The Kingdom in the Dark" (November 1934; *Redbook*, August 1935; $1,500), although the narrative is advanced to the point that Philippe finally meets the king, Fitzgerald makes it clear that if the series had gone on forever, the narrative line would have always led through an endless maze of primitive love and extreme violence. Indicative of this cycle in "The Kingdom in the Dark" is Philippe's new affair with Griselda, who has escaped from the king's entourage. After vowing to himself that he would do anything for Griselda, with whom he is now in love, he denies her first request concerning prisoners that he has taken: "Oh, don't let them torture him!" she asks, to which Philippe replies: "I won't . . . I don't like torture. Men, get a couple of heavy stones and some thongs."[51] In this episode Philippe not only establishes his position as a leader who has taken one of the king's women and made her subservient to him, but he has now also established himself as a legitimate count, recognized by the king, who in accepting Philippe as such, burns down Phillipe's fort as his punishment for taking Griselda.

Fitzgerald gives the final installment, "Gods of Darkness" (c. September 1935; *Redbook*, November 1941), a new twist in revealing that Griselda is actually a witch, and he uses the situation to comment on leadership in general. In this installment Philippe faces several crises which, without Griselda's evil supernatural power, he could not have overcome. Finally convinced that if he is to be a strong leader he too must serve the devil, Philippe attends a witch meeting at which he discovers that Griselda is "the chief priestess of the Witches of Touraine."[52]   With his new sworn allegiance to her, although he maintains half of his allegiance to God, his power becomes symbolically corrupted; it makes little difference to him which god he serves, as his last words indicate: "I'll play all their games—I'm playing to win!"[53] Ultimately Philippe's final comment suggests what the thematic intent of the "Philippe" series actually was: that leaders will always emerge, even in the presence of the greatest chaos imaginable; that leadership in an individual results from a blend of such seemingly paradoxical qualities as tenderness, callousness, warmth, and an overriding hunger for power; and that power will ultimately corrupt the one who possesses it, as Philippe was finally corrupted. In order to bend this thematic purpose to suit what Fitzgerald construed to be the intellectual and emotional level of the "average reader," he resorted to melodrama.   The brutality, violence, and primitive love is unprecedented in Fitzgerald's fiction; and based on *Redbook*'s hesitancy to publish the installments soon after they were received, the public apparently did not like the series.[54]

Arthur Mizener views the "Philippe" stories as "the clearest example there is of what Fitzgerald's work could be when he was not writing out of personal experience."[55]   But more than this, the series indicates what Fitzgerald could not be: a writer of cheap magazine serials. DeVoto contends that with such serials, the slick story "ceases to be merely entertainment," and that one who is to be successful as a serial writer must not merely cater to the biases of his audience; he must believe strongly in the simple philosophy that he preaches. And "No labor, ingenuity, or conscientiousness," DeVoto adds, "will enable a writer to produce this kind of fiction unless he naturally possesses the sentiments out of which it is made."[56] There are scores of examples to indicate that Fitzgerald did not possess such sentiments; but the "Philippe" series sharply points to the fact that Fitzgerald could never have made "the big money" that some writers made by writing slick serials.

Esquire Stories: January 1935 - July 1941

The final relationship that is important in an examination of Fitzgerald's career as a professional magazine writer is his association with *Esquire* and its editor Arnold Gingrich.[57]   In the course of this relationship Fitzgerald's work appeared in *Esquire* a total of forty-five times. Of these, thirty-six contributions were short stories[58]—nineteen of which are not closely related to each other and the remaining seventeen of which are Pat Hobby stories. Although Fitzgerald's first association with the magazine is marked by the early 1934 submission of an essay written primarily by Zelda Fitzgerald,[59] his tenure as an *Esquire* short story writer began with its publication of "The Fiend" in January 1935, less than one year after the April 1934 publication of *Tender Is the Night.*[60] It was almost by default that *Esquire* became the most dependable outlet for his work after the novel's failure. As indicated above, when Fitzgerald had seen his novel through book publication, he immediately returned to the business of writing *Post* stories; in addition, he had written the Philippe stories with the idea of a profitable serial in mind. His old market the *Post*, however, no longer served as a dependable outlet for his work, primarily because Fitzgerald was not writing the kinds of stories the magazine wanted; moreover, his Philippe serial idea was understandably received coolly by editors and readers of the other big circulation magazines who wanted typical Fitzgerald stories.

Fitzgerald's association with *Esquire*, then, grew out of the simple necessity to publish his work in any magazine that would buy it. In February 1934 when Fitzgerald had mailed Gingrich the collaborative "Show Mr. & Mrs. F. to Room—," Gingrich, excited by the prospect of sponsoring his high school idol,[61] the author of *This Side of Paradise*, accepted the article and an additional collaborative piece which appeared in July 1934.[62] Thus when Fitzgerald submitted his first *Esquire* story, "The Fiend," to the magazine, Gingrich was strongly biased in Fitzgerald's favor. Although accounts concerning Fitzgerald's relationship with Gingrich are one-sided (Gingrich has written much about it; Fitzgerald wrote little) one can be certain that Fitzgerald was aware of the fact that Gingrich would have published almost anything in *Esquire* with Fitzgerald's name attached. Regarding this, Fitzgerald wrote to Ober that *Esquire* gave him "200-250 for a mere appearance (1,000 to 2,000 words of any sort in any genre)."[63] Gingrich's suggestion to Fitzgerald in 1935 that he write "I can't write stories about young love for *The Saturday Evening Post*" five hundred times and give it to Gingrich with a by-line so he could "Say it's a manuscript that's just awaiting some revision"[64] suggests the mood of extreme tolerance characteristic of their relationship. Nor, finally, were there any restrictions as to length or subject matter imposed on Fitzgerald by Gingrich.[65] This was true of Gingrich's relations with all his authors, Hemingway included. He designed *Esquire* as a wide-open magazine, in part to pick up on odd pieces by famous authors, unsaleable elsewhere. Therefore, whatever standards Fitzgerald chose to place on his *Esquire* work were dictated only by his perception of what the *Esquire* audience would like and, no doubt, by his own feelings about making a decent showing alongside the high calibre writers that he would be appearing next to in the magazine.

When Fitzgerald began contributing to *Esquire*, the magazine boasted a fine stable of authors, among them Hemingway, John Dos Passos, André Malraux, and Theodore Dreiser.[66] Less frequent contributors included Thomas Wolfe, Ezra Pound, D. H. Lawrence, and George Jean Nathan.[67] Quite different from the *Post*, *Esquire* was conceived as a fashion magazine for men and was geared to a different audience. The group at whom it was aimed was able to pay fifty cents per issue. When Fitzgerald first contributed to *Esquire* in 1934, the circulation was 184,000; by 1937, it had passed the 600,000 mark.[68] Therefore, in the fiction that Fitzgerald contributed to *Esquire* there was no question whether it need cater to a large cross-section of middle America; instead, the magazine was squarely directed at a male, upper middle-class audience—a group for whom little censorship was necessary.

In essence, Fitzgerald could write what he wanted to write for *Esquire*, within reason, and he could be reasonably sure that the magazine would publish it. The only catch was that, regardless of the merit of any submission, Fitzgerald could not hope to make much more than the $250-per-piece price that became his regular fee for *Esquire* contributions. The result was that *Esquire* as a marketplace for his fiction became a number of things to Fitzgerald: in very hard times it was a buyer to whom he could sell a story which had been dashed off hurriedly; it became a last-resort market for those stories rejected by magazines that paid more, such as the *Post*; it was a place that enabled Fitzgerald very late in his life to use and enjoy his craft through the Pat Hobby stories, although the series, continued only at Gingrich's urging,[69] almost entirely ruled out the possibility that any single story would approach the level of high art as several *Post* stories had done; and finally, it remained the only vehicle through which Fitzgerald could keep his name before the public, though in this case it was a smaller and more limited one than his *Post* public.

The *Esquire* phase of Fitzgerald's career divides naturally into two parts: the period between February 1934 when Fitzgerald mailed Gingrich the collaborative "Show Mr. and Mrs. F. to Room—" and July 1937 when Fitzgerald left North Carolina for Hollywood; and the second period between July 1939, at which time Fitzgerald's contract with MGM expired,[70] and his death in December 1940.[71]

A fundamental characteristic of the *Esquire* stories which differentiates them from most of Fitzgerald's other commercial fiction is their length. All of the *Esquire* stories are short—an average of 2,000 words as compared with the average of 6,000 words for Fitzgerald's *Post* stories; and there are several reasons which account for this brevity. First, having written long stories for fifteen years to satisfy the requirements of the *Post*, Fitzgerald had, no doubt, come to equate length in his commercial stories with their market value; it would follow, naturally, that a $250 *Esquire* story should be shorter than a $4,000 *Post* story. And second, Fitzgerald must have realized that a central artistic weakness of his *Post* stories, which had to be long, resulted from the inclusion of too much deadwood in the form of nonessential description and distracting subplots. Thus *Esquire* provided him with the opportunity to remedy a problem which he had diagnosed already. Beginning with his first *Esquire* stories Fitzgerald became more length conscious, and thus economical, in them; and they are the primary exhibits of what is now generally regarded as his "later" style—a style marked, among other things, by spare description, economical phrasing in developing characters, and sharp focusing on relatively uncomplicated situations. That *Esquire* served as a laboratory in which he experimented with this new style is unquestionable: in many of the early *Esquire* stories Fitzgerald is consciously economizing on words to enhance the artistic value of his story. In other cases Fitzgerald, in order to make a quick $250, turned out for *Esquire* some of the weakest work of his career, the worst example of which is "Shaggy's Morning."

It is precisely the editorial *laissez faire* which characterized Fitzgerald's relationship with the magazine that accounts for the varied types of Fitzgerald stories published in *Esquire*. Each of Fitzgerald's thirty-six *Esquire* stories falls into one of four categories: (a) experimental pieces in which Fitzgerald works with various techniques of form not usually associated with the traditional "beginning, middle, and end" short story; (b) standard stories which are in many ways similar to Fitzgerald's *Post* stories, but shorter; (c) fictionalized, generally superior autobiographical pieces; and (d) the Pat Hobby series stories, which show Fitzgerald exploring with apparent enjoyment and some seriousness his new and final major subject—Hollywood. The very general rule applicable to all of Fitzgerald's fiction—that his work becomes progressively stronger as he comes closer to writing about his personal experiences—applies to the *Esquire* fiction: his fictionalized autobiography constitutes the best group of his *Esquire* contributions. But within each of the four categories of *Esquire* stories there is a wide range in quality, depending on the particular ways in which he was using his market in any given story. In some cases he wrote very short stories—true potboilers—for *Esquire* simply in order to make $250 quickly.[72] In other cases he expressly wrote stories whose brevity is artistically calculated to complement the themes of the stories: "The Lost Decade," for example. And in other cases he sold to the magazine stories that had been previously rejected by every other market that paid more than *Esquire*.[73] By examining each story within the context of the group to which it belongs, it becomes possible to determine with some precision the effects of Fitzgerald's last market—a very unselective, undemanding one—on the development of his craft and, to some degree, on the nature of his reputation in the last five years of his life.

Experimental Stories: January 1935 - November 1936

Although Fitzgerald should not be regarded as a technical or stylistic innovator in either the genre of the short story or the novel, he did on occasion perform minor experiments. In *This Side of Paradise*, for example, he blended a play, lines from Swinburne, and letters into the narrative. But during the period between *This Side of Paradise* and the beginning of his association with *Esquire* his experiments are minor: the inclusion of a play within a story as in "The Captured Shadow," for instance. In *Esquire* the experimentation becomes bolder. While all of the *Esquire* pieces differ from Fitzgerald's earlier work in length and compactness, several of the pieces stand out beyond the simple fact of their brevity as genuine experiments in form. The five pieces which represent the most radical departures from the traditional beginning, middle, end story were all written before Fitzgerald left for Hollywood. They are generally characterized by Fitzgerald's attempt to approach a dramatic immediacy while still working within the broad limits of the short story genre; however, for various reasons—among them, Fitzgerald's apparent haste in putting them together—these stories are typically weaker than any of the other *Esquire* pieces.

"The Night Before Chancellorsville" (November 1934; *Esquire*, February 1935; $250; *TAR*), the least experimental of the group, is also the most successful. In it, Fitzgerald attempts in a very short space to comment on the indifference to human suffering often felt by an observer who is inconvenienced by the suffering. This he does by establishing Nell, a callous prostitute, as the story's first person narrator. And he does not interrupt her story to describe or comment. He stands back to allow Nell the opportunity to reveal her own insensitivity; she views the train's delay, which is the main event around which the story revolves, simply as bothersome in spite of the fact that the delay enables dying men to receive medical aid. Though the story is a short one with no proper climax or dénouement, Fitzgerald is nearly as successful in this story at showing his heroine's insensitivity as he had been in demonstrating the desirability of his similarly callous heroines in the early 1920's. If these qualities—indifference and egocentricity—are less becoming to Nell than they were to some of the early heroines, it is because Fitzgerald in 1935 found them a good deal less attractive. And in this story, at least, he found an effective vehicle for his message: a story which tells itself quickly through first person narration and thus approaches the immediacy of drama.

"Shaggy's Morning" (March 1935; *Esquire*, May 1935; $250), the next experimental piece, is one of Fitzgerald's weakest stories. Like "The Night Before Chancellorsville," the story is told from the first person vantage point; but Fitzgerald fails to make it clear why this dog's morning is worth reading about. *Esquire*'s editor came as close in a headnote as any of the story's contemporary readers were apt to come in evaluating the story's purpose: "Now let the behaviorist psychologists gather around to see why dogs bury bones."[74] But in the context of Fitzgerald's use of the magazine as a laboratory for experimentation, "Shaggy's Morning" can be viewed as an experiment that did not work—a short stream of consciousness narration from a dog's point of view, the purpose of which may have been primarily to earn $250 for Fitzgerald.

In "Three Acts of Music" (February 1936; *Esquire*, May 1936; $250), Fitzgerald takes a basic idea that might well have originated as a plan for a *Post* story and executes it by leaving off the accessories that would have accompanied it in the *Post*. The story is essentially a sketch in three parts during which a young interne moves out of the life of his nurse-fiancée. The romantic tunes which provide the background for his departure and his return years later accentuate by counterpoint the fact that the two unnamed protagonists have no hope for finding romance. And so, the short drama ends with the only romance in the characters' lives relegated to the lyrics which have played at intervals through the story. In relation to Fitzgerald's other *Esquire* stories "Three Acts of Music" has significance as an experiment, the results of which Fitzgerald applied to later, more traditional contributions to the magazine: suggesting as it does a stripping away of as much detail as possible while still retaining a standard basic plot, the story is a forerunner, though more compressed, of such later *Post*-like *Esquire* stories as "The Honor of the Goon."

In the same league with "Shaggy's Morning" is "The Ants at Princeton" (*Esquire*, June 1936; $250) which is even more farfetched than "The Curious Case of Benjamin Button" (*Collier's*, 27 May 1922). Labelled as "Satire" by the editors, "The Ants at Princeton" succeeds primarily as a private joke in which Fitzgerald pokes fun at the Harvard football team, whose members "violate all the traditions of [their] families and play dirty."[75] The chief value of the story lies, not in any practical application that Fitzgerald later made of his satirical bent, but rather in the insight it provides into Fitzgerald's attitude, at that point, regarding his *Esquire* audience: at least two months after the last crack-up essay, he apparently felt that he need not always take the audience seriously.

The final experimental piece, "'Send Me In, Coach'" (October 1936; *Esquire*, November 1936; $250), is more accurately described as a drama than as a short story in the sense that the main story line is interwoven into that of a play which is being rehearsed by a group of boys at camp. In the sketch Fitzgerald moralizes that little boys must learn to play fair because, as *Esquire* editors accurately summed up Fitzgerald's message in a headnote, "all life, they say, is a game."[76] The story is undistinguished, but it points again to the fact that *Esquire* was a more versatile market than any Fitzgerald had had since the *Smart Set*. It is difficult, in fact, to imagine another magazine aside from *Esquire* which would have accepted it—a feature of all of the experimental stories which strongly suggests that Fitzgerald wrote them if not with *Esquire* in the front of his mind, then with the secure feeling that *Esquire* would like them even if they failed elsewhere. And none of these stories except perhaps "The Night Before Chancellorsville" has noteworthy redeeming value.

Traditional Stories: January 1935 - December 1937

In sharp contrast to the group of experimental pieces are the four stories which, more than any other *Esquire* pieces, resemble Fitzgerald's earlier traditional commercial stories. The first of these, "The Fiend" (September 1934; *Esquire*, January 1935; $250; *TAR*), which was also Fitzgerald's first non-collaborative contribution to *Esquire*, suggests both the strengths and weaknesses that characterize the group in general. It also raises the questions concerning Fitzgerald's use of the *Esquire* market: since these stories resemble the *Post* stories in form, were they first conceived with another audience in mind only to be trimmed down for *Esquire*, or were they written with the *Esquire* audience clearly in mind?

There is no mention in Fitzgerald's correspondence with Ober about "The Fiend," indicating perhaps that it was not submitted to another magazine first. Because it is much too short, approximately 2,300 words, to fit *Post* specifications or the specifications of magazines similar to the *Post*, it is likely that Fitzgerald wrote it for and submitted it to *Esquire* as a test case; by his admission to Perkins the story was one that he had wanted to write for six years.[77] The question which *Esquire*'s acceptance of the story answered was this: would the magazine publish stories, as the *Smart Set* had done much earlier, which were written in Fitzgerald's "second manner"—that is, stories written for his own amusement?   As a test case the story helped Fitzgerald establish the limits of acceptability for *Esquire* stories—a necessary process in feeling out his audience.

"The Fiend" represents a compromise between the old Fitzgerald story and what was to become the new one.   In its moralizing quality it resembles the late *Post* stories.   Its implied message is that when one becomes obsessed with evil, as Crenshaw Engels was obsessed with the evil of revenge, he will be destroyed by it.   In addition to the didacticism, "The Fiend's" thirty-four-year time span associates it with such longer stories as "More than Just a House," which depend on the passing of several decades for their lessons.   However, in its brevity and compactness the story differs from almost all earlier Fitzgerald stories—"Outside the Cabinet-Maker's" (*Century*, December 1928) is perhaps the only earlier story which sets a precedent for Fitzgerald's "new" style.   In "The Fiend" Fitzgerald leads the reader quickly through the bizarre murder of Mrs. Engels and her child in the first paragraph and then immediately to the revenge theme which is of primary concern in the story.   There are no digressions to confuse the reader; instead Engels is brought into focus so sharply that the reader has no doubts about either the authenticity of his obsession or the inevitability of his self-destruction.

Therefore, "The Fiend" is a transition story in which Fitzgerald begins to move away from those deeply ingrained features of his story writing such as that of providing the reader with a novel's worth of supporting characters who operate in a web of circumstances so complicated that they could never get out of them plausibly in the space of a single story; and he moves toward an abbreviated style in which circumstances are sketched in quickly while the main characters define themselves primarily through dialogue and action.   Those remnants of the old *Post* style, such as didacticism, provide the story with a link not only to Fitzgerald's earlier work, but also associate it with older romantic tales similar in some respects to Hawthorne's, whose work this story most closely resembles.   In that sense, even as a story in which Fitzgerald is working with stylistic departures from his previous work, he grounds these alterations in a tested theme which makes the story a serious, if perhaps a less than original, effort.

The three remaining stories of the group are highly improbable narratives, heavily plotted in the manner of Fitzgerald's late *Post* stories.   But in his now-characteristic *Esquire* style Fitzgerald compresses the action of each story into a very short space as he had done in "The Fiend."   The improbabilities in the three later stories, however, make them generally much weaker than "The Fiend."   "The Honor of the Goon" (April 1937; *Esquire*, June 1937; $250), for example, rests on Bomar Winlock's ability regularly to fall down full flights of stairs without hurting himself, an acrobatic trick which on one occasion causes a Malaysian student to humiliate herself by taking his fall seriously. For her concern she receives the nickname "The Goon." And subsequently, Bomar is attacked by her uncle for having brought dishonor on his niece's name. Similarly, "The Guest in Room Nineteen" (March 1937; *Esquire*, October 1937; $250) has an unlikely plot which turns finally on old Mr. Cass's apprehension that "a tough number" whom he sees in his hotel was death personified. Thus he dies from the fear that death has overtaken him when, in fact, the "tough number" was only the brother of his hotel manager. And the last of the three stories, "In the Holidays" (February 1937; *Esquire*, December 1937; $250), is also a farfetched tale—a mystery in which a detective catches the murderer, McKenna, by tracing the fingerprints McKenna left on a torn-up letter. The primary difference, then, between these stories and Fitzgerald's weakest *Post* stories is their compactness. However, when he was not bound by length requirements, Fitzgerald was able to achieve a sharper focus on his material than his late *Post* stories would indicate.

Taps at Reveille

In March 1935, a month after the appearance of Fitzgerald's *Esquire* story "The Night Before Chancellorsville," Scribners published Fitzgerald's fourth and final short story collection, *Taps at Reveille*. Fitzgerald had submitted to Perkins in May 1934 four possible alternatives for the collection to follow *Tender Is the Night*: the book could be an omnibus which included the best stories from the three previous collections and also new stories; it might include the Basil and Josephine stories plus one or two other stories; it could be simply a collection of stories chosen from those published after *All the Sad Young Men*, but excluding the Basil and Josephine stories; or it might be a collection of Fitzgerald's articles.[78] Perkins favored the second of these plans—a book consisting primarily of the Basil and Josephine stories.[79] However, Fitzgerald, after reconsidering the plan, decided that such a collection might be regarded by book buyers as his next novel, in which case he would be accused of selling "watered goods under a false name."[80] The collection finally assembled represents a compromise between Fitzgerald's second and third alternatives: it contains eight Basil and Josephine stories and ten additional stories published after the appearance of *All the Sad Young Men*.

Fitzgerald had difficulty in selecting stories for *Taps at Reveille*, and he discussed his reasons for the difficulty in his correspondence with Perkins. First, between the publication of *All the Sad Young Men* and *Taps at Reveille* fifty-six Fitzgerald stories had appeared in commercial magazines; the matter of eliminating approximately two-thirds of these from a planned collection posed a problem. Moreover, the problem was compounded by the fact that thirty-one of the fifty-six stories belonged in one of two distinct story blocks—the Basil/Josephine group (thirteen stories) or the *Tender Is the Night* cluster group (eighteen stories). Fitzgerald had reservations about including only parts from either of these blocks: the Basil/Josephine stories as a group, particularly the Basil ones, were of a high, even quality and demonstrated a sustained effort. The individual stories were simply stronger when read as a part of the group. Thus Fitzgerald naturally had reservations about publishing an isolated story from either the Basil or Josephine groups; and, for the reason indicated above that he did not want critics seeing it as his next "novel," he was also hesitant to publish them as a group. His reluctance to include stories from the second group—the *Tender Is the Night* cluster group—came from his unwillingness to serve readers with what might be regarded as warmed over fare from *Tender Is the Night*, a concern that echoes through the Fitzgerald/Perkins correspondence relating to *Taps at Reveille*.[81] The problem related to the Basil and Josephine stories was resolved by including more than half of both the Basil stories (five of the eight) and the Josephine stories (three of five), which by Fitzgerald's instruction were not "run together as units."[82] Of the eighteen cluster stories, Fitzgerald included four,[83] none of which is as closely related to *Tender Is the Night* as "One Trip Abroad" or "The Rough Crossing."

The eight Basil/Josephine stories and the five *Tender Is the Night* cluster stories constitute approximately two-thirds of *Taps at Reveille* and the five remaining stories in the book accurately represent the work Fitzgerald had been doing outside of these two groups. He had been writing long, rambling stories which mark his decline in popularity with the *Post* ("Family in the Wind"); he had worked with the idea of a doctor-nurse series ("One Interne"); he had returned to the subject of college men and women ("A Short Trip Home"), and to other early material such as the Tarleton, Georgia, setting ("The Last of the Belles"); and he had begun writing for *Esquire*, the two contributions from which were included in *Taps at Reveille* to "give people less chance to say they are all standardized *Saturday Evening Post* stories. . . ."[84]

The best stories in *Taps at Reveille* are "Babylon Revisited" and the Basil stories, and these were the stories most often singled out for praise by contemporary reviewers. A majority of the reviewers reacted favorably to the collection. Twelve of the reviews located by Bryer are "favorable," "five are 'mixed,'" and five are "unfavorable." But the reviews are Depression reviews characterized, with few exceptions, on one extreme by qualified praise and on the other by reserved criticism. As the *New York Sun's* reviewer noted, "It is hard, in these days of the depression, to be fair to Mr. Fitzgerald. The children of all ages—from 13 to 30—that decorate his pages seem as remote today as the neanderthal man."[85] One way that reviewers seem to have chosen to deal with Fitzgerald was to ignore *Taps at Reveille*; as Bryer indicates, there were fewer reviews of *Taps at Reveille* than of any previous Fitzgerald story volume.[86] Another way reviewers dealt with the collection was to neutralize their observations. What would seem to be the beginning of a totally negative review—"herein lies the petrifaction of a talent"[87]—ends with the less bitter, "All of which is not to say Fitzgerald is not entertaining. He is and slickly so."[88] Even John Chamberlain's fairly eloquent defense of Fitzgerald's material is tempered with the observation that "The trouble with Fitzgerald, to date, is that he has not found a way of offering his pictures of aspiration . . . and his pictures of aspiration defeated. . . in such a way as to convince that there is one unifying philosophy. . . ."[89] A fact that is clearer now, perhaps, than it was to Fitzgerald's contemporaries is that the volume could have been stronger if Fitzgerald had included more of the stories which are closely related to *Tender Is the Night*, such as "The Rough Crossing," "The Swimmers," "One Trip Abroad," and "A New Leaf." All of these stories are as good as either "Family in the Wind" or "One Interne," which they might have replaced. Certainly they are all superior to the *Esquire* stories in the collection.[90]

Fictionalized Autobiography: September 1936 - January 1938

If based on no other index than the varied kinds of stories that Fitzgerald published in *Esquire* during the year of publication of *Taps at Reveille*—stories ranging in seriousness of intent from "The Night Before Chancellorsville" to "Shaggy's Morning" and ranging in quality from mediocre to poor—it is clear that Fitzgerald had projected no clear image of himself to *Esquire* readers during the first year of his association with the magazine. Among other things, this meant to Fitzgerald that he need not—and obviously did not—tailor his work to reinforce whatever preconceptions the *Esquire* audience might have had about him; since most *Esquire* readers probably did not read the *Post* it is likely that they knew only that Fitzgerald had been a popular writer, and some of them, perhaps, had heard of *Tender Is the Night*. But in February 1936 Fitzgerald began to create a new image with the publication in *Esquire* of the probing, auto-analytical crack-up essays.[91] Perhaps the most important, and certainly the most talked about, of Fitzgerald's contributions to the magazine, these essays are a catalyst which precipitated a dialogue between Fitzgerald and the public, as Gingrich indicates in the June 1936 "Backstage with Esquire": "Seldom has as much interest been aroused by anything printed in our pages."[92] Based on the sample of comments on the essays recorded in Jackson Bryer's *The Critical Reputation of F. Scott Fitzgerald*, the critical response was mixed.[93] The immediate effect of Fitzgerald's dialogue with the *Esquire* public was his formulation of a new image for himself in the magazine. Quite the reverse of his early image with the *Post*, the *Esquire* Fitzgerald became an in-residence expert on failure. His new image dictated a measurable and clearly defined trend in his short story writing between mid-September 1936 and June 1937. His short stories came to provide the evidence for and the circumstances surrounding the actual event of cracking up.

Of the nine *Esquire* stories following "The Ants at Princeton," five of them are directly related to Fitzgerald's life and they are typically bleak narratives.[94] In them Fitzgerald fictionalizes autobiographical episodes and does so with extreme objectivity. Of the thirteen stories to appear in the magazine during the first phase of Fitzgerald's association with it, these are the best.

The first of these stories, "An Author's Mother" (*Esquire*, September 1936; $250), is predictably the most subjective one. In this three-column sketch, occasioned by the death of his mother, Fitzgerald alludes to her notoriously bad reading habits. The dying Mrs. Johnston, mother of famous author Hamilton J. Johnston in the sketch, prefers the works of sentimental poets like Alice and Phoebe Cary over the artistically superior works of her son. Her final words show that she has even become confused as to whether or not her son is the one who wrote "The poems of Alice and Phoebe Cary." Fitzgerald is saying through the sketch that it is one of life's ironies that the fame of a son is often completely lost on his mother. It was a sad fact, he suggests, that Johnston's books "were not vivid to her," that at the moment of her death the important image in her mind was that of Alice and Phoebe Cary coming to lead "her back gently into the country she understood."[95] In spite of the sentimental moments in the story, however—and there are few of them in the *Esquire* stories generally—"An Author's Mother" forecasts the sharp focus that Fitzgerald will achieve on his personal experiences in the autobiographical stories which follow.

In the less bleak "'I Didn't Get Over'" (August 1936; *Esquire*, October 1936; $250), Fitzgerald treats a subject that had concerned him for twenty years: the fact that he did not leave his training camp to go over and fight in World War I. He uses a double first-person narrator in this story much as Samuel Clemens does in "The Celebrated Jumping Frog of Calaveras County"; and he does so to achieve a greater objectivity toward the feelings associated with this experience. The first narrator sets the stage for Hibbing's story and, when Hibbing feels that he is boring his listeners, this unnamed narrator prompts him, by playing straight man, to continue. Fitzgerald shows Hibbing as quite reluctant to relate his adventures in the United States during the war, believing that the other men have more exciting tales to tell about their experiences in Europe. The reader, though, becomes interested in Hibbing's story, in large part because Fitzgerald's double narrator device adds suspense to it. When the wives demand that their husbands leave before Hibbing has finished his narrative, thus calling a halt to it, the reader is apt to want to hear more. Despite the subjective nature of the story's material, Fitzgerald skillfully chose the most effective manner to tell the story. Whereas a single first person narrative would, perhaps, have relayed a sour grapes attitude on Hibbing's part, the humility and matter-of-factness with which he tells of the meeting with "hero" Abe Danzer and of the sinking of the barge during which numerous men were killed emphasizes through understatement the fact that soldiers who remained at home during the war may have had a more exciting time than many who went abroad. And though the story is not a great one, it is a good, entertaining story.

In "An Alcoholic Case" (December 1936; *Esquire*, February 1937; $250) the doomed cartoonist is a fictional version of Fitzgerald as he saw himself in early 1937; and the Forest Park Hotel is a thinly disguised Grove Park Inn. Like Dick Ragland in "A New Leaf" (*Post*, 4 July 1931), the unnamed cartoonist is trapped by alcoholism; and when he, also like Ragland, breaks at the end of the story his nurse sums up Fitzgerald's deterministic message: "It's just that you can't help them and it's so discouraging—it's all for nothing."[96] But this story, one of the best *Esquire* pieces, also points up a sharp difference between such unhappy *Post* stories as "A New Leaf" and its *Esquire* counterpart. The cast of main characters in the *Post* story, both Dick and Julia, had a kind of glamour even in the midst of their misfortune; and there was always the feeling that somehow Ragland might even have been able to buy his way out of his grave. At least the world that he belonged to had a patina of unreality which made anything seem possible. Fitzgerald's cartoonist in "An Alcoholic Case," by contrast, though his fate is similar to Ragland's, had lost whatever sparkle he might have once had. His world is a dreary and depressing one in which it is appropriate that his last gesture is to cough in his hand and rub it into the braid of his trousers. The serious, autobiographical *Esquire* stories, like "An Alcoholic Case" which tell how empty life can be are typically carried off among drab, virtually hopeless characters who move through old, sparsely furnished rooms. And appropriately they die there. The personal style of the *Post* characters, then, differentiates them from their *Esquire* counterparts whose stories begin when their glamour has worn off.

In the next autobiographical story Fitzgerald returns to material very close to him: his wife's illness and her confinement in a sanitarium.[97] "The Long Way Out" (May 1937; *Esquire*, September 1937; $250) establishes parallels between "the tortures of long ago" and contemporary ones like Mrs. King's confinement in a mental institution. The torture is partly perpetrated by the bungling doctors and nurses who, in postponing the revelation to Mrs. King that her husband has been killed, miss the chance to convince her that he actually is dead. She slips into a make-believe world anticipating his arrival daily, a torture similar to the hopeless plight of Fitzgerald's "alcoholic case."

The first four autobiographical stories, therefore, reinforce the point that he was capable even in his weakest stories of objectifying material that was very close to him—that is, that his double vision rarely failed him. "Financing Finnegan" (June 1937; *Esquire*, January 1938; $250), the final personal experience story that Fitzgerald wrote before going to Hollywood in 1937, when read with the Fitzgerald-Ober correspondence in mind, provides a useful documentary study of this double vision: Fitzgerald's account of Finnegan's situation, while it parallels his own financial situation, is presented with humor in the story; but as one reads of the actual situation in the Ober correspondence there can be little doubt that it was a tragic one for Fitzgerald.

When Fitzgerald wrote "Financing Finnegan" in June 1937, he was in one of the worst artistic and financial slumps of his career. Deeply in debt to both Ober and Perkins,[98] he was having no luck selling stories to commercial magazines such as the *Post*. "Financing Finnegan" was, in fact, declined by the *Post* and offered to *Esquire*, to which Fitzgerald was also in debt for approximately $500.[99] His correspondence with Ober in the period immediately preceding the composition of "Financing Finnegan" is punctuated with telegrams which are often desperate requests for money: "TO REMAIN HERE AND EAT MUST HAVE ONE HUNDRED AND THIRTY TODAY PLEASE ASK PERKINS."[100]

Fitzgerald had little to laugh about in reflecting on either his professional or financial status in June 1937. And yet he was able to write in "Financing Finnegan" a humorous account of Finnegan's similarly unhappy plight. Just as Fitzgerald often wired Ober for money, so does Finnegan send his agent telegrams asking for money: "With fifty I could at least pay typist and get haircut and pencils life has become impossible and I exist on dream of good news desperately Finnegan."[101] And Finnegan, again like Fitzgerald, is being backed completely by his Ober and Perkins counterparts, who agree to allow Finnegan to make them beneficiaries of his life insurance policy—a humorous touch in Finnegan's case as it turns out, but unfunny in terms of Fitzgerald, who had borrowed heavily against his own life insurance policy. Essentially Fitzgerald is able to take his own lamentable condition and apply the details to Finnegan, thus pointing to the aspects of his own slump that would be funny if they were not, in fact, tragic. Even the tone of the story is light as opposed to the somber tone of "An Alcoholic Case," suggesting, perhaps, that Fitzgerald was optimistic about the prospect of his Hollywood contract materializing. An appropriate high note to end his stay in North Carolina before going to Hollywood, the last sentence of "Financing Finnegan" is prophetic—one of the only non-objective aspects of the story: "But the movies are interested in him—if they can get a good long look at him first and I have every reason to think that he will come through. He'd better."[102]

Between June 1937 and December 1938 Fitzgerald wrote no stories. When his contract with MGM expired at the end of 1938 he turned again to writing stories with the *Post* in mind; but he was unsuccessful in his attempts.[103] In July 1939, the month during which Fitzgerald separated from Ober,[104] he returned to his predictable *Esquire* market, and from then until his death—the second phase of the *Esquire* years—all but two of his stories appeared in that magazine.

Traditional Stories: December 1939 - July 1941

The twenty-two *Esquire* stories written during the last nineteen months of Fitzgerald's life point to what is, perhaps, the single indisputable generalization that one can make about his career as a writer of magazine fiction: from the beginning to the end he was a professional writer in the best sense of the phrase. In his retrospective view of his "early success" Fitzgerald had commented on his metamorphosis from amateur to professional and described it as "a sort of stitching together of your whole life into a pattern of work, so that the end of one job is automatically the beginning of another."[105] The final group of *Esquire* stories constitute Fitzgerald's next-to-last job—the job that followed his preceding job, script writing; and they are a prelude, of sorts, to the unfinished fifth act of his career, *The Last Tycoon*. Taken singly the stories are not brilliant; there is no "May Day," no "The Diamond as Big as the Ritz," no "Babylon Revisited." But there are good stories like "Design in Plaster," "The Lost Decade," and the Pat Hobby story, "A Patriotic Short." While some of the stories are weak, each of them bears the authentic stamp of a mature talent, though in many cases it appears to be the tired talent of one who still in 1939 had not yet been able to afford the luxury of "filling up" after the composition of *Tender Is the Night*. Of the twenty-two stories which Fitzgerald sold to *Esquire* between July 1939 and December 1940, five are related to the early *Post*-type *Esquire* pieces, primarily because Fitzgerald was attempting in them to break back into the high-priced magazine market, and seventeen are Pat Hobby stories.

Five of the stories resemble the early, more traditional *Esquire* pieces in their now-characteristic brevity and compactness[106] and in their standard form. In addition, they are presented in Fitzgerald's objective, detached *Esquire* manner evident in such earlier stories as "The Fiend" and the autobiographical "An Alcoholic Case." Though each of these stories shows Fitzgerald using his tools proficiently, their overall quality varies in proportion to Fitzgerald's affection for, or his closeness to, the material he is working with.

"Design in Plaster" (*Esquire*, November 1939; $250) and "The Lost Decade" (*Esquire*, December 1939; $250), the two stories written and published before the first Pat Hobby story, are the best single pieces of the last twenty-two *Esquire* stories. In "Design in Plaster" Fitzgerald concentrates on a single night in the frustrating life of Martin Harris. Confined to his bed with a broken shoulder,[107] Martin hopes for a reconciliation with his estranged wife Mary, who has come to visit him. But in the short space of that single night Fitzgerald makes it understandable that Martin's jealousy—of similar intensity to Dick Diver's jealousy over Rosemary at one point in *Tender Is the Night*—and the rage that it precipitates have not only been major factors in his estrangement from Mary, but also will make it impossible for him to win her back. Reacting to his brashness, Mary rejects him and instead chooses a freedom that she will never give up for him. The mood of intense frustration which results both from the restraint of Martin's cast on his physical freedom and from the restraint that his temperament imposes on his chance for future happiness gives "Design in Plaster" its force—a mood which links the story with its closest companion story, "Babylon Revisited."

"The Lost Decade," in an even shorter space of 1,200 words, conveys the intense feeling of loss which results from Mr. Trimble's having been "every-which-way drunk" for ten years. The starkness of the description complements the feeling of Trimble's disorientation in a world that he is really seeing for the first time in a decade. His reentry into the world, then, is complete and believable when he at last feels the texture of his coat and the building's granite at his side.

Both of these stories are good because Fitzgerald accomplishes in them what he intended to: primarily to create moods, of frustration in "Design in Plaster" and of disorientation in "The Lost Decade." The artistic effect in these two stories is carefully calculated; but that Fitzgerald's *Esquire* public gave him the incentive to write stories of this quality is doubtful. Fitzgerald indicated to Ober his feeling that *Liberty* probably would have paid $1,000 for "Design in Plaster," but because he had to dispose of it quickly he was forced to send it, as well as "The Lost Decade," to Gingrich.[108] *Esquire*, then, while it had given Fitzgerald an opportunity in the pre-Hollywood days to be more economical in his stories than he was permitted to be in the *Post*, did not finally impose a new style on Fitzgerald. The *Esquire* formula—at least as Fitzgerald apparently viewed it—called only for brevity; it did not necessarily call for brevity and quality. Understandable, then, is Fitzgerald's bemoaning the fact that he had to sell good stories like these two to *Esquire*. But this fact points to an important quality of the Fitzgerald-*Esquire* relationship. By the simple virtue of *Esquire*'s quick-acceptance, quick-payment policy it fell heir to a few of Fitzgerald's best very short stories, "Design in Plaster" and "The Lost Decade" among them. But it should be noted also this same policy had its advantages for Fitzgerald: in its rather indiscriminating stance toward Fitzgerald's work, *Esquire* bought more than its share of Fitzgerald's weakest commercial stories—"Shaggy's Morning" and "The Ants at Princeton," for instance.

The last three *Esquire* stories outside of the Pat Hobby group suggest that Fitzgerald finally took the most practical option provided for in *Esquire*'s policy regarding his work; he tailored short pieces expressly for publication in that magazine. In "Three Hours Between Planes" (*Esquire*, July 1941), Fitzgerald imposes the limited time frame indicated in the title on his material in order to get an *Esquire* sketch out of his old favorite subject, lost youth. No longer, however, is the subject viewed as tragic; instead Fitzgerald shows objectively that Donald needed even less time than three hours to discover that his attempt to recapture the past is sadly laughable; Nancy, the embodiment of his youth, kisses him sentimentally, but she does so under the mistaken impression that he is someone else. "On an Ocean Wave" (*Esquire*, February 1941), the only Fitzgerald story published under a pseudonym,[109] is also informed by an old favorite serious subject, wealth. With the authority granted him through his money, Gaston Sheer chooses to interfere in his wife's shipboard affair by paying to have her professor-suitor thrown overboard. Fitzgerald's comment on Sheer's presumption that his money can buy anything is typically objective in his *Esquire* manner: Mrs. Sheer will, no doubt, keep on playing "whatever it was they played"[110] even when her professor fails to show up for their date. His comment on wealth and corruption, though, becomes more pointed in "The Woman from Twenty-One" (*Esquire*, June 1941). In this sketch the famous author-protagonist, Raymond Torrence, who returns to New York from his adopted home Java, finds that all of the unpleasant things he had left New York to escape are still there. They are embodied in the obnoxious Mrs. Ritchbitch, a woman who spoils a Saroyan play for Torrence by telling her companion loudly and repeatedly that she would rather be at Twenty-one; after listening to her through the first two acts, Torrence decides that he and his wife will return immediately to Java.[111]

The Pat Hobby Stories: January 1940 - May 1941

The loose unity which binds together the five stories discussed above derives primarily from the fact that they are "typical" *Esquire* stories: they are short, they are compact, and they are objective. The seventeen stories centered around the "scenario hack," Pat Hobby, are all of these things; but they are, in addition, held together by a central theme of failure. Gingrich in his introduction to *The Pat Hobby Stories* indicates most of the reasons why the Pat Hobby stories deserved to be collected in book form: they show that Fitzgerald was turning out "good copy" shortly before his death; they were his "last word from his last home"; Fitzgerald cared about them and extensively revised them; and they have an impact when read together which they lack when read singly. The argument—and the tone of Gingrich's introduction is closer to argument than explanation—is sound on all points. For this study, however, it is less important that the Pat Hobby stories are unified and now collected than it is that they served a distinct economic function in Fitzgerald's life which overshadowed their literary one. As his daughter commented, "Why [Pat Hobby] sent me to Vassar."[112] And the stories were, in fact, as well suited for their economic role as anything Fitzgerald could have written for *Esquire*. In a sense they are a culmination of everything he had learned about the *Esquire* market; primarily he had found that it was not nearly as discriminating as the *Post* had been, and that, consequently, he had a great deal of leeway in what he chose to write for *Esquire*. Given the loose guidelines of the magazine, it becomes clear how the idea of the Pat Hobby series was gradually formed and why it evolved as it did in Fitzgerald's mind. The series idea itself was a good moneymaking one as Fitzgerald knew from the Basil and Josephine stories; moreover, to write a series of sketches, shorter *Esquire*-length pieces which could be completed during a single Saturday or Sunday, would have been even more appealing. When Fitzgerald took the sketch series idea and modeled it around a free-lance movie script writer who was on a failure treadmill, the combination offered unlimited possibilities: it would be as impossible for Pat to die as it would be for him to succeed.

Unlike the Basil stories in which the main character's movement was toward maturity, and unlike the Josephine stories in which hers was toward emotional bankruptcy, the Pat Hobby stories have no forward movement. Instead the stories characteristically have a triangular structure in which Pat begins as a failure, tries a new angle that almost works, and then generally sinks again into failure. That is the point at which he remains until his next adventure. Having established a basic framework with almost unlimited potential for expansion, Fitzgerald had only to make his idea entertaining enough to sustain the audience's interest month after month. In part, he did this by establishing a comic tone which is, more often than not, tempered with pathos. Fitzgerald viewed the stories as comedy,[113] though he probably would not have thought them funny himself, since it is likely that Fitzgerald was projecting through Pat his own fears about what he might become.

An overview of the series suggests how Fitzgerald limited the scope of the series to make certain that Pat would never be taken so seriously by the audience that he would lose his potential as a comic subject, a ploy which was complementary to Fitzgerald's humorous stance toward his character. This he accomplishes by reducing to a minimum those facets of Pat's personality which would give him any real complexity. He does not have a conscience, for example, as illustrated in "Pat Hobby's Christmas Wish"—a negative aspect of his personality which Fitzgerald counterpoints by giving him an essentially "good" nature; only at times is he a vicious scoundrel. To further uncomplicate his personality Fitzgerald refuses to give him anything more than the hint of a past: except for his specific memory of meeting the President in "A Patriotic Short," Pat appears to have only the vague recollection that he was a real somebody back in the silent movie days—a memory about whose actual poignancy to Pat the reader can only speculate. Moreover, Fitzgerald presents him as a man without a future, except in the very limited sense that Pat exists from two-week job to two-week job.

Whatever feeling the reader has for Pat, then, must be based mainly in the present. And in the present he is a man who is always looking for the right angle that will assure him of a two or four-week job involving as little work as possible. Thus Fitzgerald sets him up for the numerous letdowns, most of which result from his own laziness or his own bungling of opportunities which might have paid off. The final result of Fitzgerald's conception of Pat as an uncomplicated, in some ways atavistic character, is that the reader's range of reaction is sharply limited: one may see Pat's situation as humorous or sad, but never as tragic or sublime. Fitzgerald's intention is, in fact, to settle for a consistently predictable reaction from the audience when Pat is placed in either of his two possible positions: failure or near-success. Since Pat's depth of character changes very little throughout the series, Fitzgerald's portrait of him depends on the variety of situations he has to react to, each sketch adding a little more information.

In "Pat Hobby's Christmas Wish" (*Esquire*, January 1940; $250), just as Pat's four-week contract is about to expire, he is presented with an opportunity to make his future secure by blackmailing his boss. But his explosive information turns out to be false, which leaves Pat headed toward the termination of his contract at the end of the story. The audience is called on to react to this first adventure of Pat's with laughter, though it will be mingled with at least mild disapproval of the basically serious blackmail attempt, and finally with at least a touch of regret that Pat—whose contract, unknown to him, would have expired anyway—has made his chances for getting a job the next time more difficult. This predictable reaction sequence is one that Fitzgerald will set up over and over again in the remaining sixteen Pat Hobby stories; and he will vary the intensity of the called-for emotional responses very little, guaranteeing the reader sheer amusement without real challenge.

"A Man in the Way" (*Esquire*, February 1940; $250) shows Pat as an out-of-work, forty-nine-year-old veteran script writer who resorts to stealing a script idea from his boss's girlfriend; and for it he gets a movie contract. But the story closes as the girlfriend is about to innocently relate to Pat's boss the now-disclosed script that she herself had wanted to try. Again as in "Pat Hobby's Christmas Wish," the story's conclusion leaves Pat on the way to his familiar, out-of-work, position of failure. And also as in "Christmas Wish" when the humor of Pat's scheming has worn off, Fitzgerald draws the reader back into sympathy with Pat's plight by using dramatic irony: the reader knows, but Pat has no way of knowing, that events are in motion at the end of the story which will rob him of the short-lived security of knowing he has a two-week job. That is, while Pat is, no doubt, out celebrating, forces beyond his control are already undermining his cause for celebration.

Likewise "'Boil Some Water—Lots of It'" (*Esquire*, March 1940; $250) shows Pat on his way to at least minor success which is thwarted when Pat mistakes a studio executive for a dining room intruder. Pat severely injures the man for presuming to sit at "the Round Table," again setting himself up for the inevitable punishment which must follow his error. Thus the audience is moved from the humor of Pat's initial scheme—to get from a pretty, young nurse some realistic background information on his line "Boil some water—lots of it"—into sympathy for Pat who has made a fool of himself.

In "Teamed with Genius" (*Esquire*, April 1940; $250) Pat is assigned to collaborate on a script with "genius," René Wilcox, but in his fear that Wilcox will produce nothing, Pat submits a script that he has plagiarized. He is saved from complete humiliation and total failure when Wilcox produces a masterpiece and requests that Pat be his collaborator on his next assignment—a stroke of luck for Pat who was chosen, not for any merit that he had as a writer, but because Wilcox thought he might do a story about Pat. Again Pat's amusing adventure leads him finally into a sad situation in which the forces beyond his awareness and control work to undermine whatever satisfaction he will feel when he learns that he has "earned" a job.

In "Pat Hobby and Orson Welles" (*Esquire*, May 1940; $250), Pat, after scheming to gain entrance to the studio lot, agrees to allow a make-up man to disguise him for fun as Orson Welles in exchange for a ten-dollar loan. Pat winds up running from the lot to Mario's bar with his ten dollars in order to escape the humiliation that would come when it was discovered that he was masquerading as Welles. The image that Fitzgerald creates of Pat actually posing as Orson Welles provides the story's humor. But as usual Pat is driven back into his sad plight of unemployment, this time almost reduced to a wounded animal running for the shelter of Mario's Bar.

Pat almost works himself into a bargaining position in "Pat Hobby's Secret" (*Esquire*, June 1940; $250) when he succeeds in learning R. Parke Woll's valuable, secret ending for a script. But just as Pat is about to sign a contract which depends on his knowledge of the ending, everything in his mind goes black and white, a psychological blank that resulted, in part, from Pat's witnessing the murder of R. Parke Woll. Now that Pat's humorous antics have led him to become the rightful owner of valuable information, he becomes an amnesiac, which robs him of his near-success and evokes a degree of sympathy for him, an underdog with the deck stacked against him.

Essentially the same pattern is continued in the stories which lead up to "A Patriotic Short." In "Pat Hobby, Putative Father" (*Esquire*, July 1940; $250), Pat loses a $250-a-month-for-life gift from his "putative" son he had never met—an unfortunate loss which resulted, through no fault of Pat's, from Germany's declaration of war on England, causing his son's fortune to revert to the British Empire. Pat's angle for making extra money as a tour guide in "The Homes of the Stars" (*Esquire*, August 1940; $250) also fails when Pat takes a Missouri couple on an unauthorized tour of movie mogul Marcus's home. When Marcus arrives unexpectedly Pat is forced to run away, leaving his Missouri couple to explain how they happened to be there, and leaving Pat, still without money for new tires, and with "beads of gin breaking out on his forehead."[114] Still broke and in trouble for having spoiled an important take in "Pat Hobby Does His Bit" (*Esquire*, September 1940; $250), Pat is forced to act as a stunt man in order to redeem himself for having ruined a scene. His success at the end is the dubious one of having held up the picture once more by indirectly causing a star to break his leg; certainly there is little chance that it will help him in his next attempt to get a job with the studio. In "Pat Hobby's Preview" (*Esquire*, October 1940; $250) the success is again a clouded one in which Pat manages to get a screen credit only because the picture is so bad that its major author refuses to have his name associated with it, and again in "No Harm Trying" (*Esquire*, November 1940; $250) Pat has moderate success, but it all revolves around the fact that Pat has been given a "charity job" at the studio, during which time he acts beyond the call of duty and plagiarizes another script.

"A Patriotic Short" (*Esquire*, December 1940; $250) is the best single story in the series; it is also the least funny primarily because Fitzgerald gives Pat a depth which requires a more complex reaction to his situation. Against the background of Pat's current movie assignment Fitzgerald sketches in details of his past which give Pat's personality a new dimension. In fact, he ceases for the short space of this story to be simply a "scenario hack" who exists from moment to moment in hopes of finding the angle that will make his life easier for a few more weeks. Instead, juxtaposed against his specific recollection of the day the President visited the studio, a day filled with Pat's memory of what it had meant to be an insider with a swimming pool and direct personal access to the industry's giants, Pat's present situation appears more tragic than sad. Consequently, the cynicism of Pat's script line—"*Mr. President you can take your commission and go straight to hell*"[115]—indicates more than the simple sour grapes attitude which, in other stories, accompanies his self-analysis of his plight. It is clear, though, from this story that if Fitzgerald had been as graphic about Pat's past in his other adventures, the series would have been radically different. "A Patriotic Short" is unique in the series: it violates the rather rigidly set Pat Hobby formula and in doing so it stands out as artistically superior to the other sixteen stories whose amusement value relies, at least partly, on the nebulous nature of Pat's past.

The five remaining stories show Pat back in his maze, finding new angles that will sustain him for short periods and then sinking back into characteristic failure. Broke and hatless in "On the Trail of Pat Hobby" (*Esquire*, January 1941) Pat sneaks onto the studio lot after police had raided the motel where he had been a part-time clerk. Shortly after he has become secure within the gates of his studio home, Pat is painfully reminded of his earlier encounter with the police when his boss offers him fifty dollars to invent a title for a movie about tourist cabins. Thus the excitement of the prize money that he finally earns for the title "Grand Motel" is undercut by the nausea brought on partially because he has had to relive the experience of the raid. In "Fun in an Artist's Studio" (*Esquire*, February 1941) Fitzgerald's dramatic irony takes over and causes Pat's potentially funny experience of posing nude to become a sad situation in which Pat, unknown to him, has been chosen because his face is a study in failure. In "Two Old-Timers" (*Esquire*, March 1941) Pat comes out on top in a verbal exchange between Phil Macedon, a has-been actor who still has delusions of grandeur. But without anywhere to go after being released from jail, Pat gains the audience's sympathy when he salutes the mansions he "used to be able to drop into." With twenty cents in his pocket in "Mightier than the

Sword" (*Esquire*, April 1941) Pat is given an opportunity to get a screen credit but is unable to produce anything worth filming. And finally, in "Pat Hobby's College Days" (*Esquire*, May 1941) Pat's scheme for making a college movie fails when his conference with university officials is interrupted by Pat's secretary who has been caught on campus with a pillowcase full of empty liquor bottles, "the evidence of four strained weeks at two-fifty"[116]—evidence of his drinking that Pat was having removed on the eve of the expiration day of his contract.

Based on the structural repetition of the individual Pat Hobby stories, then, it is true as Gingrich maintains that they stand up better artistically when they are read as a group constituting "a full-length portrait"; and it is true that the value of the picture increases with each story added. But to compare the quality of the portrait with that of such other Fitzgerald "failures" as Gordon Sterrett would be to do Fitzgerald a disservice; no evaluation of the Pat Hobby stories should ignore the primary economic function that they initially served for Fitzgerald. Pat, after all, was conceived for the $250 Fitzgerald knew each story would bring from *Esquire*. That Fitzgerald became attached to his creation, of course, is indisputable as the introduction to *The Pat Hobby Stories* indicates. These stories, however, do point up the difference between the *Esquire* market and the other markets that Fitzgerald had previously used as outlets for his commercial short fiction. Whereas Fitzgerald could comment in 1935 that all of his stories were "conceived like novels,"[117] this was clearly not true of the *Esquire* stories. For the most part they were conceived as vignettes or sketches and, in the case of the Pat Hobby stories, they were executed according to a formula or pattern which, in advance, guaranteed a $250 price and almost precluded the possibility that they would reach the level of high art.

One of the most curious facts about the Pat Hobby stories is that while their composition dates coincide precisely with the composition date of the unfinished *The Last Tycoon*—Gingrich received the first Pat Hobby story on 16 September 1939[118] and Fitzgerald began the actual writing of *The Last Tycoon* before the end of September 1939[119]—these stories are related to the novel only in a very remote sense: both deal with Hollywood, and the stories share occasional minor details with the novel, the presence of the old executive Marcus in both, for example. But the dissimilarities between the novel and the Pat Hobby stories are much more obvious than the similarities. There is no one in the stories who resembles Monroe Stahr, though Jack Berners is in approximately his position; moreover, there is no Cecelia Brady, nor is there a Kathleen Moore. And there is no romance in the stories except the unexplored affair between Berners and Pricilla in "A Man in the Way." More importantly, however, Fitzgerald focuses in the Pat Hobby stories on failure, whereas Monroe Stahr's character is a study in success: as his mother remarked, "We always knew Monroe would be all right."[120] His only major flaw, in fact, as Fitzgerald indicates, results from his surrounding himself with "men who were very far below him."[121] But none of the characters in the novel is as inept as Pat Hobby; certainly, none of the story characters as sparkling as Stahr.

Clearly the Pat Hobby stories, written as they were during the composition of *The Last Tycoon*, did not serve the purpose of a "more orderly writer's notebook" for the novel as the *Post* stories which cluster around *Tender Is the Night* had done. Far from using *Esquire* as a workshop for his novels, Fitzgerald used it as a workshop for more *Esquire* stories. In fact, he developed an "*Esquire* form" and an "*Esquire* style" expressly for *Esquire* in view of various economic and artistic considerations discussed earlier. These facts have both positive and negative implications regarding the influence that *Esquire* exerted on Fitzgerald's career during his tenure with it. On the positive side, Fitzgerald, before his relationship with *Esquire* was established, had begun to blur the focus of his longer commercial short stories with tangential descriptions and webs of often-unrelated circumstances, perhaps in an attempt to gloss over the fact that his material was depleted. It was to his advantage to be as economical as possible in his *Esquire* work since the length of the *Esquire* stories had no bearing on the price he received for them.   Furthermore, *Esquire* published Fitzgerald's work when he was having a difficult time selling it to anyone and, in this way, it gave him the exposure to the public that most writers—this is particularly true of Fitzgerald—need as incentive to keep writing. And in the course of his association with *Esquire* he added several good stories to the body of his short fiction: "An Alcoholic Case," "Financing Finnegan," and "Design in Plaster," to name three.

The negative influences are, perhaps, more subtle and they relate back to the integral relationship which had, before *The Last Tycoon*, existed between Fitzgerald's novel writing and his short story writing: his two best novels, *Tender Is the Night* and *The Great Gatsby*, were composed in a climate of free exchange between the stories and the novels. The *Esquire* market, however, was not suited to serve a workshop function as the *Post* had been. And even if it had, it is difficult to imagine how Fitzgerald would have experimented in the framework of short *Esquire* sketches with the complex relationships that he was developing in *The Last Tycoon*. Perhaps "Dearly Beloved"

(c. January-February 1940; *Fitzgerald/Hemingway Annual 1969*), a short *Esquire*-length sketch, best illustrates this point. In it Fitzgerald was apparently attempting to see if he could use *Esquire* for *The Last Tycoon* as he had used the *Post* for *Tender Is the Night* character studies.[122]   This sketch is clearly a working through of the characterization of the black fisherman in *The Last Tycoon*. Beauty Boy in the story reads Plato and Rosicrucian literature and is the only reflective black character in the short stories, just as the fisherman is the only seriously thoughtful black character in Fitzgerald's novels. The brevity of the sketch suggests that Fitzgerald wrote it with *Esquire* in mind. But the magazine rejected it[123]—a fact which raises a question of the suitability of Fitzgerald's *The Last Tycoon* material, regardless of how he treated it, for *Esquire*: the Stahr-Kathleen relationship, for example, and certainly the Cecelia-Stahr relationship would have been as out of place in *Esquire* as "The Lost Decade" would have been in the *Post*. In short, *Esquire* was ill-suited to Fitzgerald's need for a profitable workshop for *The Last Tycoon*, a fact that is no less lamentable in view of the fact that Fitzgerald was responsible for losing his best workshop, the *Post*. It is difficult to read the *Esquire* pieces—particularly the Pat Hobby stories—without realizing that every hour that Fitzgerald spent on them could have been spent completing *The Last Tycoon*. From a practical standpoint, then, it is fair to say that the small sums which Fitzgerald worked for in writing the Pat Hobby stories may have interfered with the completion of his last novel, whereas the high prices Fitzgerald earned from the *Post* between 1925 and 1933 provided the financial climate which made it possible for him to complete *Tender Is the Night*.

The Last Tycoon Cluster Stories

Indeed, if the Pat Hobby stories, close as they were in terms of composition date to *The Last Tycoon*, marked the distance Fitzgerald had come in resolving the dichotomy between being both a professional writer and literary artist with which he had been confronted for twenty years, this study of the function of the stories in Fitzgerald's overall career would end on a bleak note. It does not, however, because of the existence of two posthumously published works which, although neither is an outstanding story, indicate that Fitzgerald was attempting to recreate the climate of free exchange between his stories and novels characteristic especially of the composition period of *Tender Is the Night*. The two stories—"Discard" and "Last Kiss" are companion pieces to *The Last Tycoon*; and, as such, they are primary exhibits of

Fitzgerald's attempt to reestablish the popular magazines as a workshop for his novels.

"Discard" (c. early August 1939; *Harper's Bazaar*, January 1948), in its marketing history as well as its content, provides a valuable commentary on this attempt. The fact that Fitzgerald directly submitted the story, originally entitled "Director's Special," to *Collier's* before attempting to sell it to the *Post,* coupled with his remarks to Ober that a concern in the first draft of the story with *Collier's* length restrictions had weakened it, suggest that the story was tailored for *Collier's*.[124] When it was rejected by that magazine Fitzgerald sent the story to the *Post*, at the same time mailing a carbon copy to Ober, who attempted to place the story elsewhere after the *Post* rejected it.

A number of interesting suggestions emerge from the Fitzgerald-Ober correspondence surrounding this story, the last one that Fitzgerald would attempt to sell through Ober. Perhaps the most valuable are those which indicate why the story was unacceptable to the *Post* editors who rejected it. Their primary complaint was that the beginning and ending of the story were obscure;[125] and even after Fitzgerald revised it, "none of them could make head nor tail out of it."[126] Ober, on the other hand, felt that the story was a good one whose only problem was that it was too subtle for *Post* readers. It is ironic, however, that the beginning and ending of "Discard," the obscure parts, contain those ingredients without which the story could, perhaps, never have been even considered by the *Post*: it is in the beginning that Dolly is established as a *grande cliente*, and it is not until the end that the hard work ethic finally pays off for her. The problem, though, for *Post* editors would have arisen from the fact that Dolly's reward is a dubious one: although she is granted a second chance, she is pictured, nonetheless, as an old-timer whose best years are gone. Based on the Fitzgerald *Post* heroines who had been Hollywood stars—Jenny Prince ("Jacob's Ladder"), for example—the *Post* audience liked starlets left with their glamour intact. Even the sugar coating of Fitzgerald's "obscure" beginning and end for "Discard" does not conceal the serious study of Hollywood superficiality that lies slightly beneath the story of Dolly's success.

When the facade is removed, "Discard" contains an early version of the corrupt Hollywood of *The Last Tycoon*, a place where only a Monroe Stahr can "turn out all right in the end"; and it is in this kinship to the novel that the primary importance of the story lies. In it Fitzgerald experiments, not specifically with any of the characters that appear in *The Last Tycoon*, but rather with the patina of glamour which covers Stahr's Hollywood world, peopled with its empty-headed actresses and inept production men. Dolly Borden, "Discard's" twenty-five-year-old heroine, has at the beginning of the story earned everything that Hollywood has to offer: an Academy Award, the best house in the valley, and a European count, Hennen de Lanclerc, who has settled in Hollywood as Dolly's husband. But she is a frustrated woman who sulkily leaves Hollywood because she is not given the role that she wants in *Sense and Sensibility*. From the beginning it is clear that, in her mid-twenties, Dolly is at once at the top of the Hollywood success ladder and, at the same time, poised for the downfall that must accompany such a rise in the movie world. Phyllis Burns, who is four years younger than Dolly and who worships her, embodies the surface beauty and cutthroat ambition that will precipitate Dolly's misfortune; she is a member of the next Hollywood generation, which is as shallow and amoral as the preceding one. Predictably, at the end of the story—in time, four years later—Phyllis owns the best house in the valley where she will live with her new husband, Hennen de Lanclerc.

Thus, just as "The Hotel Child" had succeeded in painting a picture of the decadent nobility which would later figure into *Tender Is the Night*, so is "Discard" successful in conveying a feeling of the fragility of Hollywood success which plays an important role in Stahr's Hollywood. In "Discard" there is only the relatively weak producer, Jim Jerome, by whose success one can measure that of others. Beyond this, Fitzgerald offers through the story a message which, in some respects, runs counter to the emotional bankruptcy idea expressed, among other places, in *Tender Is the Night* and the Josephine Perry stories, in which vitality that is depleted probably does not return. For "Discard" the message is that when people fail in a particular venture, they may start over on "another street" and open a new "big charge account with life,"[127] as Dolly does on her return to Hollywood. This message, though, was part of the cloak that Fitzgerald was using to disguise his *The Last Tycoon* material for a popular magazine-reading public. That he was willing to do this in an attempt to find a workshop for the novel is not surprising; that both Ober and the *Post* editors thought that he could revise the story and make it suitable for the magazine[128] is evidence on the positive side that if there had been more time, he might have succeeded.

Of "Last Kiss" (*Collier's*, 16 April 1949), the final *The Last Tycoon* cluster story, *Collier's* said, "the story seems to contain the seed that grew into the novel The Last Tycoon, which Fitzgerald was writing when he died."[129] The claim is too extravagant for the story in that it implies the sort of relationship between the story and the novel that exists between "Winter Dreams" and *The Great Gatsby*, a relationship which does not exist in the case of "Last Kiss" and *The Last Tycoon*. However, the story more closely resembles the novel than does any other story; it is closer certainly than "Discard." Mizener suggests that "about all Fitzgerald took from the story for the novel" was Kathleen's "uncertainty about Americans and her looking like pink and silver frost."[130] But the relationship is actually closer than this. In addition to the Hollywood setting and theme of Hollywood success dealt with in "Discard," Fitzgerald creates in "Last Kiss" counterparts both to Stahr and Kathleen. Jim Leonard, a thirty-five-year-old producer, is similar to Stahr in that he possesses the same kind of power: when the budding starlet, Pamela Knighton, meets Leonard, the tone of her agent's voice tells her, "This *is* somebody."[131] In fact, on the Hollywood success ladder he is, in Fitzgerald's words, "on top,"[132] though also like Stahr he does not flaunt this fact.   And although Pamela is fundamentally different from Kathleen in her self-centered coldness, she is similar in more ways than her resemblance to "pink and silver frost" and her uncertainty about Americans. Unlike Pamela, Kathleen is no aspiring actress; but her past life, like Pamela's, has an aura of mystery about it. Moreover, the present lives of both are complicated by binding entanglements: Pamela's to Chauncey Ward, and Kathleen's to the nameless man she finally marries.   There are also other parallels: the first important encounter between Leonard and Pamela, for instance, closely resembles the ballroom scene during which Stahr becomes completely enchanted by Kathleen's beauty.   In fact, Leonard's attraction to Pamela is similar to that of Stahr's to Kathleen; although there is no Minna Davis lurking in Leonard's past, he is drawn to Pamela by the kind of romantic, mysterious force which had finally, apart from her resemblance to Minna, drawn Stahr to Kathleen. Moreover, both attachments end abruptly with the same sort of finality: Pamela dies leaving Leonard with only film fragments to remember her by, and Kathleen abruptly leaves Stahr when she marries "The American."

That these parallels were the "seeds" of *The Last Tycoon* is doubtful. But the important point is that "Last Kiss" is a popular treatment of the primary material that Fitzgerald would work with in the novel: Leonard's sentimental return to the drugstore where he had once seen Pamela and his nostalgic remembrance of their last kiss earmark the story for a popular audience, an audience that Fitzgerald hoped would help pay his bills during the composition of the novel. Fitzgerald, though, was unable to sell the story; and because there is no mention of it in the Fitzgerald-Ober correspondence, the number and kind of rejections that Fitzgerald received regarding it are unknown.[133]

The story's major weakness is that neither Leonard nor Pamela generates enough interest to provoke strong or genuine emotion. Leonard, on the one hand, is simply a weak character whose rise to power lacks the motivating force necessary to make him believable; Pamela, on the other, is a thoroughly unsympathetic character whose death means very little, except to Leonard. Furthermore, Fitzgerald in "Last Kiss," as in "Discard," challenges the suitability for its role of the institution which, in Robert Sklar's words, "was now the spokesman for America's dreams": the motion picture industry.[134] Such challenges are not, of course, of the sort on which one either builds or rebuilds a popular reputation. It is sufficiently clear, however, from "Discard" and "Last Kiss" that Fitzgerald was regaining his sense of audience. Both stories in the process of demonstrating how well Fitzgerald understood Hollywood—and in the face of *The Last Tycoon* it is unquestionable that he did—also captured much of the glitter that is generally associated with it. In order to rebuild the kind of popular magazine workshop that he had had for *Tender Is the Night*, it remained for him to subordinate his understanding of Hollywood to the task of recreating its surface. Had he continued in the direction of "Discard" and "Last Kiss" he would, perhaps, have done this. It is true, of course, that if Fitzgerald had written more stories like these two during the composition period of *The Last Tycoon* he would have written fewer Pat Hobby stories—a negligible loss both in artistic and financial terms—and he might have been "unemployed" on more of his Sundays in Hollywood. But based on the climate which had in the past proven to be most favorable for his serious novel work—that is, a climate in which he wrote stories for popular magazines while the novels were taking shape—it is also possible that he might have used such stories to make *The Last Tycoon* something more than a great fragment.

Of the role of the stories in Fitzgerald's career one can finally state that they functioned as moneymakers, as proving grounds for his ideas, as workshops for his craft, and as dictators of his popular reputation. In the months following Scribner's acceptance of *This Side of Paradise* Fitzgerald paid his bills with money earned from stories, just as he did in the year preceding the publication of *The Beautiful and Damned*, a novel whose somber mood is heavily forecast in the stories preceding it. Similarly, the way to *The Great Gatsby* is paved with money earned from stories; and many of the ideas in the novel are also expressed first in the stories preceding it. *Tender Is the Night* with its cluster stories is a study in miniature of the relationship between professional writer and literary artist with which Fitzgerald lived all of his adult life: a study of the novel and of the climate from which it emerged is incomplete without an examination of the stories which cluster around it. Finally, Fitzgerald was attempting in mid-stride of the composition of *The Last Tycoon* to use the stories as a springboard into the money that would enable him to complete the novel; those stories, too, came to serve as a workshop for the novel in a limited sense.

Fitzgerald wrote most of his 178 short stories for money, and by God, Lorimer, Gingrich, and others he earned from them a small fortune—scarcely a penny of which was left at his death. Now, half a century later, with virtually all of the stories collected between hard covers, the evidence is in for all to see. And as Steven Vincent Benét said of Fitzgerald shortly after his death, "You can take off your hats now, gentlemen."[135] What we have before us in the complete short stories of F. Scott Fitzgerald is one of the richest literary fortunes of our time.

Appendix A:
List of Stories Arranged by Publication Date

The chart below lists stories by date of publication. Information about the composition dates and prices received (before Ober's commission) were taken from Fitzgerald's *Ledger* and from *As Ever*. Bracketed information about the compostion dates was taken from Bryer's *Short Stories*. When a story was collected in one of the four story volumes published in Fitzgerald's lifetime, the volume is listed in the right-hand column in abbreviated form (*Flappers and Philosophers, F&P; Tales of the Jazz Age, TJA; All the Sad Young Men, ASYM; Taps at Reveille, TAR*).

Story	Magazine	Published	Written	$	Book
I. 1919-1924: (Exploring the Market)					
1919					
Babes in the Woods	*Smart Set*	Aug.	Jan. 1917	30	
1920					
Benediction	*Smart Set*	Feb.	Oct. 1919	40	*F&P*
Dalyrimple Goes Wrong	*Smart Set*	Feb.	Sep. 1919	35	*F&P*
Head and Shoulders	*Post*	21 Feb.	Nov. 1919	400	*F&P*
Myra Meets His Family	*Post*	20 Mar.	[Apr.], Dec.1919	400	
The Camel's Back	*Post*	24 Apr.	Jan. 1920	500	*TJA*
The Cut-Glass Bowl	*Scribner's*	May	Oct. 1919	150	*F&P*
Bernice Bobs Her Hair	*Post*	1 May	Jan. 1920	500	*F&P*
The Ice Palace	*Post*	22 May	Dec. 1919	400	*F&P*
The Offshore Pirate	*Post*	29 May	[Feb. 1920]	500	
The Four Fists	*Scribner's*	June	May 1919	150	*F&P*
The Smilers	*Smart Set*	June	Sep. 1919	35	
May Day	*Smart Set*	July	Mar. 1920	200	*TJA*
The Jelly-Bean	*Metropolitan*	Oct.	May 1920	900	*TJA*
The Lees of Happiness	Chicago *Sunday Tribune*	12 Dec.	July 1920	750	*TJA*
1921					
His Russet Witch	*Metropolitan*	Feb.	Nov. 1920	900	*TJA*
Tarquin of Cheapside	*Smart Set*	21 Feb.	Feb. 1917		
1922					
The Popular Girl	*Post*	Feb.11,18	Nov. 1921	1500	
Two for a Cent	*Metropolitan*	Apr.	Sep. 1921	900	
The Curious Case of Benjamin Button	*Collier's*	27 May	Feb. 1922	1000	*TJA*
The Diamond as Big as the Ritz	*Smart Set*	June	Oct. 1921	300	*TJA*
Winter Dreams	*Metropolitan*	Dec.	Sep. 1922	900	*ASYM*

Story	Magazine	Published	Written	$	Book
1923					
Dice, Brass Knuckles & Guitar	*Hearst's International*	May	Jan. 1923	1500	
Hot & Cold Blood	*Hearst's International*	Aug.	Apr. 1923	1500	*ASYM*
1924					
Gretchen's Forty Winks	*Post*	15 Mar.	Jan. 1924	1200	*ASYM*
Diamond Dick and the First Law of Woman	*Hearst's International*	Apr.	Dec. 1923	1500	
The Third Casket	*Post*	31 May	Mar. 1924	1750	
Absolution	*American Mercury*	June	Jun. 1923		*ASYM*
Rags Martin-Jones and the Pr-nce of W-les	*McCall's*	July	Dec. 1923	1750	*ASYM*
"The Sensible Thing"	*Liberty*	5 July	Nov. 1923	1750	*ASYM*
The Unspeakable Egg	*Post*	12 July	Apr. 1924	1750	
John Jackson's Arcady	*Post*	26 July	Apr. 1924	1750	

II. 1925-1933: (The *Saturday Evening Post* Period)

Story	Magazine	Published	Written	$	Book
1925					
The Pusher-in-the-Face	*Woman's Home Companion*	Feb.	Mar. 1924	1750	
The Baby Party	*Hearst's International*	Feb.	Feb. 1924	1500	*ASYM*
Love in the Night	*Post*	14 Mar.	Nov. 1924	1750	
One of My Oldest Friends	*Woman's Home Companion*	Sep.	Mar. 1924	1750	
The Adjuster	*Red Book*	Sep.	Dec. 1924	2000	*ASYM*
A Penny Spent	*Post*	10 Oct.	July 1925	2000	
Not in the Guidebook	*Woman's Home Companion*	Nov.	Feb. 1925	1750	
1926					
Presumption	*Post*	9 Jan.	Nov. 1925	2500	
The Rich Boy	*Red Book*	Jan.,Feb.	Apr.-Aug.1925	3500	*ASYM*
The Adolescent Marriage	*Post*	6 Mar.	Dec. 1925	2500	
The Dance	*Red Book*	June	Jan. 1926	2000	
1927					
Your Way and Mine	*Woman's Home Companion*	May	Feb. 1926	1750	
Jacob's Ladder	*Post*	20 Aug.	June 1927	3000	
The Love Boat	*Post*	8 Oct.	Aug. 1927	3500	
A Short Trip Home	*Post*	17 Dec.	Oct. 1927	3500	*TAR*
1928					
The Bowl	*Post*	21 Jan.	Nov. 1927	3500	
Magnetism	*Post*	3 Mar.	Dec. 1927	3500	
The Scandal Detectives	*Post*	28 Apr.	Mar. 1928	3500	*TAR*

Story	Magazine	Published	Written	$	Book
1928 (cont.)					
A Night at the Fair	*Post*	21 July	May 1928	3500	
The Freshest Boy	*Post*	28 July	Apr. 1928	3500	*TAR*
He Thinks He's Wonderful	*Post*	29 Sep.	July 1928	3500	*TAR*
The Captured Shadow	*Post*	29 Dec.	Sep. 1928	3500	*TAR*
Outside the Cabinet-Maker's	*Century*	Dec.	[1927]	150	
1929					
The Perfect Life	*Post*	5 Jan.	Oct. 1928	3500	*TAR*
The Last of the Belles	*Post*	2 Mar.	Nov. 1928	3500	*TAR*
Forging Ahead	*Post*	30 Mar.	Jan. 1929	3500	
Basil and Cleopatra	*Post*	27 Apr.	Feb. 1929	3500	
The Rough Crossing	*Post*	8 June	Mar. 1929	3500	
Majesty	*Post*	13 July	May 1929	3500	*TAR*
At Your Age	*Post*	17 Aug.	June 1929	4000	
The Swimmers	*Post*	19 Oct.	July-Aug. 1929	4000	
1930					
Two Wrongs	*Post*	18 Jan.	Oct.-Nov. 1929	4000	*TAR*
First Blood	*Post*	5 Apr.	Jan. 1930	4000	*TAR*
A Nice Quiet Place	*Post*	31 May	Mar. 1930	4000	*TAR*
The Bridal Party	*Post*	9 Aug.	May 1930	4000	
A Woman with a Past	*Post*	6 Sep.	June 1930	4000	*TAR*
One Trip Abroad	*Post*	11 Oct.	Aug. 1930	4000	
A Snobbish Story	*Post*	29 Nov.	Sep. 1930	4000	
1931					
The Hotel Child	*Post*	31 Jan.	Nov. 1930	4000	
Babylon Revisited	*Post*	21 Feb.	Dec. 1930	4000	*TAR*
Indecision	*Post*	16 May	[Jan.-Feb.1931]	4000	
A New Leaf	*Post*	4 July	Apr. 1931	4000	
Emotional Bankruptcy	*Post*	15 Aug.	June 1931	4000	
Between Three and Four	*Post*	5 Sep.	June 1931	4000	
A Change of Class	*Post*	26 Sep.	July 1931	4000	
A Freeze-Out	*Post*	19 Dec.	Sep. 1931	4000	
1932					
Diagnosis	*Post*	20 Feb.	Oct. 1931	4000	
Six of One–	*Red Book*	Feb.	July 1931	3000	
Flight and Pursuit	*Post*	14 May	Apr. 1931	4000	
Family in the Wind	*Post*	4 June	Apr. 1932	3500	*TAR*
The Rubber Check	*Post*	6 Aug.	May 1932	3000	
What a Handsome Pair!	*Post*	27 Aug.	Apr. 1932	2500	
Crazy Sunday	*American Mercury*	Oct.	Jan. 1932	200	*TAR*
One Interne	*Post*	5 Nov.	Aug. 1932	3500	*TAR*
1933					
On Schedule	*Post*	18 Mar.	Dec. 1932	3000	

Story	Magazine	Published	Written	$	Book
1933 (cont.)					
More Than Just a House	Post	24 June	Apr. 1933	3000	
I Got Shoes	Post	23 Sep.	July 1933	2500	
The Family Bus	Post	4 Nov.	Sep. 1933	3000	
III. 1934-1940: (The *Esquire* Period)					
1934					
No Flowers	Post	21 July	May 1934	3000	
New Types	Post	22 Sep.	July 1934	3000	
In the Darkest Hour	Redbook	Oct.	Apr. 1934	1250	
Her Last Case	Post	3 Nov.	Aug. 1934	3000	
1935					
The Fiend	Esquire	Jan.	Sep. 1934	250	
The Night Before	Esquire	Feb.	Nov. 1934	250	
Chancellorsville					
Shaggy's Morning	Esquire	May	Mar. 1935	250	
The Passionate Eskimo	Liberty	8 June	Feb. 1935	1500	
The Intimate Strangers	McCall's	June	Feb.-Mar. 1935	3000	
The Count of Darkness	Redbook	June	Oct. 1934	1500	
Zone of Accident	Post	13 July	Fall 1932-May 1935	3000	
A Kingdom in the Dark	Redbook	Aug.	Nov. 1934	1500	
1936					
Too Cute for Words	Post	18 Apr.	Dec. 1935	3000	
Fate in Her Hands	American Magazine	Apr.	[June-July 1935]		
Image on the Heart	McCall's	Apr.	Sep. 1935	1250	
Three Acts of Music	Esquire	May	Feb. 1936	250	
Inside the House	Post	13 June	Apr. 1936	3000	
The Ants at Princeton	Esquire	June	[1936]	250	
An Author's Mother	Esquire	Sep.		250	
"I Didn't Get Over"	Esquire	Oct.	Aug. 1936	250	
"Send Me In, Coach"	Esquire	Nov.	Oct. 1936	250	
1937					
An Alcoholic Case	Esquire	Feb.	Dec. 1936	250	
"Trouble"	Post	6 Mar.	June 1936	2000	
The Honor of The Goon	Esquire	June	Apr. 1937	250	
The Long Way Out	Esquire	Sep.	May 1937	250	
The Guest in	Esquire	Oct.	Mar. 1937	250	
Room Nineteen					
In the Holidays	Esquire	Dec.	Feb. 1937	250	
1938					
Financing Finnegan	Esquire	Jan.	June 1937	250	
1939					
Design in Plaster	Esquire	Nov.	[July 1939]	250	
Strange Sanctuary	Liberty	9 Dec.	[1935]	250	

Story	Magazine	Published	Written	$	Book
1939 (cont.)					
The Lost Decade	*Esquire*	Dec.	[July 1939]	250	
1940					
Pat Hobby's Christmas Wish	*Esquire*	Jan.	[1939]	250	
A Man in the Way	*Esquire*	Feb.	[1939]	250	
"Boil Some Water– Lots of It"	*Esquire*	Mar.	[Sep. 1939]	250	
Teamed with Genius	*Esquire*	Apr.	[1939]	250	
Pat Hobby and Orson Welles	*Esquire*	May	[1940]	250	
The End of Hate	*Collier's*	22 June	[Aug.1936;June1939]	250	
Pat Hobby's Secret	*Esquire*	June	[1940]	250	
Pat Hobby, Putative Father	*Esquire*	July	[1939]	250	
The Homes of the Stars	*Esquire*	Aug.	[1940]	250	
Pat Hobby Does His Bit	*Esquire*	Sep.	[1940]	250	
Pat Hobby's Preview	*Esquire*	Oct.	[1939]	250	
No Harm Trying	*Esquire*	Nov.	[1939]	250	
A Patriotic Short	*Esquire*	Dec.	[1940]	250	

V. Posthumous

Story	Magazine	Published	Written
1941			
On the Trail of Pat Hobby	*Esquire*	Jan.	[1940]
Fun in an Artist's Studio	*Esquire*	Feb.	[1940]
On an Ocean Wave	*Esquire*	Feb.	[Sep. 1940]
Two Old-Timers	*Esquire*	Mar.	[1939]
Mightier than the Sword	*Esquire*	Apr.	[1939]
Pat Hobby's College Days	*Esquire*	May	[1939]
The Woman from Twenty-One	*Esquire*	June	[1940]
Three Hours Between Planes	*Esquire*	July	[1939]
Gods of Darkness	*Redbook*	Nov.	[1934]
1948			
Discard	*Harper's Bazaar*	Jan.	[1939]
1949			
Last Kiss	*Collier's*	16 Apr.	[1939-40]
1951			
That Kind of Party	*Princeton University Library Chronicle*	Summer	[1928]

Story	Magazine	Published	Written	$	Book
1969					
Dearly Beloved	*Fitzgerald/ Hemingway Annual*		[Jan.-Feb. 1940]		
1971					
Lo, the Poor Peacock	*Esquire*	Sep.	[1935]		
1979					
On Your Own	*Esquire*	30 Jan.	1931		

Appendix B:
List of Stories Arranged by Composition Date

Fitzgerald's *Ledger* provides composition dates for virtually all stories written before 1936. I have used Fitzgerald's dates when they were available. I have relied on Bryer (*Short Stories*, pp. 348-77) for dating the remaining stories. In cases where only the year of composition is known, I have ordered the stories by publication date relative to other stories. In cases where two stories were written in the same month of a given year, I have listed first the story published first. Thus while this listing is relatively accurate through 1935, the ordering from 1936-40 should be considered approximate.

The Mystery of the Raymond Mortgage	June	1909
Reade, Substitute Right Half		1909-10
A Debt of Honor		1909
The Room with the Green Blinds		1909-11
A Luckless Santa Claus		1912
The Trail of the Duke		1912-13
Pain and the Scientist		1912-13
The Ordeal		1915
The Spire and the Gargoyle		1916
Babes in the Woods	Jan.	1917
Tarquin of Cheepside	Feb.	1917
Sentiment–and the Use of Rouge		1917
The Pierian Springs and the Last Straw		1917
Myra Meets His Family	[Apr].-Dec.	1919
The Four Fists	May	1919
Dalyrimple Goes Wrong	Sep.	1919
The Smilers	Sep.	1919
Benediction	Oct.	1919
The Cut-Glass Bowl	Oct.	1919
Head and Shoulders	Nov.	1919
The Ice Palace	Dec.	1919
The Camel's Back	Jan.	1920
Bernice Bobs Her Hair	Jan.	1920
The Offshore Pirate	[Feb.	1920]
May Day	Mar.	1920
The Jelly-Bean	May	1920
The Lees of Happiness	July	1920
His Russet Witch	Nov.	1920
Two for a Cent	Sep.	1921
The Diamond as Big as the Ritz	Oct.	1921
The Popular Girl	Nov.	1921
The Curious Case of Benjamin Button	Feb.	1922
Winter Dreams	Sep.	1922
Dice, Brass Knuckles & Guitar	Jan.	1923

Hot & Cold Blood	Apr.	1923
Absolution	June	1923
"The Sensible Thing"	Nov.	1923
Rags Martin-Jones and the Pr-nce of W-les	Dec.	1923
Diamond Dick and the First Law of Women	Dec.	1923
Gretchen's Forty Winks	Jan.	1924
The Baby Party	Feb.	1924
The Third Casket	Mar.	1924
The Pusher-in-the-Face	Mar.	1924
One of My Oldest Friends	Mar.	1924
The Unspeakable Egg	Apr.	1924
John Jackson's Arcady	Apr.	1924
Love in the Night	Nov.	1924
The Adjuster	Dec.	1924
Not in the Guidebook	Feb.	1925
The Rich Boy	Apr.-Aug.	1925
A Penny Spent	July	1925
Presumption	Nov.	1925
The Adolescent Marriage	Dec.	1925
The Dance	Jan.	1926
Your Way and Mine	Feb.	1926
Outside the Cabinet-Maker's		1927
Jacob's Ladder	June	1927
The Love Boat	Aug.	1927
A Short Trip Home	Oct.	1927
The Bowl	Nov.	1927
Magnetism	Dec.	1927
That Kind of Party		1928
The Scandal Detectives	Mar.	1928
The Freshest Boy	Apr.	1928
A Night at the Fair	May	1928
He Thinks He's Wonderful	July	1928
The Captured Shadow	Sep.	1928
The Perfect Life	Oct.	1928
The Last of the Belles	Nov.	1928
Forging Ahead	Jan.	1929
Basil and Cleopatra	Feb.	1929
The Rough Crossing	Mar.	1929
Majesty	May	1929
At Your Age	June	1929
The Swimmers	July-Aug.	1929
Two Wrongs	Nov.	1929
First Blood	Jan.	1930
A Nice Quiet Place	Mar.	1930
The Bridal Party	May	1930
A Woman with a Past	June	1930
One Trip Abroad	Aug.	1930
A Snobbish Story	Sep.	1930
The Hotel Child	Nov.	1930
Babylon Revisited	Dec.	1930
On Your Own		1931
Indecision	Jan.-Feb.	1931
A New Leaf	Apr.	1931

Flight and Pursuit	Apr.	1931
Emotional Bankruptcy	June	1931
Between Three and Four	June	1931
A Change of Class	July	1931
Six of One–	July	1931
A Freeze-Out	Sep.	1931
Diagnosis	Oct.	1931
Crazy Sunday	Jan.	1932
Family in the Wind	Apr.	1932
What a Handsome Pair!	Apr.	1932
The Rubber Check	May	1932
One Interne	Aug.	1932
Zone of Accident	Fall 1932 - May	1935
On Schedule	Dec.	1932
More than Just a House	Apr.	1933
I Got Shoes	July	1933
The Family Bus	Sep.	1933
In the Darkest Hour	Apr.	1934
No Flowers	May	1934
New Types	July	1934
Her Last Case	Aug.	1934
The Fiend	Sep.	1934
The Count of Darkness	Oct.	1934
The Night before Chancellorsville	Nov.	1934
The Kingdom in the Dark	Nov.	1934
Gods of Darkness	[Dec.]	1934
Lo, the Poor Peacock!		1935
Strange Sanctuary		1935
The Passionate Eskimo	Feb.	1935
The Intimate Strangers	Feb.-Mar.	1935
Shaggy's Morning	Mar.	1935
Fate in Her Hands	June-July	1935
Image on the Heart	Sep.	1935
Too Cute for Words	Dec.	1935
The Ants at Princeton		1936
An Author's Mother		1936
Three Acts of Music	Feb.	1936
Inside the House	Apr.	1936
"Trouble"	June	1936
"I Didn't Get Over"	Aug.	1936
The End of Hate	Aug.	1936
"Send Me In, Coach"	Oct.	1936
An Alcoholic Case	Dec.	1936
In the Holidays	Feb.	1937
The Guest in Room Nineteen	Mar.	1937
The Honor of the Goon	Apr.	1937
The Long Way Out	May	1937
Financing Finnegan	June	1937
Design in Plaster	July	1939
The Lost Decade	July	1939
Discard	July	1939
Pat Hobby's Christmas Wish		1939
A Man in the Way		1939

"Boil Some Water–Lots of It"	Sep.	1939
Teamed with Genius		1939
Pat Hobby, Putative Father		1939
Pat Hobby's Preview		1939
No Harm Trying		1939
Two Old-Timers		1939
Mightier than the Sword		1939
Pat Hobby's College Days		1939
Three Hours between Planes		1939
Last Kiss		1939-40
Dearly Beloved	Jan.-Feb.	1940
Pat Hobby and Orson Welles		1940
Pat Hobby's Secret		1940
The Homes of the Stars		1940
Pat Hobby Does His Bit		1940
A Patriotic Short		1940
On the Trail of Pat Hobby		1940
Fun in an Artist's Studio		1940
On an Ocean Wave	[Sep.]	1940
The Woman from Twenty-One		[1940]

Notes

Chapter One Notes

1. T. S. Matthews, *New Republic*, LXXXII (10 April 1935), p. 262. Matthews, however, saw "no real difference in kind between 'Taps at Reveille' and 'Tender Is the Night'; the creatures whom he has sold down the river for a good price are a little cruder, that's all."

2. Margaret Marshall, "Notes By the Way," *The Nation*, CLII (8 February 1941), pp. 159-160.

3. Arthur Mizener, *The Far Side of Paradise* (Boston: Houghton Mifflin, 1951), p. 94.

4. These and all figures relating to Fitzgerald's earnings may be located in *F. Scott Fitzgerald's Ledger* (Washington: Bruccoli Clark/NCR, 1972). In this study, figures are rounded off to the nearest dollar.

5. Matthew J. Bruccoli, ed., and Jennifer McCabe Atkinson, *As Ever, Scott Fitz–, Letters Between F. Scott Fitzgerald and His Literary Agent Harold Ober, 1919-1940* (New York: Lippincott, 1971), p. 36. Hereafter cited as *As Ever*.

6. Ernest Hemingway, *A Moveable Feast* (New York: Scribners, 1964), p. 153.

7. As Richard Lehan notes, "To discuss Fitzgerald's stories . . . involves a discussion of the major themes of his novels–the theme of youthful cynicism and disillusionment that characterized *This Side of Paradise* and *The Beautiful and Damned*, the theme of romantic limits that characterized *The Great Gatsby*, the theme of cultural and personal decline that characterized *Tender Is the Night*, and the theme of romantic betrayal that characterized the unfinished *The Last Tycoon*." See "The Romantic Self and the Uses of Place in the Stories of F. Scott Fitzgerald" in *The Short Stories of F. Scott Fitzgerald*, ed. Jackson R. Bryer (Madison: University of Wisconsin Press, 1982), p. 3.

8. The "cluster story" concept was developed by Bruccoli and is discussed in Matthew J. Bruccoli, *The Composition of Tender Is the Night* (Pittsburgh: University of Pittsburgh Press, 1963). John Higgins notes some of the connections in *F. Scott Fitzgerald: A Study of the Stories* (Jamaica: St. John's University Press, 1971).

9. Bryer lists the 178 stories in alphabetical order in *The Short Stories of F. Scott Fitzgerald*, pp. 348-377. Bruccoli comments on the numbering of the stories in this way: "The Fitzgerald story canon includes some 160 published stories, including his school writings. (The 'some' is necessitated by the borderline essay/fiction pieces.)." "Preface," *The Short Stories of F. Scott Fitzgerald*

(New York: Scribners, 1989), p. xii. For discussion of the lost and unpublished stories, see Jennifer McCabe Atkinson's "Lost and Unpublished Stories by F. Scott Fitzgerald," *Fitzgerald/Hemingway Annual*, III (1971), pp. 32-63, and also Ruth Prigozy's "The Unpublished Stories: Fitzgerald in His Final Stage," *Twentieth Century Literature* XX (April 1974), pp. 69-90.

10. F. Scott Fitzgerald, "Early Success," *American Cavalcade*, I (October 1937), reprinted in *The Crack-up*, ed. Edmund Wilson (Norfolk, Conn.: New Directions, 1945), p. 86.

11. William Charvat, *The Profession of Authorship in America, 1800-1870*, ed. Matthew J. Bruccoli (Columbus: Ohio State University Press, 1968), p. 3.

12. Here the earnings from the book publishing industry include royalties from novels and short story volumes, the latter of which earned a total of approximately $15,000. Earnings from the magazine market here do not include novel serializations, nor do the figures relating to the movie industry include sales of novels and stories sold to the movies. The figures are approximations intended to indicate the relative importance of each of the three markets.

13. Alan Margolies in "The Hollywood Market" in Bryer's *Short Stories*, pp. 65-73, tells how Fitzgerald tried early to take advantage of the Hollywood market by writing stories that would also interest Hollywood, but failed. Hollywood earnings came largely from his work under contract to MGM in the late thirties.

14. Steven Wayne Potts's dissertation, "F. Scott Fitzgerald: His Career in Magazines" (University of California, Berkeley, 1980) is the only study to date which closely examines Fitzgerald's stories in the context of the editorial policies and audience tastes of the magazines in which the stories appeared.

15. Frances Fitzgerald Lanahan, introduction to *Six Tales of the Jazz Age and Other Stories* by F. Scott Fitzgerald (New York: Scribners, 1960), p. 9.

16. *The Saturday Evening Post* will be referred to in the text as the *Post*.

Chapter Two Notes

1. Matthew J. Bruccoli, *Some Sort of Epic Grandeur* (New York: Harcourt Brace Jovanovich, 1981), p. 70.

2. *The Apprentice Fiction of F. Scott Fitzgerald*, ed. John Kuehl (New Brunswick, N. J.: Rutgers, 1965), p. 15.

3. "The Crack-Up," (*Esquire*, February, 1936) in *Afternoon of an Author*, ed. Arthur Mizener (New York: Scribners, 1958), p. 69.

4. *The Letters of F. Scott Fitzgerald*, ed. Andrew Turnbull (New York: Scribners, 1963), p. 19.

5. *Afternoon of an Author*, p. 132.

24. Reprinted in *Profile of F. Scott Fitzgerald*, comp. Matthew J. Bruccoli (Columbus: Merrill, 1971), p. 11.

Chapter Three Notes

1. James Playstead Wood, *Magazines in the United States* (New York: Ronald, 1956), pp. 192-193. See Potts, pp. 15-39, for a discussion of the influences of the British aesthetic movement of the turn of the century and of the conflicting tastes of Mencken and Nathan on the editorial policies of the *Smart Set*.

2. Wood, p. 154.

3. *Dear Scott/Dear Max: The Fitzgerald-Perkins Correspondence*, ed. John Kuehl and Jackson R. Bryer (New York: Scribners, 1971), p. 28.

4. *Dear Scott/Dear Max*, p. 28.

5. *As Ever*, p. 34.

6. When each story is mentioned for the first time in the text, it will be followed, in parentheses, by date written, place of publication, date of publication, price received, and major story volume in which it was collected in Fitzgerald's lifetime–if it was collected. "Babes in the Woods," for example, was not collected in any of Fitzgerald's four major story collections. All references to the stories in the text are to the magazine versions, unless otherwise indicated.

7. "Myra Meets His Family," *Post* (20 March 1920), p. 40.

8. "Babes in the Woods," *Smart Set* (August, 1919), p. 69.

9. First published as "The Ordeal" in the June 1915 issue of *Nassau Literary Magazine*.

10. "Benediction," p. 42.

11. "Benediction," p. 39.

12. "Dalyrimple Goes Wrong," p. 11.

13. "Dalyrimple Goes Wrong," p. 115.

14. *As Ever*, p. 5. As Fitzgerald's neglected stories receive increasing attention, Fitzgerald's assertion about this story will be thoroughly debated. Ruth Prigozy is one who makes a strong case for "Dalyrimple Goes Wrong" in her dissertation "The Stories and Essays of F. Scott Fitzgerald: A Critical Study" (City University of New York, 1969), pp. 61-62.

15. *As Ever*, pp. 6-7.

16. The story was first titled "A Smile for Sylvo" and was rejected by *Scribner's Magazine*, to whom it was first submitted. See *As Ever*, p. 4.

6. *The Romantic Egoists: A Pictorial Autobiography from the Scrapbooks and* *of F. Scott and Zelda Fitzgerald*, ed. Scottie Fitzgerald Smith, Joan P. K(
Matthew J. Bruccoli (New York: Scribners, 1974), p. 27.

7. *Apprentice Fiction*, p. 31.

8. *Apprentice Fiction*, p. 38.

9. *Apprentice Fiction*, p. 48.

10. *Apprentice Fiction*, p. 48.

11. *Apprentice Fiction*, p. 54.

12. Fitzgerald's first *Nassau Literary Magazine* contribution, *Shadow Laurels*,
play in which Fitzgerald dealt with the ambivalent feelings of a son for his
eloquent father.

13. *Apprentice Fiction*, p. 140. The *Smart Set* version reads, "'Damn!' mut
Isabelle as she explored the cold sheets cautiously. 'Damn!'" In *This Si(*
Paradise Fitzgerald combines the two versions: "'Damn!' muttered Isat
punching the pillow into a luxurious lump and exploring the cold sl
cautiously. 'Damn.'"

14. *Apprentice Fiction*, p. 136.

15. *Apprentice Fiction*, p. 158.

16. *Apprentice Fiction*, p. 144.

17. James L. W. West III details the ways in which Fitzgerald used *The Nassau*
and *Smart Set* material in the composition of *This Side of Paradise* in his *1*
Making of This Side of Paradise (Philadelphia: University of Pennsylvania Pr(
1983).

18. R. V. A. S., *New Republic*, (12 May 1920), p. 362. Reprinted in *The Critic*
Reception of F. Scott Fitzgerald, ed. Jackson Bryer (New York: Burt Frankl
1978), p. 22.

19. F. S. F. to Frances Turnbull, 9 November 1938, in *Letters of F. Scott Fitzgeral*
p. 578.

20. *This Side of Paradise* (New York: Scribners, 1920), p. 305.

21. Edmund Wilson, *The Shores of Light* (New York: Farrar, Straus and Young
Inc., 1952), p. 28.

22. *This Side of Paradise*, p. 304.

23. "Third Act and Epilogue," *The New Yorker* (30 June 1945) reprinted in *F. Scott*
Fitzgerald: A Collection of Critical Essays, ed. Arthur Mizener (Englewood Cliffs,
N.J.: Prentice-Hall, 1963), p. 64.

17. *As Ever*, p. 7.

18. "The Cut-Glass Bowl," p. 582.

19. "The Cut-Glass Bowl," p. 591.

20. James E. Hart, *Oxford Companion to American Literature*, 4th ed. (New York: Oxford University Press, 1965), p. 753. Potts (p. 180) calls it "one of a quartet" of high quality magazines in 1920 (*Atlantic, Harper's*, and *Century* being the other three) to carry on in "the highbrow genteel tradition of the previous century."

21. *Dear Scott/Dear Max*, p. 44.

22. The *Post* bought "Head and Shoulders" late in 1919 (c. November), approximately five months before *This Side of Paradise* was published on 3 April 1920.

23. Theodore Peterson, *Magazines in the Twentieth Century* (Urbana: University of Illinois Press, 1964), p. 181.

24. Wood, p. 154.

25. Wood, p. 154.

26. John Tebbel, *George Horace Lorimer and the Saturday Evening Post* (Garden City: Doubleday, 1948), p. 51.

27. Tebbel, p. 45.

28. DeVoto, "Writing for Money," p. 4.

29. Leon Whipple, "SatEvePost, Mirror of These States," *Survey*, 1 March 1928. Reprinted in part in *Magazines in the United States*, p. 156.

30. Wood, p. 158.

31. Robert Sklar sees the duality as a result of Fitzgerald's, from the beginning, having "one foot planted in the past and one foot stepping toward the future." *The Last Laocöon* (New York: Oxford University Press, 1967), p. 109.

32. Edwin S. Fussell in "Fitzgerald's Brave New World" *ELH: A Journal of English Literary History* XIX (December 1952), p. 292, identifies the two symbolic goals of the Fitzgerald hero as "the search for eternal youth and beauty" and "money."

33. *As Ever*, p. 48.

34. Introduction, *The Portable F. Scott Fitzgerald* (New York: Viking, 1949). Reprinted in *Profile of F. Scott Fitzgerald*, p. 15.

35. "Head and Shoulders," p. 82.

36. "Myra Meets His Family," p. 40.

37. "Myra Meets His Family," p. 53.

38. *As Ever*, p. 7. Fitzgerald acknowledges the letter in another letter dated 30 December 1919.

39. *As Ever*, p. 6.

40. *As Ever*, p. 13.

41. "Dice, Brassknuckles & Guitar" (*Hearst's International*, May 1923) is a Tarleton, Ga. spin-off story. Jim Powell is a native of Tarleton.

42. "The Offshore Pirate," p. 10.

43. "The Offshore Pirate," p. 10.

44. Rochelle S. Elstein in Fitzgerald's "Josephine Stories: The End of the Romantic Illusion," *American Literature* LI (1979), p. 70, sees Ardita and Kismine Washington of "The Diamond as Big as the Ritz" as representing the most "captivating of Fitzgerald's heroines," "confident in their own charm and beauty."

45. "The Offshore Pirate," p. 109.

46. "The Popular Girl" is a two-part story. The $1500 Fitzgerald received for it represents a $250 per story raise. The next single *Post* story brought $1200.

47. *As Ever*, p. 34.

48. Bryer cites twenty-six contemporary reviews. Of these, twelve are favorable, four are mixed, and nine are unfavorable. See Jackson R. Bryer, *The Critical Reputation of F. Scott Fitzgerald* (Hamden, Conn.: Arcon, 1967), pp. 13-17.

49. H. L. Mencken, *Smart Set*, LXIII (December 1920), p. 140. Reprinted in *F. Scott Fitzgerald: The Critical Reception*, ed. Jackson R. Bryer (New York: Burt Franklin, 1978), p. 48.

50. Heywood Broun, "Books," *New York Tribune* (1 November 1920), p. 10. Reprinted in *F.S.F.: The Critical Reception*, pp. 45-46.

51. Wilson, *The Shores of Light*, p. 32.

52. F. Scott Fitzgerald, *Tales of the Jazz Age* (New York: Scribners, 1922), p. viii.

53. *As Ever*, p. 27.

54. *McCall's* was a major women's magazine whose circulation in 1910 was over a million. By 1927 it had reached the two-million mark. See Peterson, p. 202.

55. *As Ever*, p. 29.

56. *As Ever*, p. 29.

57. "May Day," p. 3.

58. *Smart Set* (June 1922).

59. "The Diamond as Big as the Ritz," *Smart Set*, (June 1922), p. 5.

60. In *TJA* Philip Cory becomes Philip Dean and Gloria Hudson becomes Jewel Hudson.

61. In the *TJA* version Sterrett does shoot himself through the temple.

62. *As Ever*, p. 29.

63. The first full treatment of Fitzgerald's use of fantasy is Laurence Buell's "The Significance of Fantasy in Fitzgerald's Short Fiction" in Bryer's *Short Fiction*, pp. 23-38.

64. In *Metropolitan* the setting is Mississippi; in *Tales of the Jazz Age* it is Tarleton, Ga.

65. For full discussions of the Tarleton stories, see C. Hugh Holman's "Fitzgerald's Changes of the Southern Belle: The Tarleton Trilogy" in Bryer's *Short Fiction*, pp. 53-64, and Scott Donaldson's "Scott Fitzgerald's Romance with the South," *Southern Literary Journal*, V (Spring 1963), pp. 3-17.

66. "The Jelly-Bean," p. 15.

67. "His Russet Witch," p. 51.

68. "Winter Dreams," Fitzgerald's last *Metropolitan* story, which was written after the publication of *The Beautiful and Damned* and which deals with the subject of lost youth, will be discussed in connection with *The Great Gatsby*.

69. Hart, *Oxford Companion to American Literature*, p. 169.

70. *Tales of the Jazz Age*, p. ix.

71. Blue ribbon fiction section, pp. 1, 3, 7. This story was written under contract.

72. *Critical Reputation of F.S.F.*, pp. 40-47.

73. "'Tales of the Jazz Age' Both Silly and Profound," *Baltimore News*, 30 September 1922, p. 9. Reprinted in *F.S.F.: The Critical Reception*, p. 139.

74. "Too Much Fire Water," *Minneapolis Journal* (10 December 1922), Women's Section, p. 12. Reprinted in *F.S.F.: The Critical Reception*, p. 162.

75. *F.S.F.: The Critical Reception*," p. 162.

76. Stephen Vincent Benét, "Plotting an Author's Curve," *New York Evening Post Literary Review*, 18 November 1922, p. 219. Reprinted in *F.S.F.: The Critical Reception*, p. 156.

77. Although the contract was negotiated with Hearst's *Cosmopolitan*, the stories were actually published in *Hearst's International*. See *As Ever*, p. 51.

78. Peterson, p. 214.

79. *As Ever*, p. 59.

80. "Dice, Brassknuckles & Guitar," p. 8.

81. "Dice, Brassknuckles & Guitar," p. 145.

82. "Dice, Brassknuckles & Guitar," p. 12.

83. "Hot & Cold Blood," p. 150.

84. "Hot & Cold Blood," p. 83.

85. "Hot & Cold Blood," p. 80.

86. Peterson, p. 83.

87. "'The Sensible Thing,'" p. 10.

88. George Rollins's name is changed to George O'Kelly in *All the Sad Young Men*.

89. "'The Sensible Thing,'" p. 14.

90. "'The Sensible Thing,'" p. 14.

91. "Rags Martin-Jones and the Pr-nce of W-les," p. 50.

92. Peterson, p. 202.

93. Wood, p. 126.

94. "Rags Martin-Jones and the Pr-nce of W-les," p. 6.

95. "The Third Casket," p. 78.

96. "John Jackson's Arcady," p. 105.

97. *Dear Scott/Dear Max*, p. 112.

98. See Higgins, pp. 60-62 for a discussion of similarities.

99. It is the Sherry Island Golf Club in *ASYM*. Also, Dillard becomes Black Bear in *ASYM*.

100. "Winter Dreams," p. 14.

101. "Winter Dreams," p. 107.

102. *The Great Gatsby*, p. 112.

103. *The Great Gatsby*, p. 194.

104. *Dear Scott/Dear Max*, p. 69.

105. Turnbull, *Letters of F.S.F.*, p. 509.

106. See, for example, James E. Miller, Jr., *F. Scott Fitzgerald: His Art and His Technique* (New York: New York University Press, 1964), pp. 103-05; Richard D. Lehan, *F. Scott Fitzgerald and the Craft of Fiction* (Carbondale: Southern Illinois University Press, 1966), p. 105; Lawrence D. Stewart, "'Absolution' and *The Great Gatsby*." *Fitzgerald/Hemingway Annual* V (1973), pp. 181-87; Joan M. Allen, *Candles and Carnival Lights: The Catholic Sensibility of F. Scott Fitzgerald* (New York: New York University Press, 1978) pp. 93-101; and André Le Vot, *F. Scott Fitzgerald: A Biography*, trans. William Byron (Garden City, NY: Doubleday, 1983), pp. 139-41.

107. *Epic Grandeur*, p. 259.

108. *Stories*, p. 259.

109. See Piper, p. 104.

110. "Absolution," p. 144.

111. "Absolution," p. 144.

112. "Absolution," p. 149.

113. Alice Hall Petry provides a thorough account of the critical debate on "Absolution" in *Fitzgerald's Craft of Short Fiction: The Collected Stories 1920-1935* (Ann Arbor, MI: UMI Research Press, 1989), pp. 210-211.

114. "Absolution," p. 145.

115. *F.S.F.: A Collection of Critical Essays*, p. 81.

116. "His Russet Witch," p. 12.

117. "Rags Martin-Jones and the Pr-nce of W-les," p. 50.

118. *As Ever*, p. 9.

Chapter Four Notes

1. Introduction, *The Portable F. Scott Fitzgerald*. Reprinted in *Profile of F. Scott Fitzgerald*, p. 16.

2. Wood, p. 123.

3. *As Ever*, p. 51.

4. *As Ever*, p. 59.

5. *As Ever*, p. 59.

6. "Your Way and Mine," p. 81.

7. *As Ever*, p. 76.

8. Arthur Mizener, *The Far Side of Paradise*, p. 334n.

9. "The Baby Party," p. 37.

10. "The Baby Party," p. 33.

11. The *Red Book* prices in 1925 and 1926 ranged from $2,000 to $3,500, more than the *Post* was paying during these years.

12. Peterson, p. 208. In 1929 McCall bought *Red Book* and it became *Redbook*.

13. *As Ever*, p. 82.

14. Fitzgerald wrote Ober, "I'm sending you a story . . . called the *Adjuster* for the Red Book order you wrote me of." See *As Ever*, p. 70.

15. *Red Book*, September 1925, p. 4. Fitzgerald's name is spelled F-tzgerald.

16. "The Adjuster," p. 47.

17. Cristianne Johnson, whose treatment of the story is the most thorough to date, sees the story as "not devoid of interest," though lacking the complexity of contemporaneous stories like "Absolution." "Freedom, Contingency, and Ethics in 'The Adjuster'" in Bryer's *Short Stories*, p. 240.

18. "Six of One–," p. 22.

19. His name is Dr. Moon in *All the Sad Young Men*.

20. "The Adjuster," p. 147.

21. "The Adjuster," p. 50.

22. *Red Book*, XLVI (January 1926).

23. "The Rich Boy," January 1926, p. 27.

24. "The Rich Boy," January 1926, p. 28.

25. "The Rich Boy," February 1926, p. 76.

26. "The Rich Boy," January 1926, p. 27.

27. "The Rich Boy," February 1926, p. 126.

28. "The Rich Boy," February 1926, p. 126.

29. *As Ever*, p. 84. Actually, his first detective story was "The Mystery of the Raymond Mortgage."

30. *As Ever*, p. 85. Fitzgerald also asked Ober not to offer the story to *Red Book*.

31. *All the Sad Young Men*, published in February 1926.

32. "The Dance," p. 39.

33. "The Dance," p. 186.

34. "Six of One–" is subtitled "A story of *Youth.*" p. 22.

35. "Six of One–," p. 88.

36. "Six of One–," p. 88.

37. *Critical Reputation of F. Scott Fitzgerald*, pp. 7-77.

38. William Rose Benét, "Art's Bread and Butter," *Saturday Review of Literature* (3 April 1926), p. 682. Reprinted in *F.S.F.: The Critical Reception*, p. 267.

39. *Dear Scott/Dear Max*, p. 122.

40. He called "The Baby Party" "A fine story" and "Hot and Cold Blood" a "good story." See *Dear Scott/Dear Max*, pp. 112-113.

41. In the preliminary table of contents Fitzgerald called this story "Fantastic Jazz." See *Dear Scott/Dear Max*, p. 112.

42. A reason that he gave for including "Gretchen's Forty Winks," though he disagreed, is that "Farrar, Christian Gauss and Jesse Williams thought it my best." See *Dear Scott/Dear Max*, p. 113.

43. *Dear Scott/Dear Max*, p. 112.

44. *Dear Scott/Dear Max*, p. 112.

45. *As Ever*, p. 192. This is contained in Ober's sworn statement to the Internal Revenue Service.

46. Also, because distinct patterns emerge from the 1925-1933 *Post* stories, the strict chronological ordering has been broken. Within the following various groups, however, the particular stories are discussed in chronological sequence.

47. *As Ever*, p. 175. These remarks were made specifically about "The Hotel Child."

48. "The Rough Crossing," "Majesty," "The Swimmers," "Two Wrongs," "One Trip Abroad," "Babylon Revisited," "Indecision," and "A New Leaf" also have European settings, but their major similarity to the novel does not lie primarily in their common settings.

49. *Red Book*, XLVI (February 1926), p. 75.

50. "A Penny Spent," p. 166.

51. "Majesty," p. 58.

52. "Majesty," p. 62.

53. "Majesty," p. 62.

54. "Majesty," p. 62.

55. *As Ever*, p. 134.

56. "Majesty," p. 6.

57. "Majesty," p. 6.

58. The Conte di Minghetti, Mary's husband, was the ruler-owner of manganese deposits in southwestern Asia; Emily's husband, King Gabriel Petrocobesco, is important to the Queen of England only because his country has magnesium deposits ("Majesty," p. 62). Thus this story establishes an early link between Emily and Mary North Minghetti.

59. "The Bridal Party," p. 114.

60. "The Bridal Party," p. 114.

61. *As Ever*, p. 175. Paradoxically Costain added, "However, it is such a splendid picture of this kind of life that we had no hesitation in adding it to our list."

62. "The Hotel Child," p. 8.

63. "The Hotel Child," p. 69.

64. "The Hotel Child," p. 9.

65. Fitzgerald noted to Ober that "The Hotel Child" was based on a true story and that Fifi was patterned after an acquaintance, Mimi Cohn. *As Ever*, p. 174.

66. "The Hotel Child," p. 9. It is noteworthy that Fitzgerald, by using a foreign setting and an atypical American, was able to discuss without fanfare a topic such as cocaine use, generally tabooed by the *Post*.

67. See "The Hotel Child," p. 75 and *Tender Is the Night* (New York: Scribners, 1934), p. 350.

68. "Jacob's Ladder," p. 64.

69. *As Ever*, p. 98.

70. Scribners would not allow the Modern Library to anthologize "The Rich Boy," and Fitzgerald suggested "Jacob's Ladder" with the following comment: "It will look rather sentimental beside Conrad E. M. Forster etc." *As Ever*, p. 130.

71. "Magnetism," p. 76.

72. "Magnetism," p. 76.

73. "Magnetism," p. 74. Compare with *Tender Is the Night*, p. 262.

74. "Magnetism," p. 6.

75. Bruccoli, *Composition of Tender Is the Night*, p. 69.

76. "The Rough Crossing," p. 13.

77. "The Rough Crossing," p. 75.

78. "The Rough Crossing," p. 12.

79. John Higgins comments about the ending of "The Rough Crossing": "The typical *Post* reader might accept this ending at face value, but the irony behind it is potent." *F. Scott Fitzgerald: A Study of the Stories* (Jamaica: St. John's University Press, 1971), p. 111.

80. "The Swimmers," p. 154.

81. "The Swimmers," p. 154.

82. "Two Wrongs," p. 113.

83. "One Trip Abroad," p. 56.

84. "One Trip Abroad," p. 48.

85. "One Trip Abroad," p. 51.

86. Tommy, like Dick, flirts with "ickle durls," a touch which suggests this superficial similarity between the two characters. See *Tender Is the Night*, p. 226.

87. "A New Leaf," p. 91.

88. Dick's dissipation is linked with his expatriation–he has been in Paris for five years; largely because of this the story manages to be a *Post* story.

89. *As Ever*, p. 176.

90. "The Love Boat," p. 141.

91. "At Your Age," p. 80.

92. "At Your Age," p. 90.

93. This story is examined out of chronological sequence in order that the three lost youth stories discussed above could be studied together.

94. Refer to *The Composition of Tender Is the Night*, p. 73.

95. The only story which corresponds to "Babylon Revisited," in this sense, is "Winter Dreams." "Babylon Revisited" has received more critical attention than any other Fitzgerald story. Bryer lists some forty articles in scholarly journals as of 1979 which deal with "Babylon Revisited." Since 1979 there have been five more articles.

96. "Babylon Revisited," p. 4.

97. "Babylon Revisited," p. 82.

98. See *The Composition of Tender Is the Night*, p. 84.

99. *As Ever*, p. 181.

100. *As Ever*, p. 189.

101. Bruccoli, *Composition of Tender Is the Night*, p. 73.

102. In the 1925-1933 period Fitzgerald earned $226,341. Of this total, $157,250 was made from the sale of stories to magazines. $47,475 of this came from Fitzgerald's sale of the seventeen *Post* cluster stories.

103. *As Ever*, p. 168.

104. "The Adolescent Marriage," p. 7.

105. Although the male characters in these stories are all approximately twenty years old, their actions suggest they are much younger, perhaps sixteen.

106. "A Short Trip Home," p. 58.

107. There are nine stories in the Basil series, eight of which appeared in the *Post*.

108. John Kuehl and Jackson R. Bryer, eds., introduction to *The Basil and Josephine Stories* (New York: Scribners, 1973), p. xvi.

109. This first story in the series was reportedly rejected by the *Post* because "its editors did not care to believe that children played kissing games." See Kenneth Eble, *F. Scott Fitzgerald* (New York: Twayne, 1963), p. 24. The Ober correspondence indicates that it was first offered to *Ladies' Home Journal*, which replied in its rejection, "I regret having to return F. Scott Fitzgerald's THAT KIND OF PARTY to you as I'd very much like to buy a Fitzgerald piece. It seemed to us, though, that the children involved in the story were both precocious and rather unpleasant. . . ." See *As Ever*, p. 317.

110. *As Ever*, p. 317.

111. "The Scandal Detectives," p. 181.

112. "The Scandal Detectives," p. 182.

113. "The Scandal Detectives," p. 3.

114. "The Scandal Detectives," p. 181.

115. "The Freshest Boy," p. 73.

116. Malcolm Cowley, ed., *The Stories of F. Scott Fitzgerald* (New York: Scribners, 1951), p. 308.

117. "The Captured Shadow," p. 51.

118. "The Freshest Boy," p. 68.

119. *As Ever*, p. 116.

120. See *As Ever*, p. 118.

121. "First Blood," p. 8.

122. "A Snobbish Story," p. 36.

123. Elstein, p. 70, makes the point that Josephine marks Fitzgerald's turn away from the young and glamorous females for whom youth and beauty are enough.

124. "A Snobbish Story," p. 42.

125. "First Blood," p. 84.

126. "A Nice Quiet Place," p. 101.

127. "A Woman with a Past," p. 8.

128. "A Woman with a Past," p. 9.

129. "A Snobbish Story," p. 42.

130. "Emotional Bankruptcy," p. 60.

131. "Emotional Bankruptcy," p. 60.

132. "Emotional Bankruptcy," p. 65.

133. "A Woman with a Past," p. 137.

134. Higgins, *A Study of the Stories*, p. 148.

135. Graeme Lorimer to Bryant Mangum in conversation, 10 April 1971.

136. Turnbull, *Letters of F.S.F.*, p. 118.

137. DeVoto, "Writing for Money," p. 20.

138. "The Ice Palace" and "The Jelly-Bean" are the other two. Jim Powell ("Dice, Brassknuckles & Guitar") is also from Tarleton, Georgia.

139. "The Last of the Belles," p. 78.

140. Higgins, p. 105, considers "The Last of the Belles" successful primarily because of Fitzgerald's ironic stance toward the first person narrator who, Higgins asserts, is presented as foolish, thus affirming Fitzgerald's rejection of "the romantic attitude" characteristic of "The Ice Palace."

141. "The Last of the Belles," p. 78.

142. "A Freeze-Out," p. 89.

143. "Flight and Pursuit," p. 16.

144. "Family in the Wind," p. 3.

145. The novel was published in April 1934. It began appearing in installments in *Scribner's Magazine* (January 1934).

146. DeVoto, "Writing for Money," p. 4.

147. "The Rubber Check," p. 44.

148. "The Rubber Check," p. 44.

149. "What a Handsome Pair!" p. 64.

150. "One Interne," p. 90.

151. "More than Just a House," p. 34.

Chapter Five Notes

1. See Matthew J. Bruccoli, "*Tender Is the Night*–Reception and Reputation," *Profile of FSF*, pp. 92-106.

2. *As Ever*, p. 209.

3. But it is true that his popular reputation had not, since *This Side of Paradise*, rested on his novels. See Bruccoli, "*TITN*–Reception and Reputation," *Profile of FSF*, p. 94.

4. *Post*, 4 November 1933.

5. See *As Ever*, p. 315.

6. *Post*, 21 July 1934.

7. *As Ever*, p. 193.

8. At this time Thomas B. Costain was an associate editor of the *Post*.

9. *As Ever*, p. 189.

10. In 1932 Lorimer had become Chairman of Curtis Publishing Company, but he also retained his *Post* editorial powers until his retirement on 1 January 1937. See Wood, p. 186. Costain, Graeme Lorimer (George H. Lorimer's son), and Adelaide Neall worked as associate editors beginning in early 1932.

11. *As Ever*, p. 195.

12. With the Gwen series Fitzgerald became so careless that Ober began making suggestions as to how Fitzgerald could eliminate inconsistencies. See *As Ever*, pp. 258-259.

13. *As Ever*, p. 198.

14. *As Ever*, p. 208.

15. "New Types," p. 17.

16. "New Types," p. 16.

17. "New Types," p. 81.

18. The other three are "One Interne," 5 November 1932; "Zone of Accident," 13 July 1935; and Fitzgerald's last *Post* story, "'Trouble,'" 6 March 1937.

19. "Her Last Case," p. 61.

20. In "One Interne" he was William Tulliver V, probably a careless error on Fitzgerald's part. George Shoatze is also in both stories.

21. "Zone of Accident," p. 52.

22. *As Ever*, p. 237.

23. A third Gwen story, first called "Make Yourself at Home," was published in *Liberty*, 9 December 1939 under the title "Strange Sanctuary." The fourth and final Gwen story "The Pearl and the Fur" was sold but never published. See Jennifer McCabe Atkinson, "Lost and Unpublished Stories by F. Scott Fitzgerald," *Fitzgerald/Hemingway Annual 1971*, ed. Matthew J. Bruccoli (Washington, D. C.: Microcard Editions, 1971), p. 33.

24. *As Ever*, p. 232.

25. "One Interne" and "Zone of Accident."

26. *As Ever*, p. 276.

27. "'Trouble,'" p. 89.

28. *As Ever*, p. 275.

29. Turnbull, *Letters of F.S.F.*, p. 118.

30. *As Ever*, p. 253.

31. *As Ever*, p. 221. He remarked also in a letter to Zelda Fitzgerald in 1940 that, "As soon as I feel I am writing to a cheap specification my pen freezes and my talent vanishes over the hill. . . ." See Turnbull, *Letters of F.S.F.*, p. 118.

32. This story is not mentioned in the Fitzgerald-Ober correspondence.

33. "The Passionate Eskimo," p. 13.

34. "The Passionate Eskimo," p. 18.

35. The other two in this group listed by Fitzgerald are "Crazy Sunday" and "Philippe." See *As Ever*, p. 315. In her excellent overview of Fitzgerald's stories of the Depression, Ruth Prigozy characterizes "The Intimate Strangers" as "the poorest story" of the group of marriage stories and "the most illustrative of Fitzgerald's problems." See "The Short Stories of the Depression," in Bryer's *Short Stories*, p. 115.

36. There is no record of when Fitzgerald wrote this story, nor is there an indication in his correspondence with Ober of the magazines to which it was submitted. The first title for the story was probably "What You Don't Know." See *As Ever*, p. 220.

37. "Fate in her Hands," p. 172.

38. "Fate in her Hands," p. 168.

39. This story was first entitled "A Course in Languages." See *As Ever*, p. 315.

40. This story, first called "Make Yourself at Home," was rejected by the *Post* and bought by *Pictorial Review* along with the fourth Gwen story, "The Pearl and the Fur," but the magazine died before publishing either of the stories. See *As Ever*, p. 239 and 246. The latter was never published. In "Strange Sanctuary" Gwen's name becomes Dolly Haines.

41. This story was rejected by the following magazines: *American, Collier's, Cosmopolitan, Country Gentleman, Delineator, Ladies' Home Journal, McCall's, Pictorial Review, Redbook, Post, Woman's Home Companion,* and *This Week*. It was also entitled "When this Cruel War–" and "Dentist Appointment." Refer to *As Ever*, p. 278. Scott Donaldson calls this story "the last serious story published in Fitzgerald's lifetime. See "Fitzgerald's Romance with the South," *Southern Literary Journal*, V (Spring 1963), p. 16

42. *Dear Scott/Dear Max*, p. 208.

43. *Dear Scott/Dear Max*, p. 221.

44. *Dear Scott/Dear Max*, p. 254. Fitzgerald does not elaborate elsewhere on his idea of basing Philippe on Hemingway and making "The real modern man." Philippe's similarity to Hemingway arises from the fact that he is at once a physical man and also a sensitive one. By the term "modern man," Fitzgerald perhaps means a lost generation man: one who has grown up to find that there is nothing left to believe in. Philippe returns to France at a time when all institutions have been destroyed and he follows a ninth century version of the Hemingway code: he acts as if his life matters, he is hedonistic, and he plays to win.

45. *The Crack-up*, p. 177.

46. *Dear Scott/Dear Max*, p. 254.

47. p. 92.

48. See DeVoto, "Writing for Money," p. 22.

49. "In the Darkest Hour," p. 17.

50. "The Count of Darkness," p. 21.

51. "The Kingdom in the Dark," p. 68.

52. "Gods of Darkness," p. 90.

53. "Gods of Darkness," p. 91.

54. "Gods of Darkness," for example, was delivered in September 1935 and was not published until November 1941. See *As Ever*, p. 225.

55. Mizener, *The Far Side of Paradise*, p. 252.

56. DeVoto, "Writing for Money," p. 22.

57. The most comprehensive study of Fitzgerald's relationship with *Esquire* is James L. W. West III's "Fitzgerald and *Esquire*," in Bryer's *Short Stories*, pp. 149-66.

58. The term is used in a loose sense here and includes all of those pieces which have a fictional protagonist. *Esquire* has, unless otherwise indicated, labelled all of the pieces included here as "Fiction" or "Satire."

59. "Show Mr. and Mrs. F. to Room–," *Esquire*, May and June 1935.

60. The three Fitzgerald pieces to appear in *Esquire* before "The Fiend" were articles–not stories–written in collaboration with his wife.

61. See Arnold Gingrich, *Nothing But People: The Early Days at Esquire: A Personal History 1928-1958* (New York: Crown, 1971), p. 285.

62. "Auction–Model 1934," *Esquire* II (July 1934), pp. 20, 153, 155.

63. See *As Ever*, p. 291.

64. *Nothing But People*, p. 242.

65. Letter from Gingrich to John Higgins, *A Study of the Stories*, p. 192.

66. Curiously enough, Fitzgerald's contributions outnumber those of any other writer in *Esquire*'s history except Jesse Stuart who made seventy-nine contributions. Hemingway contributed thirty-three times in the 1930's and Dos Passos, nineteen. See *Nothing But People*, pp. 307-309.

67. Peterson, p. 276.

68. Peterson, pp. 260-65.

69. "Introduction," *The Pat Hobby Stories*, ed. Arnold Gingrich (New York: Scribners, 1962), p. xiv.

70. In December 1938 the contract was not renewed.

71. The publication dates of Fitzgerald's *Esquire* contributions are slightly different because of the normal time lag between the submission of a piece and its publication. In the second period particularly, Fitzgerald was ahead on his contributions and Gingrich was left with eight unpublished stories, six of which were Pat Hobby stories, at Fitzgerald's death.

72. He told Ober, for example, that he had written "3 little Esquire pieces (two of them mediocre) to live on." And in the context of this statement "mediocre" means better than his usual *Esquire* pieces; that is, Fitzgerald hated to forfeit even his mediocre work to *Esquire*. He was not concerned that his weakest work went to the magazine. See *As Ever*, p. 302.

73. One way to determine if any given *Esquire* story was first offered to another magazine is to check it against the index in *As Ever*. This is not foolproof, however, since Fitzgerald had come to submit his stories directly to editors; it is conceivable that an *Esquire* story which had been submitted first to another magazine might not show up in Fitzgerald's correspondence to Ober. The only *Esquire* story which can be documented as a *Post* rejection by using *As Ever* is "Financing Finnegan." See *As Ever*, p. 320.

74. "Shaggy's Morning," p. 26.

75. "The Ants at Princeton," p. 201.

76. "'Send Me In, Coach,'" p. 55.

77. *Dear Scott/Dear Max*, p. 213.

78. *Dear Scott/Dear Max*, pp. 195-98.

79. *Dear Scott/Dear Max*, pp. 198-99.

80. *Dear Scott/Dear Max*, p. 196.

81. Fitzgerald's fear of repeating himself is most evident in his remarks about revising galley proofs of *TAR*. He told Perkins, for example, ". . . the slow thing is to look through 'Tender Is the Night' and see what phrases I took out of the stories." See *Dear Scott/Dear Max*, p. 202.

82. *Dear Scott/Dear Max*, p. 212.

83. "Crazy Sunday," "Two Wrongs," "Majesty," and "Babylon Revisited."

84. *Dear Scott/Dear Max*, p. 215.

85. N. H., "Short Stories," *New York Sun* (5 April 1935), p. 30. Reprinted in *F.S.F.: The Critical Reception*, p. 346.

86. *F.S.F.: The Critical Reception*, p. xxiii.

87. Arthur Coleman, "Stories by F. Scott Fitzgerald Are Merely Entertaining," *Dallas Morning News*, 24 March 1935, p. 8. Reprinted in *F.S.F.: The Critical Reception*, p. 328.

88. *F.S.F.: The Critical Reception*, p. 339.

89. "Books of the Times," *New York Times*, 27 March 1935, p. 19. Reprinted in *F.S.F.: The Critical Reception*, p. 341.

90. "The Fiend" and "The Night Before Chancellorsville" were the two *Esquire* stories in *TAR*.

91. "The Crack-up," February 1936; "Putting It Together," March 1936; and "Handle with Care," April 1936.

92. VI (June 1936), p. 28.

93. See Bryer, *Critical Reputation of F. Scott Fitzgerald*, pp. 200-201.

94. "An Author's Mother," VI (September 1936), 36; "'I Didn't Get Over,'" VI (November 1936), 46, 194-195; "An Alcoholic Case," VII (February 1937), 32, 109; "The Long Way Out," VIII (September 1937), 45, 193; and "Financing Finnegan," IX (January 1938), 41, 180, 182, 184.

95. "An Author's Mother," p. 36.

96. "An Alcoholic Case," p. 109.

97. He may also have had in mind Ring Lardner's story "Mamma" (*Good Housekeeping*, June 1930). See Matthew J. Bruccoli, "A Source for 'The Long Way Out,'" *Fitzgerald Newsletter* (Washington: Microcard Editions, 1969), p. 229.

98. For his debt to Ober in June 1937 see *As Ever*, p. 320.

99. *As Ever*, p. 323.

100. 11 May 1937, *As Ever*, p. 314.

101. "Financing Finnegan," p. 41.

102. "Financing Finnegan," p. 184.

103. "Temperature" for example is one such story. It was submitted through Ober to the *Post*; they declined it, and it was never published.

104. See *As Ever*, pp. 404-06.

105. "Early Success," *The Crack-Up*, p. 86.

106. Each of the five is approximately 2,000 words. "The Lost Decade," approximately 1,200 words, is the shortest.

107. This detail links the story with "Financing Finnegan" and more directly with Fitzgerald's own broken shoulder experience.

108. See *As Ever*, pp. 403, 408. Ober did not handle Fitzgerald's *Esquire* contributions, thus stories such as "Design in Plaster" would have been sold without Ober's ever having seen them.

109. In order to increase his market, Fitzgerald persuaded Gingrich to allow him to publish work under a pen name. The idea was that Fitzgerald would be able to contribute two stories to *Esquire* per single issue; one under his name and another under a pseudonym. This was, in fact, done, but only after Fitzgerald's death. The February 1941 issue carried "On an Ocean Wave" and "Fun in an Artist's Studio," a Pat Hobby story. See Gingrich's introduction to *The Pat Hobby Stories*, p. xix.

110. "On an Ocean Wave," p. 141.

111. This is the second incident in Fitzgerald's stories in which a woman talked during a performance. In the first, Charles David Stuart pushed the woman in the face ("The Pusher-in-the-Face," *Woman's Home Companion*, February 1925).

112. Gingrich, "Introduction," *The Pat Hobby Stories*, p. xxi.

113. See the "Introduction," *The Pat Hobby Stories*, p. ix.

114. "The Homes of the Stars," p. 121.

115. "A Patriotic Short," p. 269.

116. "Pat Hobby's College Days," p. 169.

117. Turnbull, *Letters of F.S.F.*, p. 399.

118. "Introduction," *The Pat Hobby Stories*, p. x.

119. Mizener, *The Far Side of Paradise*, p. 287.

120. *The Last Tycoon* (New York: Scribners, 1941), p. 147.

121. *Last Tycoon*, p. 146.

122. For the dating of the composition of this story, see James L. W. West III, "F. Scott Fitzgerald to Arnold Gingrich: A Composition Date for 'Dearly Beloved,'" *Papers of the Bibliographic Society of America* LXVII (Fourth Quarter 1973), pp. 452-54.

123. *Epic Grandeur*, p. 473.

124. *As Ever*, p. 411.

125. *As Ever*, p. 410.

126. *As Ever*, p. 413. *Cosmopolitan* editors rejected the story for no specific reason, stating "It's really heart-breaking to return a Scott Fitzgerald story." See *As Ever*, p. 415.

127. "Discard," p. 149.

128. Ober was even optimistic about the story after the second *Post* rejection; and although Ober, no doubt, wanted to be optimistic at this time when the professional relationship between the two was particularly strained, Ober was

not in the habit of deceiving Fitzgerald as to his estimated worth of any given piece. See *As Ever*, p. 416.

129. "Last Kiss," p. 16. See the headnote.

130. Mizener, *The Far Side of Paradise*, p. 348 note. Compare "pink and silver frost" on p. 34 of "Last Kiss" with p. 116 of *The Last Tycoon*.

131. "Last Kiss," p. 34.

132. "Last Kiss," p. 34.

133. A safe guess is that Fitzgerald sent it directly to *Collier's* as he had done in the case of "Discard."

134. Sklar, p. 334.

135. "Fitzgerald's Unfinished Symphony," *Saturday Review of Literature* XXIV (6 December 1941), p. 19. Reprinted in Bryer, *Critical Reception*, p. 375.

Bibliography

A. Primary—Works by F. Scott Fitzgerald

"Absolution," *The American Mercury*, II (June 1924), 141-149.
"The Adjuster," *The Red Book Magazine*, XLV (September 1925), 47-51, 144-148.
"The Adolescent Marriage," *The Saturday Evening Post* CXCVIII (6 March 1926), 6-7, 229-230, 233-234.
Afternoon of an Author, ed. Arthur Mizener. New York: Scribners, 1958.
"An Alcoholic Case," *Esquire*, VI (February 1937), 32-109.
All The Sad Young Men. New York: Scribners, 1926.
"The Ants at Princeton," *Esquire*, V (June 1936), 35, 201.
The Apprentice Fiction of F. Scott Fitzgerald, ed. John Kuehl. New Brunswick, N. J.: Rutgers, 1965.
As Ever, Scott Fitz—Letters Between F. Scott Fitzgerald and his Literary Agent Harold Ober 1919-1940, ed. Matthew J. Bruccoli with the assistance of Jennifer McCabe Atkinson. New York: Lippincott, 1971.
"At Your Age," *The Saturday Evening Post*, CCII (17 August 1929), 6, 7, 79, 80.
"An Author's Mother," *Esquire*, VI (September 1936), 36.
"Babes in the Woods," *The Smart Set*, LX (September 1919), 67-71.
"The Baby Party," *Hearst's International*, XLVII (February 1925), 32-37.
"Babylon Revisited," *The Saturday Evening Post*, CCIII (21 February 1931), 3, 4, 5, 82, 83, 84.
"Basil and Cleopatra," *The Saturday Evening Post*, CCI (27 April 1929), 14, 15, 16, 166, 170, 173.
The Beautiful and Damned. New York: Scribners, 1922.
"Benediction," *The Smart Set*, LXI (February 1920), 35-44.
"Bernice Bobs Her Hair," *The Saturday Evening Post*, CXCII (1 May 1920), 14-15, 159, 163, 167.

"Between Three and Four," *The Saturday Evening Post*, CCIV (5 September 1931), 8, 9, 69, 72.

"'Boil Some Water—Lots of It,'" *Esquire*, XIII (March 1940), 30, 145, 147.

"The Bowl," *The Saturday Evening Post*, CC (21 January 1928), 6, 7, 93, 94, 97, 100.

"The Bridal Party," *The Saturday Evening Post*, CCIII (9 August 1930), 10, 11, 109, 110, 112, 114.

"The Camel's Back," *The Saturday Evening Post*, CXCII (24 April 1920), 16-17, 157, 161, 165.

"The Captured Shadow," *The Saturday Evening Post*, CCI (29 December 1928), 12, 13, 48, 51.

"A Change of Class," *The Saturday Evening Post*, CCIV (26 September 1931), 6-7, 37-38, 41.

"The Count of Darkness," *Redbook Magazine*, LXV (June 1935), 20-23, 68, 70, 72.

The Crack-Up, ed. Edmund Wilson. New York: New Directions, 1945.

"Crazy Sunday," *The American Mercury*, XXVII (October 1932), 209-220.

"The Curious Case of Benjamin Button," *Collier's*, LXIX (27 May 1922), 5, 6, 22-28.

"The Cut-Glass Bowl," *Scribner's Magazine*, LXVII (May 1920), 582-592.

"Dalyrimple Goes Wrong," *The Smart Set*, LXI (February 1920), 107-116.

"The Dance," *The Red Book Magazine*, XLVII (June 1926), 39-43, 134, 136, 138.

Dear Scott/Dear Max: The Fitzgerald-Perkins Correspondence, eds. John Kuehl and Jackson R. Bryer. New York: Scribners, 1971.

"Dearly Beloved," *Fitzgerald/Hemingway Annual 1969*, ed. Matthew J. Bruccoli. Washington, D. C.: Microcard Editions, 1969, pp. 1-3.

"Design in Plaster," *Esquire*, XII (November 1939), 51, 169.

"Diagnosis," *The Saturday Evening Post*, CCIV (20 February 1932), 18-19, 90, 92.

"The Diamond as Big as the Ritz," *The Smart Set*, LXVIII (June 1922), 5-29.

"Diamond Dick and the First Law of Woman," *Hearst's International*, XLV (April 1924), 58-63, 134, 136.

"Dice, Brassknuckles & Guitar," *Hearst's International*, XLIII (May 1923), 8-13, 145-149.

"Discard," *Harper's Bazaar*, LXXXII (January 1948), 103, 143-144, 146, 148-149.

"Early Success," *American Cavalcade*, I (October 1937), 74-79. Reprinted in *The Crack-Up*, pp. 85-90.

"Emotional Bankruptcy," *The Saturday Evening Post*, CCIV (15 August 1931), 8-9, 60, 65.

"The End of Hate," *Collier's*, CV (22 June 1940), 9, 10, 63, 64.

F. Scott Fitzgerald's Ledger. Washington, D. C.: Bruccoli Clark/NCR, 1972.

"The Family Bus," *The Saturday Evening Post*, CCVI (4 November 1933), 8-9, 57, 61-62, 65-66.

"Family in the Wind," *The Saturday Evening Post*, CCIV (4 June 1932), 3, 4, 5, 71, 72, 73.

"Fate in Her Hands," *American Mercury*, CXXI (April 1936), 56-59, 168-172.

"Flight and Pursuit," *The Saturday Evening Post*, CCIV (14 May 1932), 16, 17, 53, 57.

"The Fiend," *Esquire*, III (January 1935), 23, 173-174.

"Financing Finnegan," *Esquire*, IX (January 1938), 41, 180, 182, 184.

"First Blood," *The Saturday Evening Post*, CCII (5 April 1930), 8, 9, 81, 84.

Flappers and Philosophers. New York: Scribners, 1921.

Forging Ahead," *The Saturday Evening Post*, CCI (30 March 1929), 12, 13, 101, 105.

"The Four Fists," *Scribner's Magazine*, LXVII (June 1920), 669-680.

"A Freeze-Out," *The Saturday Evening Post*, CCIV (19 December 1931), 6, 7, 84, 85, 88, 89.

"The Freshest Boy," *The Saturday Evening Post*, CCI (28 July 1928), 6-7, 68, 70, 73.

"Fun in an Artist's Studio," *Esquire*, XV (February 1941), 64, 112.

"Gods of Darkness," *Redbook Magazine*, LXXVIII (November 1941), 30-33, 88-91.

The Great Gatsby. New York: Scribners, 1925.

"Gretchen's Forty Winks," *The Saturday Evening Post*, CXCVI (15 March 1924), 14-15, 128, 130, 132.

"The Guest in Room Nineteen," *Esquire*, VIII (October 1937), 56, 209.

"He Thinks He's Wonderful," *The Saturday Evening Post*, CCI (29 September 1928), 6-7, 117-118, 121.

"Head and Shoulders," *The Saturday Evening Post*, CXCII (21 February 1920), 16-17, 81-82, 85-86.

"Her Last Case," *The Saturday Evening Post*, CCVII (3 November 1934), 10-11, 59, 61-62, 64.

"His Russet Witch," *Metropolitan Magazine*, LIII (February 1921), 11-13, 46-51.

"The Homes of the Stars," *Esquire*, XIV (August 1940), 28, 120-121.

"The Honor of the Goon," *Esquire*, VII (June 1937), 53, 216.

"Hot & Cold Blood," *Hearst's International*, LXIV (August 1923), 80-84, 150-151.

"The Hotel Child," *The Saturday Evening Post*, CCIII (31 January 1931), 8-9, 69, 72, 75.

"'I Didn't Get Over,'" *Esquire*, VI (October 1936), 45, 194-195.

"I Got Shoes," *The Saturday Evening Post*, CCIV (23 September 1933), 14-15, 56, 58.

"The Ice Palace," *The Saturday Evening Post*, CXCII (22 May 1920), 18-19, 163, 167, 170.

"Image on the Heart," *McCall's*, LXII (April 1936), 7-9, 52, 54, 57-58, 62.

"In the Darkest Hour," *Redbook Magazine*, LXIII (October 1934), 15-19, 94-98.

"In the Holidays," *Esquire*, VIII (December 1937), 82, 184, 186.

"Indecision," *The Saturday Evening Post*, CCIII (16 May 1931), 12-13, 56, 59, 62.

"Inside the House," *The Saturday Evening Post*, CCVIII (13 June 1936), 18-19, 32, 34, 36.

"The Intimate Strangers," *McCall's*, LXII (June 1935), 12-14, 36, 38, 40, 42, 44.

"Jacob's Ladder," *The Saturday Evening Post*, CC (20 August 1927), 8-9, 134, 139, 141.

"The Jelly-Bean," *Metropolitan Magazine*, LII (October 1920), 15-16, 63-67.

"John Jackson's Arcady," *The Saturday Evening Post*, CXCVII (26 July 1924), 8-9, 100, 102, 105.

"The Kingdom in the Dark," *Redbook Magazine*, LXV (August 1935), 58-62, 64, 66-68.

"Last Kiss," *Collier's*, CXXIII (16 April 1949), 16-17, 34, 38, 41, 43-44.

"The Last of the Belles," *The Saturday Evening Post*, CCI (2 March 1929), 18, 19, 75, 78.

The Last Tycoon. New York: Scribners, 1941.

"The Lees of Happiness," *Chicago Sunday Tribune*, III (12 December 1920), blue ribbon fiction section, 1, 3, 7.

The Letters of F. Scott Fitzgerald, ed. Andrew Turnbull. New York: Scribners, 1963.

"Lo, the Poor Peacock!" *Esquire*, LXXVI (September 1971), 154-158.

"The Long Way Out," *Esquire*, VIII (September 1937), 45, 193.

"The Lost Decade," *Esquire*, XII (December 1939), 113, 228.

"The Love Boat," *The Saturday Evening Post*, CC (8 October 1927), 8-9, 134, 139, 141.

"Love in the Night," *The Saturday Evening Post*, CXCVII (14 March 1925), 18-19, 68, 70.

"Magnetism," *The Saturday Evening Post*, CC (3 March 1928), 5, 6, 7, 74, 76, 78.

"Majesty," *The Saturday Evening Post*, CCII (13 July 1929), 6, 7, 57, 58, 61, 62.

"A Man in the Way," *Esquire*, XIII (February 1940), 40, 109.

"May Day," *The Smart Set*, LXII (July 1920), 3-32.

"Mightier than the Sword," *Esquire*, XV (April 1941), 36, 183.

"More than Just a House," *The Saturday Evening Post*, CCV (24 June 1933), 8, 9, 27, 30, 34.

"Myra Meets His Family," *The Saturday Evening Post*, CXCII (20 March 1920), 40, 42, 44, 46, 49-50, 53.

"A New Leaf," *The Saturday Evening Post*, CCIV (4 July 1931), 12-13, 90-91.

"New Types," *The Saturday Evening Post*, CCVII (22 September 1934), 16-17, 74, 76, 78-79, 81.

"A Nice Quiet Place," *The Saturday Evening Post*, CCII (31 May 1930), 8, 9, 96, 101, 103.

"A Night At the Fair," *The Saturday Evening Post*, CCI (21 July 1928), 8-9, 129-130, 133.

"The Night before Chancellorsville," *Esquire*, III (February 1935), 24, 165.

"No Flowers," *The Saturday Evening Post*, CCVII (21 July 1934), 10-11, 57-58, 60.

"No Harm Trying," *Esquire*, XIV (November 1940), 30, 151-153.

"Not in the Guidebook," *Woman's Home Companion*, LII (November 1925), 9-11, 135-136.

"The Offshore Pirate," *The Saturday Evening Post*, CXCII (29 May 1920), 10-11, 99, 101-102, 106, 109.

"On Schedule," *The Saturday Evening Post*, CCV (18 March 1933), 16-17, 71, 74, 77, 79.

[pseud. Paul Elgin]. "On an Ocean Wave," *Esquire*, XV (February 1941), 59, 144.

"On the Trail of Pat Hobby," *Esquire*, XV (January 1941), 36, 126.

"On Your Own," *Esquire*, XCI (30 January 1979), 57-66.
"One Interne," *The Saturday Evening Post*, CCV (5 November 1932), 6-7, 86, 88-90.
"One of My Oldest Friends," *Woman's Home Companion*, LII (September 1925), 7-8, 120-122.
"One Trip Abroad," *The Saturday Evening Post*, CCIII (11 October 1930), 6, 7, 48, 51, 53, 54, 56.
"Outside the Cabinet-Maker's," *The Century Magazine*, CXVII (December 1928), 241-244.
"The Passionate Eskimo," *Liberty*, XII (8 June 1935), 10-14, 17-18.
"Pat Hobby Does His Bit," *Esquire*, XIV (September 1940), 41, 104.
"Pat Hobby and Orson Welles," *Esquire*, XIII (May 1940), 38, 198-199.
"Pat Hobby, Putative Father," *Esquire*, XIV (July 1940), 36, 172-174.
"Pat Hobby's Christmas Wish," *Esquire*, XIII (January 1940), 45, 170-172.
"Pat Hobby's College Days," *Esquire*, XV (May 1941), 55, 168-169.
"Pat Hobby's Preview," *Esquire*, XIV (October 1940), 30, 118, 120.
"Pat Hobby's Secret," *Esquire*, XIII (June 1940), 30, 107.
"A Patriotic Short," *Esquire*, XIV (December 1940), 62, 269.
"A Penny Spent," *The Saturday Evening Post*, CXCVIII (10 October 1925), 8-9, 160, 164, 166.
"The Perfect Life," *The Saturday Evening Post*, CCI (5 January 1929), 8, 9, 113, 115, 118.
"The Popular Girl," *The Saturday Evening Post*, CXCIV (11 February and 18 February 1922), 3-5, 82, 84, 86, 89; 18-19, 105-106, 109-110.
"Presumption," *The Saturday Evening Post*, CXCVIII (9 January 1926), 3-5, 226, 228-229, 233-234.
The Price Was High: The Last Uncollected Stories of F. Scott Fitzgerald, ed. Matthew J. Bruccoli. New York: Harcourt, Brace Jovanovich/Bruccoli Clark, 1979.
"The Pusher-in-the-Face," *Woman's Home Companion*, LII (February 1925), 27-28, 143-144.
"Rags Martin-Jones and the Pr-nce of W-les," *McCall's*, LI (July 1924), 6-7, 32, 48, 50.
"The Rich Boy," *The Red Book Magazine*, XLVI (January and February 1926), 27-32, 144, 146; 75-79, 122, 124-126.
The Romantic Egoists: A Pictorial Autobiography from the Scrapbooks and Albums of F. Scott and Zelda Fitzgerald, ed. Joan P. Kerr and Matthew J. Bruccoli. New York: Scribners, 1974.

"The Rough Crossing," *The Saturday Evening Post*, CCI (8 June 1929), 12, 13, 66, 70, 75.

"The Rubber Check," *The Saturday Evening Post*, CCV (6 August 1932), 6-7, 41-42, 44-45.

"The Scandal Detectives," *The Saturday Evening Post*, CC (28 April 1928), 3, 4, 178, 181, 182, 185.

"'Send Me In, Coach,'" *Esquire*, VI (November 1936), 55, 218-221.

"'The Sensible Thing,'" *Liberty*, I (5 July 1924), 10-14.

"Shaggy's Morning," *Esquire*, III (May 1935), 26, 160.

The Short Stories of F. Scott Fitzgerald. Ed. Matthew J. Bruccoli. New York: Scribners, 1989.

"A Short Trip Home," *The Saturday Evening Post*, CC (17 December 1927), 6-7, 55, 57-58.

"Six of One—," *Redbook Magazine*, LXVIII (February 1932), 22-25, 84, 86, 88.

"The Smilers," *The Smart Set*, LXII (June 1920), 107-111.

"A Snobbish Story," *The Saturday Evening Post*, CCIII (29 November 1930), 6, 7, 36, 38, 40, 42.

"Strange Sanctuary," *Liberty*, XVI (9 December 1939), 15-20.

"The Swimmers," *The Saturday Evening Post*, CCII (19 October 1929), 12, 13, 150, 152, 154.

Taps at Reveille. New York: Scribners, 1935.

Tales of the Jazz Age. New York: Scribners, 1922.

"Tarquin of Cheapside," *The Smart Set*, LXIV (February 1921), 43-46.

"Teamed with Genius," *Esquire*, XIII (April 1940), 44, 195-197.

Tender Is the Night. New York: Scribners, 1934.

"That Kind of Party," *The Princeton University Library Chronicle*, XII (Summer 1951), 167-180.

"The Third Casket," *The Saturday Evening Post*, CXCVI (31 May 1924), 8-9, 78.

This Side of Paradise. New York: Scribners, 1920.

"Three Acts of Music," *Esquire*, V (May 1936), 39, 210.

"Three Hours Between Planes," *Esquire*, XVI (July 1941), 41, 138-139.

"Too Cute for Words," *The Saturday Evening Post*, CCVIII (18 April 1936), 16-18, 87, 90, 93.

"'Trouble,'" *The Saturday Evening Post*, CCIX (6 March 1937), 14-15, 81, 84, 86, 88-89.

"Two for a Cent," *Metropolitan Magazine*, LV (April 1922), 23-26, 93-95.

"Two-Old Timers," *Esquire*, XV (March 1941), 53, 143.

"Two Wrongs," *The Saturday Evening Post*, CCII (18 January 1930), 8, 9, 107, 109, 113.
"The Unspeakable Egg," *The Saturday Evening Post*, CXCVII (12 July 1924), 12-13, 125-126, 129.
"What a Handsome Pair!" *The Saturday Evening Post*, CCV (27 August 1932), 16-17, 61, 63-64.
"Winter Dreams," *Metropolitan Magazine*, LVI (December 1922), 11-15, 100-102, 104-107.
"The Woman from Twenty-One," *Esquire*, XV (June 1941), 29, 164.
"A Woman with a Past," *The Saturday Evening Post*, CCIII (6 September 1930), 8, 9, 133, 134, 137.
"Your Way and Mine," *Woman's Home Companion*, LIV (May 1927), 7-8, 61, 64, 67, 68.
"Zone of Accident," *The Saturday Evening Post*, CCVIII (13 July 1935), 8-9, 47, 49, 51-52.

B. Secondary Works

Allen, Joan M. *Candles and Carnival Lights: The Catholic Sensibility of F. Scott Fitzgerald*. New York: New York University Press, 1978.
Atkinson, Jennifer McCabe. "Lost and Unpublished Stories by F. Scott Fitzgerald," *Fitzgerald/Hemingway Annual 1971*, ed. Matthew J. Bruccoli. Washington, D. C.: Microcard Editions, 1971, pp. 32-63.
Bruccoli, Matthew J. *The Composition of Tender Is the Night: A Study of the Manuscripts*. Pittsburgh: University of Pittsburgh Press, 1963.
——. *F. Scott Fitzgerald: A Descriptive Bibliography*. Pittsburgh: University of Pittsburgh Press, 1972.
——, ed. *Fitzgerald Newsletter*. Washington, D. C.: Microcard Editions, 1969.
——. "'A Handful Lying Loose'—A Study of F. Scott Fitzgerald's Basil Duke Lee Stories," unpublished M. A. thesis. University of Virginia, 1955.
——, ed. "Introduction," F. Scott Fitzgerald, *The Great Gatsby: A Facsimile of the Manuscript*. Washington, D. C.: Microcard Editions, 1973, pp. xiii-xxxv.
——. "A Source for 'The Long Way Out,'" *Fitzgerald Newsletter*, p. 229.
——, comp. *Profile of F. Scott Fitzgerald*. Columbus: Merrill, 1971.

———. *Some Sort of Epic Grandeur: The Life of F. Scott Fitzgerald.* New York: Harcourt Brace Jovanovich, 1981.

———. "Tender is the Night—Reception and Reputation," *The Composition of Tender Is the Night.* Pittsburgh: University of Pittsburgh Press, 1963. Revised and reprinted in *Profile of F. Scott Fitzgerald*, pp. 92-106.

Bryer, Jackson R. *The Critical Reputation of F. Scott Fitzgerald.* Hamden, Connecticut: Archon, 1967.

———, ed. *F. Scott Fitzgerald: The Critical Reception.* New York: Burt Franklin, 1978.

———, ed. *The Short Stories of F. Scott Fitzgerald: New Approaches in Criticism.* Madison: University of Wisconsin Press, 1982.

Bryer, Jackson R. and Kuehl, John, eds. "Introduction," *The Basil and Josephine Stories.* New York: Scribners, 1973, pp. vii-xxvi.

Charvat, William. *The Profession of Authorship in America, 1800-1870*, ed. Matthew J. Bruccoli. Columbus: Ohio State University Press, 1968.

Cowley, Malcolm, ed. "Introduction," *The Stories of F. Scott Fitzgerald.* New York: Scribners, 1951.

Donaldson, Scott. "Scott Fitzgerald's Romance with the South." *Southern Literary Journal* V (Spring 1963), pp. 3-17.

DeVoto, Bernard. "Writing for Money," *Saturday Review of Literature.* XVI (9 October 1937), 3-4, 20, 22.

Ebel, Kenneth. *F. Scott Fitzgerald.* New York: Twayne, 1963.

Elstein, Rochelle S. "Josephine Stories: The End of the Romantic Illusion," *American Literature* LI (1979), pp. 69-83.

Fussell, Edwin S. "Fitzgerald's Brave New World." *ELH: A Journal of English Literary History* XIX (December 1952), pp. 291-306.

Gingrich, Arnold, ed. "Introduction," F. Scott Fitzgerald, *The Pat Hobby Stories.* New York: Scribners, 1962, pp. ix-xxiii.

———. *Nothing but People: The Early Days at Esquire: A Personal History 1928-1958.* New York: Crown, 1971.

Hart, James E. *Oxford Companion to American Literature*, 4th ed. New York: Oxford University Press, 1965.

Hemingway, Ernest. *A Moveable Feast.* New York: Scribners, 1964.

Higgins, John A. *F. Scott Fitzgerald: A Study of the Stories.* Jamaica: St. John's University Press, 1971.

Jones, Howard Mumford. "Foreword," *The Profession of Authorship in America, 1800-1870*, ed. Matthew J. Bruccoli. Columbus: Ohio State University Press, 1968, pp. v-xvi.

Kazin, Alfred, ed. *F. Scott Fitzgerald: The Man and His Work.* Cleveland and New York: World, 1951.

Lanahan, Frances Fitzgerald. "Introduction," F. Scott Fitzgerald, *Six Tales of the Jazz Age and Other Stories*. New York: Scribners, 1960, pp. 5-11.

Le Vot, André. *F. Scott Fitzgerald: A Biography*. Trans. William Byron. Garden City, NY: Doubleday, 1983.

Lehan, Richard D. *F. Scott Fitzgerald and the Craft of Fiction*. Carbondale: Southern Illinois University Press, 1966.

Long, Robert Emmet. "B & D: Nathan and Mencken as Maury Noble," *Fitzgerald Newsletter*. Washington, D. C.: Microcard Editions, 1969, p. 203.

Lorimer, Graeme. Interview, 10 April 1971.

Mangum, Bryant. "The Reception of 'Dearly Beloved,'" *Fitzgerald/Hemingway Annual 1970*, ed. Matthew J. Bruccoli. Washington, D. C.: Microcard Editions, 1970, pp. 240-244.

Marshall, Margaret. "Notes By the Way," *The Nation*, CLII (8 February 1941), 159-160. Reprinted as "On Reading Fitzgerald" in Kazin, *Fitzgerald*, pp. 112-114.

Matthews, T. S. Review of *Taps at Reveille*, *New Republic*, LXXXII (10 April 1935), p. 62. Reprinted in Kazin, *Fitzgerald*, p. 107.

Miller, James E., Jr., *F. Scott Fitzgerald: His Art and His Technique*. New York: New York University Press, 1964.

Mizener, Arthur, ed. *F. Scott Fitzgerald: A Collection of Critical Essays*. Englewood Cliffs, N. J.: Prentice-Hall, 1963.

——. *The Far Side of Paradise*. Boston: Houghton Mifflin, 1951.

O'Hara, John. "Introduction," *The Portable F. Scott Fitzgerald*, selected by Dorothy Parker. New York: Viking, 1945. Reprinted in *Profile of F. Scott Fitzgerald*, comp. Matthew J. Bruccoli. Columbus: Merrill, 1971, pp. 11-20.

Perosa, Sergio. *The Art of F. Scott Fitzgerald*, trans. Charles Matz and the author. Ann Arbor: University of Michigan Press, 1965.

Peterson, Theodore. *Magazines in the Twentieth Century*. Urbana: University of Illinois Press, 1964.

Petry, Alice Hall. *Fitzgerald's Craft of Short Fiction: The Collected Stories 1920-1935*. Ann Arbor, MI: UMI Reserach Press, 1989.

Potts, Steven Wayne. "F. Scott Fitzgerald: His Career in Magazines." Ph.D. diss., University of California, Berkeley, 1980.

Prigozy, Ruth M.. "The Stories and Essays of F. Scott Fitzgerald: A Critical Study." Ph.D. diss. City University of New York, 1969.

——. "The Unpublished Stories by F. Scott Fitzgerald," *Twentieth Century Literature* XX (April 1974), pp. 69-90.

Sklar, Robert. *F. Scott Fitzgerald: The Last Laocöon*. New York: Oxford University Press, 1967.

Stewart, Lawrence D. "'Absolution' and *The Great Gatsby*." *Fitzgerald/Hemingway Annual* V (1973), pp. 181-87.

Tanselle, G. Thomas and Bryer, Jackson R. "*The Great Gatsby*—A Study in Literary Reputation," *New Mexico Quarterly*, XXXIII (Winter 1963-1964), 409-425. Reprinted in *Profile of F. Scott Fitzgerald*, pp. 74-91.

Tebbel, John. *George Horace Lorimer and The Saturday Evening Post*. Garden City: Doubleday, 1948.

Turnbull, Andrew. *Scott Fitzgerald*. New York: Scribners, 1962.

West, James L. W. III, "F. Scott Fitzgerald to Arnold Gingrich: A Composition Date for 'Dearly Beloved,'" *Papers of the Bibliographic Society of America* LXVII (Fourth Quarter 1973), pp. 452-54.

——. *The Making of This Side of Paradise*. Philadelphia: University of Pennsylvania Press, 1983.

Whipple, Leon. "SatEvePost, Mirror of These States," *Survey* (1 March 1928). Reprinted in part, Wood, *Magazines in the United States*, pp. 155-156.

Wilson, Edmund, ed. "Editor's Notes," *The Crack-Up*. New York: New Directions, 1945.

Wilson, Edmund. *The Shores of Light*. New York: Farrar, Straus and Young, 1952.

Wood, James Playstead. *Magazines in the United States*. New York: Ronald, 1956.

Wycherly, Alan. "An Early View of Mencken—and a Query," *Fitzgerald Newsletter*. Washington, D. C.: Microcard Editions, 1969, pp. 129-130.

Index